D0878367

Social Democracy
& Welfare Capitalism

A Century of Income Security Politics

ALEXANDER HICKS

CORNELL UNIVERSITY PRESS   ITHACA AND LONDON

Cornell University Press gratefully acknowledges a subvention from Emory University, which aided in publication of this book.

First published 1999 by Cornell University Press
First printing, Cornell Paperbacks, 1999

Printed in the United States of America

Cornell University Press strives to use environmentally responsible suppliers and materials to the fullest extent possible in the publishing of its books. Such materials include vegetable-based, low-VOC inks, and acid-free papers that are recycled, totally chlorine-free, or partly composed of nonwood fibers. Books that bear the logo of the FSC (Forest Stewardship Council) use paper taken from forests that have been inspected and certified as meeting the highest standards for environmental and social responsibility. For further information, visit our website at www.cornellpress.cornell.edu.

Library of Congress
Cataloging-in-Publication Data

Hicks, Alexander M.
Social democracy and welfare capitalism : a century of income security politics / Alexander Hicks.
    p.   cm.
Includes bibliographical references and index.
ISBN 0-8014-3568-4 (cloth).—ISBN 0-8014-8556-8 (pbk.)
1. Capitalism.   2. Welfare economics—History.
3. Welfare state—History.   4. Corporate state—History.   5. Socialism—History.
6. Capitalism—History.   7. Income maintenance programs—History.   8. Social security—History.
9. Public welfare—History.   10. Labor movement—History.   I. Title.
HB846.H53   1999
330.15'56—dc21   99-41664

Cloth printing
10 9 8 7 6 5 4 3 2 1
Paperback printing
10 9 8 7 6 5 4 3 2 1

®

TO

NANCY

AND

RYAN

Contents

The object of government is the welfare of the people. The material progress and prosperity of a nation are desirable chiefly so far as they lead to the moral and material welfare of all citizens.

Theodore Roosevelt (1910)

Preface

The United States has one of the highest poverty rates of the twenty or so most affluent democracies. This is true even if poverty lines are drawn to a single standard of consumption provided by the prosperous United States. It is true despite the fact that the U.S. poverty rate is not unusually high among comparable affluent democracies if the rate is tallied before the give-and-take of government taxing and spending has had its impact. So why is there so much poverty in the United States?

A free-market conservative might impute the deterioration of the United States's relative egalitarian standing once government finances are accounted for to a counterproductive government involvement in setting personal income. Data suggest, however, that poverty figures tend to shrink after governmental taxes and transfers are tallied. Indeed, this book shows that U.S. spending for income-security purposes is relatively low. As Gosta Esping-Andersen's *Three Worlds of Welfare Capitalism* has famously shown, the extent to which the United States buffers people against the economic vicissitudes of old age, illness, and unemployment is slight in comparison with the public protections provided citizens of other affluent democracies.

Government income security spending appears to reduce poverty. Indeed, the economic shortfalls associated with old age, sickness, and lack of work (though they hurt) do not always drop one into poverty. Thus, it appears that governmental social spending allays an income problem more general than the problem of poverty alone. Why is the U.S. income security state not larger and more effective? What determines the size and effectiveness of income security states? This book addresses these questions for the affluent capitalist democracies over the last century.

Social Democracy and Welfare Capitalism began as an investigation into the causes of those state policies that help secure working families against economic anxiety, shortfalls, poverty, and inequity within the relatively affluent capitalist democracies. It developed into a study of the solidaristic politics and institutions of working citizens over the last century or so, and into a study of industrial working-class politics and institutions in particular.

The book's broadest conclusion is that the political organizations and organizational politics of employees—of workers into parties and unions, of parties into governing coalitions, and of unions into participation in those centralized national labor markets often dubbed "neo-corporatist"—are the most persistently powerful forces operating to advance income security policy. A more refined conclusion is that labor organizations and their politics built the welfare state by exploiting— sometimes quite fortuitously, sometimes most deliberately—the political opportunities offered to them. Militant social democrats pressed anxious autocrats such as Otto von Bismarck into bidding for employee loyalties with social insurance programs. Moderate labor parties turned votes into similar concessions from Herbert Asquith to Clement Attlee. Strong labor unions have helped set the stage for centrist as well as leftist reforms throughout post–World War II Europe. The most reformist centrist governments have often seemed to advance, when their parade was noteworthy, to a social democratic drummer.

As an author, I stood on the shoulders of many recent students of the welfare state—Chris Hewitt, Gosta Esping-Andersen, Geoffrey Garrett, Peter Lange, Adam Przeworski—when I began work in 1991. Furthermore, my work has been illuminated by examples out of the halcyon 1970s at the Department of Sociology, University of Wisconsin, Madison. So much is possible with a graduate education aided by such persons as Michael Aiken, Robert Alford, Jerald Hage, Rogers Hollingsworth, Erik Olin Wright, and Maurice Zeitlin, to mention senior 1970s political sociologists alone, and (to invoke the names of some fellow graduate students) Gosta Esping-Andersen, John Myles,

Neil Fligstein, and Roger Friedland, and, just down Bascom Hill, Leon Lindberg and the legend of Douglas A. Hibbs Jr.

In a sense this book's origins date back even farther into my New Frontier–era life and, later, Allende-years sojourn in Chile, during its last, tragic realization of Second International Social Democracy. Or perhaps they date back even to the casual household political commentary of my father, Nathaniel W. Hicks, earnest ideologue of several successive stripes: Norman Thomas Socialist, Tom Dewey Republican, Chilean Christian Democrat—and George McGovernite after a prescient 1971 surmise that Richard Nixon was about to compound his brutal Vietnamese "endgame" with Chilean dirty tricks.

For less distant origins of the book I must look, first, to the inspiration received from the perfect intellectual collaborator, Duane H. Swank, who while still a graduate student embarked with me on the study of comparative public policy in the affluent democracies. For the idea of a book as such, perhaps the proddings of Alvin Boskoff and Richard Rubinson were most crucial. For feedback on one or another chapter, I thank Richard Doner, Thomas Lancaster, Michael Mann, Leslie Martin, Lisa Meyer, Tang Nah Ng, Janos Pontusson, Sidney Tarrow, and members of the Department Seminar of the Department of Sociology, Emory University; the Political Economy Seminar, Department of Government, Cornell University; and members of the Department of Sociology, New York University. For generous access to important data, I thank stateside colleagues Duane H. Swank and Michael Wallerstein and Swedes Walter Korpi and Joakim Palme of the Stockholm Institute for Social Research. For reading large portions of manuscript drafts, I am greatly indebted to Robert Alford, Alvin Boskoff, Terry Boswell, Nancy Traynor Hicks, Lane Kenworthy, Frank Lechner, Kristin March, Joya Misra, John Myles, Richard Rubinson, Duane Swank, Jill Quadagno, Michael Wallerstein, and a trio of anonymous reviewers. Linda Beer, Alma Idiart, Cathy David, Lisa Meyer, Joya Misra, Maggie Stephens, and Julie Squires have provided invaluable help with data management and word processing.

Many have provided less direct or intangible (yet invaluable) support along the road to this book's completion. They include deans David Minter and Steven Sanderson of Emory University (generous with leaves of absence); Christopher Jencks and Jane Mansbridge (inspirational friends); Robert Alford, Richard Rubinson, and Jill Quadagno (who liked the manuscript first); Valerie Bunce and Roger Friedland (who demanded and expedited completion); Joya Misra (unhesitatingly helpful); Randy Malamud and Wendy Simond (who extended my library resources to Georgia State); Emory students (who make teaching refreshing); Roger Haydon, my editor at Cornell University Press (who provided three years of invaluable assistence and encouragement); and Nancy and Ryan Hicks, who make everything possible.

Social Democracy and Welfare Capitalism may not be your routine thriller, but let's start off at the movies.

ALEXANDER HICKS

INTRODUCTION

Background and Synopsis

We live in a relatively affluent, liberal democratic, free-market capitalist world. Yet stories of economic insecurity and hardship have been close at hand throughout the past century. The irony is not large, for capitalism is well known to breed insecurity as well as affluence, and democratic politics are well known to allay insecurity. Ironic or not, stories of economic insecurity, like the topic they illuminate, are interesting.

Soon after Antonio Ricci, the protagonist of Vittorio De Sica's 1948 film *The Bicycle Thief*, reports the theft of his bicycle to a Rome police station, a journalist dropping by the station desk asks the on-duty officer if there is any news. "No, nothing. Just a bicycle," responds the officer.

The film audience, however, knows that Ricci's life hangs in the balance. Ricci's new job, pasting up film publicity posters across the length and breadth of Rome, ends a desperate period of unemployment. Keeping this job depends on recovering the bicycle. Just one day earlier, Ricci had liberated his bicycle from hock. Its retrieval had signaled resumption of his role as breadwinner after humiliating dependence on the pittance earned by his son Bruno as a gas station attendant. In celebration, he had seated Signora Ricci and Bruno on the bicycle's handlebars and had ridden them about the streets of Rome. Now unemployment looms again, and yesterday's triumph looks like a fool's paradise.

A day's search by father and son for the stolen bike deepens their relationship, but it proves futile. A church mission thwarts Antonio's request for a free meal with the unpalatable demand that, before eating, he be sheared bald (for possible lice) and bathed. The police reject Antonio's identification of the thief on grounds of insufficient evidence. Then Antonio attempts to steal a bicycle from the bike racks along La Via Panica. However, both the attempt and its subsequent failure forfeit his son's respect.

Whether Antonio Ricci's Roman odyssey is a quest for recovery of the lost bike or a search for amelioration of the consequences of the loss, surrounding circumstances—police, church, crime—frustrate Ricci's resolve at every turn. The elusiveness of employment and the unavailability of public relief hang like storm clouds over Antonio and Bruno's inexorable movement through the streets of Rome. This portrayal is consistent with the economic and political conditions of Italy circa 1950, when the Italian unemployment rate was more than 10 percent (Flora 1983, 470) and when state unemployment compensation covered less than 20 percent of the Italian labor force (Table I.1). At the film's end, Antonio and Bruno are moving forward with palpable courage but little basis for hope. Their fate is written in the character of Italian society rather than in their individual characters, but their unyielding resolve to overcome adds a note of tragic dignity to the prevailing pathos of the film's close.

If *The Bicycle Thief* dramatizes the failures of Italian institutions circa 1950 with regard to employment and unemployment, *Umberto D.* extends De Sica's Italian *purgatorio* to the informal social relations and the problem of old age. Signore Umberto's struggle with aging is as doomed and dignified as is Antonio's with unemployment. "We have worked all our lives," proclaims the placard of an old man protesting the inadequacy of public pensions at the outset of the film. The protesters are scolded and dispersed by the police for demonstrating without a permit. De Sica uses Umberto's encounters with an affluent fellow protester (who won't buy his gold watch), a landlady (who demands owed rent), and a young unwed mother (whose filial affection toward Umberto is insufficient to bring her to form an economically efficient quasifamily with him) to dramatize Umberto D.'s essential dependence on a state unable to meet his needs. Specifically, the Italian state around 1950 provided public pensions for less than one third of its population, and these pensions on average replaced

Table 1.1. Indicators of Income-Security Policy in 1950 and 1980

	Public Pensions[a]				Unemployment Compensation[b]		
	1950		1980		1950	1980	Peak
	C	R	C	R	C	C	Unemployment[c]
Germany	50	41	74	61	35	79	9 (1994)
Italy	31	18	69	75	18	72	14 (1991)
Netherlands	49	50	92	68	—	87	9 (1989)
Sweden	100	27	100	89	34	81	8 (1994)
United Kingdom	67	28	78	50	—	64	12 (1985)
United States	40	39	74	67	39	62	10 (1983)

[a] Data on coverage (C) and income replacement rates (R) for public pension programs from Palme 1990 (29–34).
[b] Data on coverage for unemployment compensation programs from Flora 1987, vol. 4 and (for 1980) from Korpi 1988.
[c] Highest unemployment figure, 1950–1994, with year in parentheses. See OECD, 1960–1995a, esp. 1982.

less than a fifth of the income earned by recipients just before retirement. Still, the state offers Umberto more than the stern police and judges that greets the little tramp in Charlie Chaplin's films set in the United States of a few decades earlier.

There is a lesson to be drawn from these cinematic allusions: If you are not wealthy, you had better have a good job or a responsible government. If you cannot draw subsistence or income from property (dividends, self-employment, savings, insurance, and so on) and are not blessed by the bounty of family, friends, neighbors, or charitable institutions, you'd better have steady employment or a well-developed welfare state.[1]

Economic insecurity has been endemic throughout history, from such things as "invaders' depredations . . . the sudden loss of harvest, the unpredictable vagaries of the weather, the unforeseen death of cattle" (Doyal and Gough 1991, 210). Of course, the spread of modernity has raised aggregate and average living standards. The Industrial Revolution constituted the greatest surge ever achieved in the collective power of the human race over nature. In Britain, the leading early industrializer, by the end of "first wave" industrialization around 1850, "most labor and investment had switched to towns, commerce, and manufacturing. There had never been such a prolonged period of agrarian growth as over the previous three centuries; never such commercial

[1] Although this view obscures overlapping source of goods and services, it is, as we shall see, a modest and useful stylization of the industrialized world.

growth as over [the previous] two centuries; and never the emergence of an urban, manufacturing-centered economy" (Mann 1993, 93–94). By the time of World War I, Michael Mann continues, "the entire West was becoming industrial. Britain and Belgium already were so, most countries were unevenly balanced between industry and agriculture, and agriculture was also thoroughly commercialized." Capitalism's second industrial spurt, from the 1880s on, enhanced the material conditions of all classes and both sexes, enabling "the conquest of bare subsistence and the near doubling of the human life span" (723).

Despite these gains, the nineteenth century's extension of markets and industrial capitalism added new sources of economic insecurity while eroding some traditional solutions to insecurity. Before advanced "commodification" of labor and industrialization, hardship had been cushioned by traditional practices and institutions, including subsistence farming and what Karl Polanyi (1944) has called "social reciprocity and redistribution." The "capitalist system" has added, in the words of Doyal and Gough (1991, 210–211), "a new source of income insecurity," namely, the loss by the "proletariat of access to the means of production, the utter dependence on securing waged labor and, hence, the overwhelming threat of unemployment." More generally, in modern market-oriented society, the material well-being of the typical person, and all that is conditional on it, has depended on (a) personalistic familial and community support, (b) private material assets, (c) employee compensation, and (d) political, or more specifically, state subsidies.

As recently as two centuries ago, assets (above), buoyed by family and community largesse (above), were commonplace, but state and labor market income were scant. According to George Macauley Trevelyan (1937, 22–23), in Britain's preindustrial village, subsistence agriculture, "was the theory and practice of our fathers from the earliest times until the Industrial Revolution." In fact "Subsistence agriculture was still the rule in the first years of George III . . . all over England."

Indeed, all sources of material provision were complemented by family and community in the forms of Karl Polanyi's precapitalist, communal norms of "social reciprocity and redistribution," or what economic historians call the "traditional social wage" (Polanyi 1944, 270). On large estates such as Prussia's, subsistence plots and patriarchal responsibility filled in for gaps in familial and village care (Hamerow 1983, chap. 2). Thus, farmer support from land, kin, and neighbor appears to have been prevalent across agrarian Europe in preindustrial and early industrializing times. The traditional "social wage" disbursed by family and community appears to have been nearly universal in agricultural society (Polyani 1944, 270–279). So, of the various sources of personal security discussed earlier—item (a) personalistic security—prevailed in traditional society. Narrowly *state* income maintenance—or security from source (d)—was scarce. Before its 1880s Bismarckian inauguration, the welfare state was at best an unreliable, begrudging affair mostly confined to means-tested relief measures for the poor of the sort immortalized in the poorhouses of Dickens novels.

This traditional world vanished and a new one advanced. Some sense of the advance is presented in Table I.2. There, for example, we see that between 1850 and 1950, the average percentage of people in the small rural places of fewer than 2000 inhabitants that I have catalogued dropped by about half, from 74.4 percent to 34.6 percent (Table I.2). By the late nineteenth century, massive shifts from agriculture to industry helped generate these changes (Flora 1986a, 252–280, 449–527). Indeed, by the turn of the century, Britain's agricultural labor force had fallen to about 10 percent of its total labor force and its rural population to less than a quarter of total population (Flora 1985, 252–280, 449–527).

Some think of modern capitalism as a society of the self-reliant. Perhaps this is an unequivocal view for early modern capitalism before the turn of the century.[2] However, between 1850 and 1950 the independent share of the labor force constituted by the self-employed fell from more than a quarter to less than a fifth (Table I.2 and Flora 1985, 449–524). Also, the shares of income coming from assets declined in both Britain and the United States between the 1890s and the 1950s. For example, across this period, entrepreneurial and property income from profits, interest, and rents dropped from nearly a quarter of income to about a seventh of income in these nations.[3] As might be deduced, reliance on employer compensation roughly offsets the decline in entrepreneurial and wealth-holding self-sufficiency. From 1890 to 1898 to 1949 to 1958, compensation's share of income rose from just over 50 percent in both nations to just over 70 percent (U.S. Department of Commerce 1971, 238).

[2] Perhaps we also do so correctly if we happen to have familiar circles of small-business persons in mind, for the most decisive decline in the small urban proprietor did not occur until the mid-twentieth century (Mann 1993, 557).

[3] From 1890–1898 to 1949–1958, entrepreneurial and property income fell from 18.8 percent and 27.9 percent, respectively, to 10.2 percent and 17.8 percent, respectively, in the United Kingdom, and they fell from 21.5 percent and 25.7 percent, respectively, to 14.5 percent and 12.4 percent, respectively, in the United States.

Table 1.2. Changing Sites and Sources of Labor Market Independence and Dependence in Selected Nations

	Rural Population[a] (% of Total)		Independent Labor Force[b] (% of Total)		Real GDP per capita[c] ($1980)		Governmental Civilian Employees[d] (% of Population)	
	1850	1950	1850	1950	1870	1950	1880	1950
Germany	63.9	27.6	25.7	14.8	1571	3339	1.42 (1881)	4.03 (1952)
Italy	38.0	7.0	44.1	22.2	1300	2819	1.50 (1881)	3.13 (1851)
Netherlands	—	15.2	—	18.6	1210	4706	1.28 (1889)	2.34 (1947)
Sweden	91.2	53.5	32.4	19.3	1190	5331	1.03 (1890)	3.90
United Kingdom	76.2	19.6	12.8[e]	7.3	1848	5651	—	5.41
United States	—	39.3	—	—	2610	8610	1.51 (1900)	2.58
Unweighted average	74.4	34.6	27.9	16.2	1621	4300	1.35	3.56

[a] European data on residential places of less than 2000 population are from Peter Flora 1985, (252–280) for European nations; U.S. data on residential places of less than 2500 population are from U.S. Department of Commerce 1971, (11) for the United States.
[b] Data from Flora 1985, (449–524) for European nations; U.S. Department of Commerce 1973 for the United States.
[c] From Maddison 1991, Table 1.1.
[d] From Flora 1985, (449–527). (GDP, gross domestic product)
[e] Data point is 1880 for U.K.

However much self-employment and the dispersion of asset income may have spread as the first waves of capitalist modernization rolled back traditional society, self-employment and asset sources of income appear to have contracted over the last hundred years, leaving people to their earnings and state subsidies. As unemployment and retirement circumscribe employee compensation and traditional social relations no longer safeguard large shares of societies from destitution, state subsidies become widely necessary. Fortunately, the same economic revolution that engendered the need for extensive state income support brought forth resources that states could tax to meet this need. Between 1870 and 1950, real income per person increased two- to four-fold and state civilian employment as a share of population grew at a similar pace in the six illustrative cases in Table I.2.

Fortunately, the contemporary welfare state now largely averts the human disasters risked by economic insecurity. Public safeguards for Bruno Ricci's income stability around 1980 far exceeded those available to Antonio Ricci, or Umberto D. in 1950. By 1980, Bruno's chances of eligibility for unemployment benefits, simply as a member of the Italian labor force, would have approached three out of four—a big improvement over the less than one in five (or 18 percent) confronting Antonio Ricci in 1950 (Table I.1). By 1980 the chance that Antonio Ricci would have been eligible for public retirement benefits would have risen to 0.69, more than twice the chance available to Umberto D. in 1950, treating Antonio and Umberto, respectively, as average 1980 and 1950 retirees (Table I.1). Antonio's income replacement rate would have reached nearly 75 percent—four times the rate Umberto might have expected. Antonio's public medical coverage would have improved as well. True, in Sweden, the most developed post–World War II welfare state, we see a less restrained pattern. We see unemployment coverage soar from 34 percent to 81 percent, and we see pension coverage already at 100 percent in 1950. We see income replacement rates jump from 27 percent to 89 percent for retirement insurance. We also see that unemployment rates, commonly over 15 percent in the interwar years, have seldom exceeded 10 percent in the postwar period, although they are now growing increasingly likely to do so (Table I.1).

Indeed, by 1990, levels of welfare spending that varied between 15 and 35 percent of gross domestic product (GDP) substantially reduced poverty, as Kenworthy (1998) definitively shows (Table I.3). Percentages of households (cross-nationally comparable) below poverty lines drawn at 40 percent of national median household incomes are similar, hovering between 20 and 26 percent, when household income is measured "pre-fisc," without adjustment for govermental taxes or income transfers. However, these percentages are far lower—as well as far more variable—"post-fisc," that is, once government taxes and income transfers are taken into account.[4] For the small sample of nations that I am using to convey a sense of cross-national variations in well-being among affluent capitalist democracies, less than 4 percent of Swedish households were poor in 1991, but more than 12 percent of U.S. households were poor post-fisc. If we turn to the income-maintenance function of government for average wage and salary earners—wage earners at median income—we see a more volatile degree of government effectiveness. The "social wage"—the income provided average

---

[4] The technical term is *pre-fisc* and refers to income and income distributions purged of government transfer payments and unaffected by (at least direct) tax levies. Pre-fisc figures are illuminating but imprecise, counterfactual constructs. Exactly what a recipient's income might be if all state fiscal impacts on it, direct or indirect, short-term or long-term, is elusive. Precisely what such an income might be in a world without any government (property laws, police, and so on) is inestimable (Reynolds and Smolensky 1977).

Table 1.3. Percentage Indicators of Income-Security Policy Circa 1990

	Welfare[a] Effort	Pre-Fisc[b] Poverty	Post-Fisc Poverty	Social[c] Wage
Germany	22.2	21.3	6.4	37.0
Italy	22.5	21.8	4.7	15.0
Netherlands	27.7	20.5	4.3	70.0
Sweden	33.4	20.6	3.8	87.0
United Kingdom	16.1	25.7	5.3	18.0
United States	11.7	21.0	11.7	20.0

[a] See ILO 1960–1995 and Chapter 7, Table 7.1.
[b] Relative poverty, percent below 40% of median income from Kenworthy 1998.
[c] See OECD forthcoming; estimates of income replacement from Korpi forthcoming substantially higher.

workers by state income transfer programs during a first year of unemployment and tabulated as a percentage of the median earnings—varies between 15 percent for Italy and over 87 percent for Sweden.

In short, the governments of affluent democratic capitalist nations now provide substantial, and dramatically varying, income subsidies to those at risk of shortfalls in income. The liberal, democratic, free-market capitalist nations, despite essential tilts toward individual and proprietorial freedom, have been moderated by more than the minimal "umpire" state of classical liberal and libertarian theory. Income-security spending alone provides a notable departure from that legendary state.

I stress income security programs that maintain income above some minimal, if less than average, level at times when income falls short of need or precedent and that do so by means of public income transfers and service provisions. A focus on such income security programs has virtually monopolized recent studies of welfare states (Wilensky 1975; Flora and Heidenheimer 1982; Castles 1982; Myles 1989; Friedland and Sanders 1985; Weir, Orloff and Skocpol 1985; Quadagno 1988; Pempel and Williamson 1989; Korpi 1989; Esping-Anderson 1990; Baldwin 1990; Hicks and Swank 1992; but see Cameron 1978, 1984; Weir and Skocpol 1985). This is not surprising if income maintenance is an elementary problem of free-market capitalism. Nonetheless, programs bearing the label of "income maintenance" ("income security," "income supplement," "social security," or "social insurance") address the problem of income insecurity in ways that may concurrently advance goals as far-ranging as status differentiation; class fragmentation; clientelistic dependence; curtailment of market distortions; self-reliance; human capital investment; recommodification; decommodification; social and economic rights; redistribution; and worker, employee, partisan, or citizen solidarity (Esping-Andersen 1990; Janoski 1992).

In particular, Von Arnheim and Schotsman (1982) and Hicks and Swank (1984a) have stressed income redistribution, citing the more than transitionally redistributive nature of income maintenance measures. Korpi (1989, 1991), Esping-Andersen (1990), and others (Palme 1990; Kangas 1991), although focusing on the coverage and income-sustaining capabilities of income maintenance programs, have reinterpreted these in terms of citizen rights. For example, Korpi has reconceptualized rates of program income replacement as social rights in the tradition of Titmuss (1983) and Marshall (1964). Esping-Andersen (1990, Book I) has extended both arguments by stressing political and ideological ends embedded within income maintenance programs.[5]

Esping-Andersen (1990, 21–23) has conceptualized income maintenance programs primarily in terms of the rights embodied in them that realize a measure of "decommodification," which refers to the extent to which a program empowers a citizen to "maintain a livelihood without reliance on the market." However, because state income replacement and subsidization are principal procedures constituting "decommodification," this concept closely resembles that of income maintenance. Table I.4 lists figures for Esping-Andersen's index of decommodification (due to social insurance) to convey some idea of how the most relevant nations rank. Alongside decommodification the table displays how nations stand in terms of the most used measure of income security—welfare effort, or income security as a proportion of GDP.

Esping-Andersen's (1990) conceptualization of welfare programs stresses program consequences other than income maintenance. These include liberal market preservation and a residual for any and all extramarket income; conservative defense and reelaboration of hierarchical social stratification; and social democratic "solidarity" (Esping-Andersen 1990, 26–47). Program features such as universality

---

[5] Attention to such additional or alternative goals of what are at least nominally "income maintenance" programs might cast doubt on the theoretical merits of a focus on income maintenance. Nonetheless, the semantic tautology between the label and functions of "income maintenance" programs is materially compelling: All such programs entail some buoying of lapsed or depressed income as their price for use in additional functions. Most spending- (as opposed to taxing-) based redistribution can be thought of as a by-product of income maintenance.

Table 1.4. Indicators of Cross-National Differences in 1980 Income Maintenance Performance for Eighteen Nations (Percentages)

	Welfare Effort[a]	Decommodification[b]
Australia	11.7	13.0
Austria	22.4	31.1
Belgium	25.9	32.4
Canada	11.6	22.0
Denmark	26.9	38.1
Finland	18.6	29.2
France	26.8	27.5
West Germany	23.0	27.7
Ireland	21.9	23.3
Italy	19.7	24.1
Japan	10.1	27.1
Netherlands	28.9	32.4
New Zealand	16.6	17.1
Norway	20.3	38.3
Sweden	32.3	39.1
Switzerland	13.8	29.8
United Kingdom	15.1	23.4
United States	12.7	17.1

[a] Hicks and Misra 1993, Table 2. Social spending as a percent of GDP is measured.
[b] Esping-Andersen 1990, Table 2.2. Decommodification scales and refers to the extent to which social insurance programs empower a citizen to "maintain a livelihood without reliance in the market" (1990, p. 22)

or particularism of coverage, high or low income replacement rates, and the like, underlie the pervasive income maintenance function of more nationally idiosyncratic stratification and political functions. That is, the sine qua non of income maintenance may be manipulated toward the realization of the diverse additional ends that characterize diverse (e.g., liberal, conservative and social democratic) political projects.[6] In this work I focus on income maintenance, or income security programs, social insurance programs in particular.

The purpose of this work is to explain the variable course of income security programs and benefits in relatively affluent, democratic capitalist nations from their origins in 1880s social insurance reforms of German Chancellor Bismarck until just recently. In Chapter 1 I review and formulate theory concerning the causes of income security policy.

[6] In Esping-Andersen (1990), each of the three political projects entails a matching mode of politics and culminates in a matching policy "regime."

I argue for the promise of class mobilization as a core element in the explanation of income security policy's differential development across democratic capitalism over the last hundred-plus years. In line with work on class mobilization in the rational Marxist and social democratic traditions of work associated with Przreworski (1985) and Garret (1998a), the chapter stresses the empirical concreteness, theoretical range, and historical realism of organizationally specified conceptions of class mobilization. Nonetheless, I stress class action in state context, following leads in Skocpol's (1992) "polity centered" view that nation-states and their policy legacies mediate the influence of group politics—including class politics—on state policy and in line with Mann's (1993) view of the "entwining" of class with state and ideological sinews of power, even within such class-driven domains as industrializing Europe. I anticipate a century-long polyphony of class, state, and income security instruments developed around the central working class theme.

In Chapter 2, I pursue systematic, structured, cross-national comparisons of 1920 consolidations of major types of social insurance programs (aided by qualitative comparative analysis; Ragin 1987). I find that mobilized workers and the state—Social Democrats and Bismarck's state; Labour and Liberal governments; Catholic workers and Catholic governments—variously combine to define routes to early welfare consolidation. A novel view of pervasive, state-contingent worker pressures behind early social insurance reform emerges.

In Chapter 3 I move to the 1930s and 1940s, the era of widespread social democratic participation in, indeed leadership of, governments. I reveal that Social Democrats, typically touted for *post*–World War II reforms, dominated reform in these decades of what I dub the "social democratic ascendance."

Chapter 4 summarizes my argument for the (roughly) 1880 to 1950 period; presents evidence of an underlying labor-union motor for the era's reforms; and offers a recount of Esping-Anderson's *Three Worlds of Welfare Capitalism* (1990).

Chapter 5 turns to the emergence of democratic neocorporatism, which has become a bulwark of the late-twentieth century welfare state and a bridge between eras of social democratic ascendance and welfare state crisis.

In Chapter 6 I chart the course and analyze the causes of core welfare policies since around 1960. Recognizing the volume and variety of the literature on social policy in this era, I introduce an ancillary "political resources" framework to help organize and adjudicate among the sundry facets of this literature. I find that many factors influenced the ebb and flow of welfare spending but that neocorporatism powerfully shaped many of these influences, while partially eclipsing one of the recently most favored—social democratic government.

In Chapter 7, I address questions of welfare state "retrenchment" and economic globalization in some detail. Retrenchment proves a fact to which globalization has contradictory relations. Social democratic governments contest retrenchment.

In Chapter 8, I twice summarize and integrate the welfare history accruing from preceding chapters, the second time with a novel "social movement" account. I end discussing some implications of employee movements and of this work for general theory, future research, and welfare state futures.

Overall, I find that successive national manifestations of a transnational social democratic working class movement—its early mobilizations, its governing roles, and its neo-corporatist incorporation into labor-market policy making—have driven welfare state development from Bismarck until today. Sundry political contingencies importantly help route the drive, but sustained working class steering integrates the journey. Revolutionary transformation at times motivated the drive. However, in the end the historical mission of Western worker politics is the realization of a Progressive liberal agenda that remains relatively unrealized where employee mobilization never much materializes.

CHAPTER ONE

Explanatory Theory and Research Methods

Whether one likes it or not, heuristic structures and canons of method constitute an *a prior.*
(Lonergan 1960, 104)

During the 1880s, German Chancellor Bismarck spearheaded the passage of social insurance programs for victims of industrial accidents, as well as for the sick, the elderly, and disabled retirees and their dependents (Rimlinger 1971, 115–122; Alber 1986, 5–7). The system spread quickly, in part because its principles were easily realigned to serve various interests. The principle of public insurance could be shaped to cater to patriarchal or socialist interests, as in the Germany of 1883 and of 1919, respectively. The contributory principle readily catered both to liberal interests in the subordination of public income to earlier labor market activity and to state-bureaucratic interests in an easily legitimated and administered mode of financing. Money tended to flow to people with low transitional or permanent incomes, so the system tended to redistribute income and allay poverty. The welfare state might be set explicitly to such progressively redistributive purposes. These purposes, like the goal of income security, could be used to aid political mobilization, particularly working-class mobilization. Amid this welter of possible motives for welfare state development, a general principle can be seen at work from Bismarckian conservatives to social democrats: the stabilization of the flow of income (and basic services) for substantial portions of populations at risk of serious income loss. A vast literature has emerged on the origins and development of this income-security state, or welfare state, which ranges over causal forces as varied as the developmental issues discussed in this work's introduction, the policy initiatives of states leaders such as Bismarck, and the pressures exerted on policymakers by working-class organizations and economic conditions.

I begin this chaper with a theoretically oriented review of this literature, continue by devising a theoretical perspective of my own, and end the chapter by outlining the research methods that, along with my theoretical perspective, will discipline the empirical investigation of subsequent chapters. Those indifferent to theory may jump after some perusing to a very substantive Appendix 1 and to Chapter 2.

Theories of the Welfare State

Welfare state literature may be divided at various levels of abstraction and in terms of various perspectives within each level. At a rather abstract level, we can distinguish socioeconomic theories and political ones. Recent debates over the welfare state include discussions of a variety of politically oriented theories, which separate rather nicely into several rudimentary theoretical approaches and other, more synthetic ones.

One rudimentary political approach is a class analytical perspective that stresses, in its most relevant social democratic variant, the reformist effects of left parties rooted in labor unions (Stephens 1979; Przeworski 1985; and Figure 1.1, panel B). From this perspective these unions are, along with left parties, the chief vehicles of working-class mobilization and welfare reform. A second basic approach is the statist one, which stresses the interests and initiatives of politicians, as conditioned—constrained and empowered—by state institutions, albeit in more general societal context (see Heclo 1974; Ashford 1986; and Figure 1.1, panel C). A third is a pluralist approach that casts a conceptual net to harvest possible influences of every strain of group and group association, parties and state factions included, from every remotely democratic society (see Dahl 1982; Laumann and Knoke 1987; and Figure 1.1, panel D).

One synthetic approach consists of a set of neo-Marxist theories that seeks to tame statist and nonclass forces by stressing their class aspects and relevancies (Jessop 1979; Block 1977; Therborn 1979; and Figure 1.1, panel E). A second approach is a polity-centered one that seeks to order a perceived entropy in group and class theories by subordinating their actors to a set of political shaping forces (Skocpol 1985; Skocpol 1992; and Figure 1.1, panel F).

Figure 1.1 Industrial Development, Politics, and the Welfare State

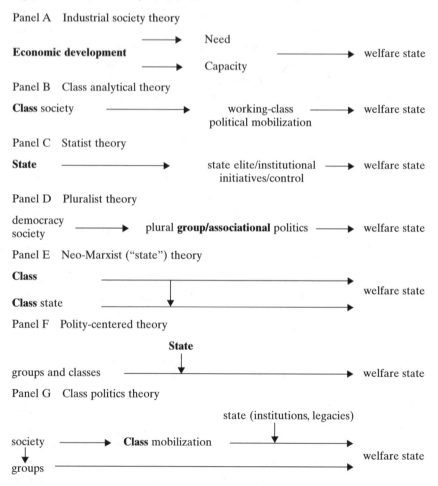

Panel A   Industrial society theory

Economic development ———→ Need / Capacity ———→ welfare state

Panel B   Class analytical theory

Class society ———→ working-class political mobilization ———→ welfare state

Panel C   Statist theory

State ———→ state elite/institutional initiatives/control ———→ welfare state

Panel D   Pluralist theory

democracy society ———→ plural **group/associational** politics ———→ welfare state

Panel E   Neo-Marxist ("state") theory

Class
Class state ———→ welfare state

Panel F   Polity-centered theory

State
groups and classes ———→ welfare state

Panel G   Class politics theory

state (institutions, legacies)
society ———→ **Class** mobilization ———→ welfare state
groups ———→ welfare state

I draw on these theories somewhat eclectically, selecting working variables and hypotheses that I further articulate, aided by my inductive encounter with the history of the welfare state. By so doing, I devise a class-centered but state-mediated theory of the welfare state.[1]

[1] I do this mindful that class theory, to invoke Dahrendorf (1959), may "merely" be an historical instantiation of group theory, perhaps Dahrendorf's own rather elitist as well as pluralistic theory of conflict between bosses and subordinates within "imperatively coordinated" associations and between additional associations of such elites and masses. I also do it without dwelling on Dahrendorf's premature "class" autopsy, indeed with one eye to the possibility that rumors of the Social Democratic demise are much exaggerated.

Before this synthesis of several politically oriented theories is possible, however, theories must be reviewed. Before turning to specific political theories of the type stressed for the last decade or two, some discussion of once prominent and heavily socioeconomic developmental theories, and of industrial society theory in particular, will prove useful. Indeed, some more general theoretical issues bear discussion as well. These introduce some methodological issues to which I return at the end of this chapter.

Literature Review

Literature on the causes of income security policy and, thus, welfare states, bifurcates. One branch focuses on general causes of quantitative dimensions of welfare state programs, whereas the other focuses on more historically specific sources of individual programs, pre– as well as post–World War II. The more generalizing, quantitative literature is narrowly focused on relatively affluent post–World War II democracies and conceptually fragmented by the wide array of theoretical perspectives that underlie the literature. At the same time, the qualitative, historical literature is more historically and geographically far-flung. Moreover, this last literature's inquiries into, at most, a few handfuls of historical cases are disparately conceived. Thus, the qualitative portion of the literature intensifies the impression that work on the welfare state is theoretically fragmented, begging for integration.

I fold brief reviews of the more generalizing and quantitative branch of the literature into reviews principally stressing the more historical branch. (For a full review of the former branch, along with my own quantitative analysis of post–World War II data, see Chapter 6.) For now, my stress is on theory that will be especially useful for the broad sweep of my analysis of 1980s to 1950 program innovations and adoptions or the even broader sweep of my full 1880s to 1990s purview. Let us turn, then, to long-run developmental theories of welfare state development that stick with the kinds of developmental consideration stressed in the introduction.

Industrial Society Theory

Giddens (1973, 217–219) has argued that a theory of industrial society centers the strong functional-structuralist tradition of sociology that runs from Comte through Parsons. In this theory new needs, such as those for income security sketched in the introduction, arise because of transitions from agriculture to industrialism, rural life to urban life, and personal relations to abstract exchange relations. Fortunately, they emerge complemented by imperatives for the efficient and stable operation of the new industrial system. Principal among the structures thrown up by society to satisfy these imperatives are a qualitatively expanded state for which the new system of production provides plentiful resources (Kerr et al. 1964). Integral to the new state is the welfare state, whose major programs should arise more or less inexorably (Myles 1989, 91–93).

In summary, economic development generates welfare states. This development may be capitalist development as well as industrial development. True, theories of capitalist development posit distinct types of policy imperatives, such as "capital accumulation" instead of "societal differentiation" and "legitimation" instead of "consensus," and they foreground different influential social actors, for example, class actors over ethnic actors, but they share with theories of industrial development a focus on underlying economic forces as root causes of social policy. See Table 1.1, Panel A.

The Class Analytical Tradition. Inspired by the "German workers' . . . use of universal suffrage" Engels (1960, 22) wrote that "if it [electoral progress] continues in this fashion, by the end of the century we . . . shall grow into the decisive power in the land before which all other powers will have to bow, whether they like it or not." These are enthusiastic words considering that Germany had not yet attained either representative ascendance over the Prussian monarchs or universal *male* suffrage (Therborn 1977).

Yet the socialist union and party movement was clearly a force to be reckoned with by the time Engels wrote. Although insurance reform was merely tolerated in early socialist manifestos, passage of such reforms appears to have been a hallmark of conservative and liberal appeals to working-class voters and responses to socialist threat at least in Germany and the United Kingdom (Zollner 1982, 1–92; Alber 1986; Ogus 1982, 150–264; Perry 1986). Indeed, socialist skepticism concerning the details and salience of social insurance legislation appears to have been a by-product of more urgent and lofty goals such as work and labor legislation. Nonetheless, once in or close to power, German "Social Democrats and trade unionist" would see "social insurance as 'their' business and one which was worthy of their defense" (Zollner 1982, 1–92). Austrian Social Democrats would crowd their first (1919–1920) participation in government with reforms of extant social insurance laws and passage of the "Unemployment Insurance Law of 20 March 1920."

The Marxian tradition of class analytical thought about capitalist reforms may have had no single engine for capitalist development, but so far as social policy is concerned, it had one principal helmsman. This was the organized working class, the culmination of processes of working-class mobilization and formation in which an interplay between workers' political practices and social organization yielded class identification, understandings, projects, and organizational capabilities for effective collective action (Stephens 1979; Korpi 1983; Przeworski 1985; Hicks and Swank 1984b, 1992; Flora and Alber 1983). A close second for principal relevant actor was the capitalist class, which might, according to its degree of political organization and circumstance, resist, vitiate, or advance social reform (Domhoff 1967; Quadagno 1988).[2]

In works stressing working-class actors, worker militancy, union organization, electoral mobilization, and worker representation by broadly socialist parties (i.e., Social Democratic, Socialist, Labour, and, more marginally, Communist), have been highlighted as sources of income maintenance reform. To date, evidence for reforms by left governments predating the Depression, or even in midcentury, has appeared scattered and unsystematic (Przeworski 1985; Rimlinger 1971; Luebbert 1991). For pre-Depression reforms, the relevance of class analytical approaches—particularly working-class reformers— has appeared limited by a paucity of sustained Left governance (Mackie and Rose 1982; Hicks, Misra and Ng 1995).[3] However, Social Democrats led governments in Denmark, France, New Zealand, Norway, Sweden, and arguably, Spain during the 1930s. Furthermore, even a near-absence of social democratic governments from the welfare state's formative years hardly purges them of working-class influence. On the contrary, each of the two most widely recounted

[2] Works stressing strategic reformist responses of capitalists to perceived popular threats have come under forceful criticism for exaggeration of capitalist control of policy formulations and false identification of particular capitalist reformers with more general capitalist classes or class fractions (e.g., Skocpol and Amenta 1985; Amenta and Parikh 1991; Skocpol 1992). Swenson's (1989) sophisticated reading of Swedish capitalists and reform, which might get beyond these criticisms, has not yet been generalized.

[3] Although class analytical investigators have tended to stress the post-Depression decades of this century (Stephens 1979; Korpi 1983), Mann's (1993, 597–793) 1815–1914 account of economic and political "entwining" in processes of working-class formation parallels our account of working-class "entwinings" with political institutions in pre-Depression welfare state formation. "Entwining" means that causes operate "not like billiard balls, which follow their own trajectories, changing directions as they hit one another" (Mann 1993, 2).

episodes in the early history of income security policy involves a crucial role for working-class mobilization.

During the 1880s German Kaiser Wilhelm signed into law legislation for the world's first national compulsory health, industrial accident, and old age insurance programs. Engineered by Bismarck, these initiatives made use of a large, neoabsolutist bureaucracy (developed mainly for military and tariff administration) to diffuse liberal and, most especially, socialist challenges to traditional, patriarchal rule (Rimlinger 1971; Zollner 1982; Alber 1986; Esping-Andersen 1990; Williamson and Pampel 1993; Mann 1993). The Bismarckian initiatives addressed "Socialist demands which . . . can be realized within the present order of society" (Zollner 1982, 13; Rimlinger 1971). These initiatives involved *a strategic response of a patriarchal state to the growing strength of the socialist workers' movements* (Rimlinger 1971; Zollner 1982; Williamson and Pampel 1993).

In 1906 Britain, Herbert Asquith's Liberal Party and Ramsay MacDonald's Labour Representation Committee (or LRC, the original Labour Party) agreed to ally themselves in the common pursuit of Liberal-Labour parliamentary majorities, governments, and social reforms (Marwick 1967; Ogus 1982; Luebbert 1991). The national pension, health, and unemployment insurance laws of 1908 to 1911 figured importantly among resulting social reforms. The Asquith government of 1906 to 1914 provides a prominent example of the type of turn-of-the-century liberal government engineered by liberals with labor union and labor party assistance that Mann (1993) and others have termed *Lib-Lab*. Although some authors have stressed the importance of such middle-class associations as the National Pension Committee and the Fabians, putting an interest-group spin on the Lloyd George reforms (Kloppenberg 1986; Williamson and Pampel 1993), the United Kingdom is reasonably judged to have taken a Lib-Lab route to the welfare state. This emerged from *the strategic responses of Liberal government to growing labor strength* (Marwick 1967; Ogus 1982; Mann 1993).

Both Bismarckian and Lib-Lab roads to the early welfare state may be generalizable beyond single cases. They warrant the general hypothesis that *working-class mobilization, combined with various political-institutional conditions, was a pervasive source of early welfare state formation.*

Historically oriented works indicate that early working-class mobilization affected social policy largely insofar as working-class actions were mediated by state paternalism and political democracy. Some works highlight the strategic responses of paternalistic rulers like Bismarck to incipient socialist organization (Draper 1977 and Esping-Andersen 1990). Others underline the liberating functions of democracy and state centralization for socialist reforms (Engels [1890] 1960; Stephens 1979; Przeworski 1985). Yet other works focus on the Depression and immediate post–World War II years, indicating a period of great social democratic reformist efficacy.

Such combinatory causes as Bismarckian preemptions of worker movements and Lib-Lab synergy have recently been recast in the "entwining" formulations of Mann (1993), the "mediations" of Wright (1978) and the "configurative" arguments of Ragin (1987). Mann (1993) has theorized causal pathways to the incorporation of industrial workers into industrial capitalist power networks in terms of the interaction (or "entwining") of underlying economic forces (e.g., market-oriented economies, industrial capitalist firms) and "political crystallizations" (e.g., "semiauthoritarian" in Germany, "Liberal-representative" in France and the United Kingdom).[4] More abstractly, "mediation" or interactive modes of determination have been extensively used following the model of Wright (1978); and Ragin (1987, 1993a) has claimed a central role for configurative causation in historically intensive, case-oriented investigations.

Consistent, then, with class analytical traditions that date back to Engels ([1890] 1960) and Marx ([1969]), *democracy and working-class mobilization* (class consciousness, labor and party organization, and so on) have been found to advance welfare state reform. Recent studies indicate that even though democracy did not open the floodgate to demands for mass redistribution, it did, at least, function as a sluice gate that permitted an ample flow of income security reforms (Pampel and Williamson 1985). Affirmation of the reformist clout of labor and social democratic movements rings sharply through the empirical literature on the welfare state, although temporally specific claims for working-class efficacy seldom apply to pre-Depression years. Also, Marxists have stressed capitalist development as a source of changing class forces and their balance of power (Rueschemeyer, Stephens, and Stephens 1991). Finally, *working-class mobilization, combined with various political-institutional conditions, appears to have been a pervasive source of early welfare state formation.*

Before further discussion of "combinatory" causation, it is best to

---

[4] Instead, "they entwine, that is, their interactions change one another's inner shape as well as their trajectories" (Mann 1993, 2), going beyond "monocausality," independent causes, or even "interaction." (See Note 3 on "entwining.")

turn to the statist and pluralist perspectives, which will extend our range of prospective causes. See Table 1.1, Panel B.

Statist Approaches. Statist approaches direct our attention to the self-aggrandizing propensities of state actors and the policymaking capabilities and orientation of state institutions (Hicks and Swank 1992). With regard to both these topics, attention has been especially focused on the self-aggrandizing and empowering actions of paternalistic state autocrats. Rimlinger (1971), Heclo (1974), Flora and Alber (1983), and many others have narrated the strategic response of Bismarck to early socialist workers movements. Esping-Andersen (1990, 59–60) has stressed the tendencies of "etatist paternalism" to "endow civil servants with extraordinarily lavish welfare provisions . . . extend basic guarantees of income protection . . . to grant relief . . . informed by the age old principle of *noblesse oblige*." He has grounded these policy tendencies in a readiness to "grant social rights albeit conditional upon morals, loyalties or conventions . . . a strong opposition to individualism and liberalism . . . and an absolutist model of paternal-authoritarian obligation for the welfare of its [the state's] subjects" (p.40).

The focus on state capabilities has been wide-ranging. It has encompassed attention to all of the following: the capacities of states for sophisticated diagnoses and prescriptions for social problems (Weir and Skocpol 1985); strong administrative precedents and policy legacies (Skocpol 1985; Ashford 1986); reform of state clientelistic and patronage systems (Orloff and Skocpol 1984); majoritarian parliamentary government (Lijphart 1984); program-specific centralization of policy administration (Hage, Gargan, and Hanneman 1989; Amenta and Carruthers 1988); veto points for the frustration of state initiatives that move swiftly in unitary, hierarchical organizations of state jurisdictions (Hicks and Swank 1992; Mann 1993); and the concentration of popular mobilizations for reform at the apexes of centralized, unitary states (Lijphart 1984; Hage, Gargan, and Hanneman 1989; Hicks and Swank 1992; Mann 1993).

For the most part, the statist emphasis on policymaking and implementation is a focus on state organizational forms affecting state policymaking and administering capabilities (Amenta and Carruthers 1988). A principal stress is on state centralization in its various jurisdictional, administrative, and governmental modes (Blondel 1969, 283–320; Lijphart 1984). By focusing reformist demands on a national state, expediting their translation into reform, and serving as sources of, as well as channels for, reform impulses, centralization advances the programmatic constitution and development of the welfare state.

I simplify the statist picture of state capacities by focusing on state centralization.

Statist works have also stressed policy legacies and policy-relevant ideas (Orloff and Skocpol 1984). The British legacies of fiscal conservatism and classical economic orthodoxy (from the collapse of the gold standard until World War II) and of periodic deficit financing and Keynesian macroeconomic theory (a few decades thereafter) may serve as examples of the power of such ideas and legacies (Skidelsky 1967, 1982; Weir and Skocpol 1985).[5]

Consistent with statist, elitist, and managerial traditions dating back to Pareto (1935) and before, *autocracy and such state structural capabilities as unitary state organization* have been found to advance welfare state reform. Not only have diffuse operations of state elites been recorded (e.g., Mosca 1939; Higley and Burton 1989), notable contributions of patriarchal elites and institutions to income security reform have also been documented (Rimlinger 1971; Flora 1986b; Esping-Andersen 1990; Hicks and Swank 1992; and Hicks and Misra 1993). In addition, state centralization has been found to facilitate state responsiveness to income security demands by reducing veto points for the potential obstruction of national reforms (Pampel and Williamson 1989; Hage et al. 1989; Hicks and Swank 1992; Hicks and Misra 1993; Huber, Stephens, Ragin 1993). Indeed, unitary democracy may be a crucial state structural variable for the realization of early social insurance reforms. In democratic polities, unitary state structures appear to facilitate reform by limiting the opportunities for antireformist policy vetoes provided by multiple levels and branches of government (Hicks and Swank 1992; Huber et al. 1993), whereas in nondemocracies, autocratic power may suffice to override ostensibly federal dispersions of state authority (Taylor 1946, 119; Blondel 1969). Indeed, at a glance, early social policy reforms in political democracies appear to have been concentrated in unitary states such as Great Britain and Denmark but to have been rare in federal democracies such as Switzerland and the former British settler colonies (Castles 1985; Baldwin 1990). Thus, we expect to find that *autocratic states and unitary democracies*—if only in conjunction with such other factors as early working-class mobilization—accelerated early welfare state formation.

Statist students of the postwar era continue in a similar vein. They

---

[5] Recently, some "state-centered" theorists have broadened their focus to encompass political as well as more formal executive, legislative, judicial, and administrative facets of political institutions (Weir, Orloff, and Skocpol 1988; Amenta and Carruthers 1988; Skocpol 1992).

argue that welfare effort is generated by relatively autonomous state institutions and elites and, in particular, by relatively centralized, clientelistic states and liberal states and elites (DeViney 1984; Orloff and Skocpol 1984).

Pluralist Theory. Democratic pluralists focus on the historical liberation of popular political rights and demands from authoritarian fetters by the institution of democracy (Dahl 1971, 1982; Pampel and Williamson 1989). They also focus on the vision of a plurality of social bases for political demands and practices. These bases include economic sectors as well as classes, cultural (e.g., ethnic, religious, regional, linguistic) as well as narrowly economic groupings, state as well as societal social locations, and identifications as well as interests (Dahl 1982; Lijphart 1984).

The approach's proliferation of the sources of political demands and practices yields fine-grained but rather open-ended expectations about the sources of income maintenance policy. For many pluralists, theory can only complete the specification of forces affecting a particular outcome in combination with empirical information of the situations and orientations of particular actors in particular settings (Alford and Friedland 1985, 22, esp. n. 4). Subjective preferences, whether viewed as fundamentally personal attributes or merely personal reflections of objective cultural schema, are privileged over objective interests as causes of action and are viewed as substantially independent of social structure.

Still, some expectations are provided. Given prevalent social insecurity, democracy (competitive politics, electoral enfranchisement and turnout, and so on) should produce group pressures for income security. For example, it should facilitate the effective mobilization of the elderly (Pampel and Williamson 1989). Moreover, a range of centrist and interclass, as well as working-class, parties advance demands for income maintenance. This is so in part because of the variety of demographic and other nonclass situations that give rise to income insecurity, indeed the almost societal reach of economic risk (Pampel and Williamson 1989; Baldwin 1990). *Democracy (or nonautocracy) tends, at least in combination with certain other factors, to advance welfare reform.*

Consistent with the wide scope of pluralist theory, *centrist governments as well as Left democratic governments* have been found to advance welfare state reform (Castles and McKinlay 1978; Pampel and Williamson 1985, 1989; Esping-Andersen 1990; Hicks and Misra 1993; Huber et al. 1993; Ragin 1993b). In particular, government by Liberal and cross-class Catholic parties preceding World War II, and by Christian Democratic parties since then, appears to have enacted substantial income security reform (Berghman, Peters, and Vranken 1987; Roebroek and Berben 1987; Baldwin 1990; Huber et al. 1993). Various interest groups and reform movements, nonpartisan as well as partisan, also seem to have been important (Skocpol 1992; Williamson and Pampel 1993). Pluralists have stressed the impacts of development as a process of social differentiation and empowerment generating social needs and state capabilities, as well as political demands conducive to the provision of income security (Wilensky and Lebeaux 1958; Wilensky 1975; Williamson and Pampel 1993).

According to pluralist conceptions, welfare effort, placed on the political agenda by the development of new socioeconomic resources and needs, tends to be directly driven by the demands of groups able to wield "swing votes," by the lobbying activities of interest organizations more generally, and by the routine administration of statutorily encoded entitlements (Pampel and Williamson 1988). In addition, a range of broadly similar attempts to synthesize more parochial perspectives argues that political institutions and actors encompass, or at least mediate effects of, the full array of forces determining welfare policy (Skocpol 1992; Hicks and Misra 1993; Mann 1993).

Critiques and Synthetic Alternatives

Marxist and statist theories tend to belie each other: In juxtaposition each looks too narrow. For example, Huber and Colleagues' (1993) claims for the worker-inclusive consequences of proportional representation reach beyond class analysis. To turn the coin over, Crepaz and Birchfield's (1998) claims for the pro-welfarism of consensual government reach beyond statism. Pluralism is likewise narrow, as when pluralist celebrants of American diversity expunge class, or it risks being too open-ended, as when Dahl (1982) constructs a pluralism that, although hyperfragmented in the United States, may be dyadic in Sweden or tripartite in Austria. Industrialization may indirectly promote welfare states, but automatic state responses to new "industrial society" needs ring hollow in the light of theoretical discussions of actual politics.

Neo-Marxist state theory and polity-centered theory offer us candidate syntheses (Prezeworski 1990; Skocpol 1992), but are syntheses that ignore industrial society theory credible? How can we choose between neo-Marxist state theory and polity-centered theory? Have we no other choice? I turn now to the first of these questions.

Industrial Society Theory and Its Political Competitors: Development, Politics, and Welfare State

It has been shown for recent decades that the level of economic development strongly correlates with levels of social spending (normed on GDP) across global populations of nations but that it hardly does so within the subpopulation of more developed nations (Pampel and Williamson 1989; Williamson and Williamson 1993). Indeed, there are indications that development—or some threshold of it—may be merely a permissive background condition, a necessary but quite insufficient condition for democracies and the democratic politics that steer welfare state development (Collier and Messick 1967). Development might even function as a mere necessary condition for welfare state emergence, roughly paralleling the impact hypothesized by Dahl (1971) for the emergence of polyarchies. That is, it might determine the candidates for welfare state emergence and then step aside for politics to choose among these.

In these analyses developmental (and political) variables are cross-tabulated and correlated with measures of social insurance program consolidation, or *early welfare state consolidation*. This is the adoption of at least three of the four major social insurance programs—those for victims of work injury, retirees, the sick, and the unemployed—by the end of the post–World War I political reorganization. Such consolidation is regarded as a programmatic foundation for subsequent welfare state development and, in fact, it is: a simple dummy variable for the adoption of three or more social insurance programs by 1920 correlates 0.620 with welfare effort (social spending as a percent of GDP) in 1980 and 0.446 with Esping-Andersen's (1990) "decommodification" measure of social insurance quality in 1980![6] And development, indeed, seems to nominate the candidates for welfare state emergence and then leave their final selection to politics.

This is what the original analyses presented in Appendix 1 suggest. Without a substantial level of economic development, here specified as per capita income over $2000 (in 1982 dollars), welfare states do not

---

[6] Here, consolidation is accounted by using the dating of programs devised for measuring of 1920 consolidation that was constructed for the extensive analyses of Chapter 2 (see Appendix 2.1). (This is a dating that requires that a program have either "substantial" coverage or funding.) Decommodification is drawn directly from Esping-Andersen (1990, 52). Nations analyzed are the fifteen nations for which such detailed dating were compiled for the Boolean comparisons of Chapter 2 (see Appendix 2.1). Correlation between a measure of cumulative social insurance program experience (Cutright 1965) and 1980 measures of decommodification and welfare effort are 0.698 and 0.552, respectively.

consolidate basic programs. That is, the adoption of at least three of the four major social insurance programs—those for victims of work injury, retirees, the sick, and the unemployed—by the end of the post–World War I political reorganization period was not clearly achieved by any nation that had not exceeded a per capita GDP level of $2000 (in real 1980 dollars) by shortly before that. At that time, an undeveloped nation was almost certain to have no substantial welfare states (see Table A1.2). A developed nation was more likely than an undeveloped one to have achieved a degree of welfare state consolidation, to be a Britain rather than a Canada (see Table A1.2). However, knowing the degree of development *within* the globally developed nations provides no more help in distinguishing 1920 consolidators.

Working-class mobilization proves to be a potent correlate of welfare state consolidation among just such developed nations (see Table A1.3). Quantitative analysis of these data indicates working-class mobilization (and nonmobilization) postdicts welfare state consolidation (and nonconsolidation) around 1920 quite well. Fully seven of eight developed nations with socialist voter or union membership levels over my mobilization thresholds of 20 percent (of voters and labor force participants, respectively) consolidated welfare states. Only one of seven developed nations without such class organizational resources did so, that being the dubiously "consolidated" Romania. In short, economic development looks as though it served as a mere gateway to the arena within which substantial welfare state emergence was possible and not as a determinant of final emergence. Among developed nations, it is *politics* that seems to have determined which nations actually consolidated early welfare states.

This arena of early economic developers closely approximates the domain of early "proto democracies" and later, long-standing democracies (delineated later in this chapter) that I single out for study in this book. Politics seems crucial to early welfare state development within this domain, at least as crucial as it does to the extremely well studied subject of post–World War II welfare states. Accordingly, my theoretical focus is a relatively political one that concentrates on the class analytical, statist, and pluralist theories reviewed earlier, as well as on recent politically orientated attempts at explanatory synthesis. My own attempt at original synthesis will be likewise political, as well as middle-range and open to historical evidence and inductive insights. I draw on empirical evidence guided by some larger assumptions and expectations, however.

One assumption is that social democratic and statist approaches are dangerously overfocused, and pluralist ones are open-minded to the verge of indeterminancy. A second assumption is that social actors, albeit at every point institutionally constrained as well as empowered, must be driving forces for an institutional (i.e., welfare state) development. A third is that the social democratic actors, as constituted by insecurity and disadvantage and political orientation, are the actors most likely to drive the development of a redistributive income security state. A fourth is that the most pertinent constraints on this political project, at least within the confines of polities, are likely to be best identified by statist—and polity-centered—writings. I also assume that historical serendipity (theoretically aided) will be as useful as theoretical deduction in the quest for explanatory accuracy.

On the basis of these assumptions, I develop a class politics theory, that is, a class-centered, if state-mediated, theory of the welfare state. This stresses a central, dynamic, persistent, and unifying role of working-class mobilization, yet it views class action as fundamentally framed by the state (Figure 1.1, panel G). It stresses a powerful, if historically delimited, role for class (see note 1). Before attempting my own synthesis, I examine neo-Marxist and "polity-centered" ones.

Neo-Marxist theories of the state incorporate statist and nonclass forces by stressing their class aspects, and their particular causal relevance to focal issues. The central claim here is that the state and (more particularly) certain state institutions make the state a *capitalist* state that cannot transgress the essential interests of those who own the productive wealth of society (Przeworski 1990, 65). Briefly and abstractly, the argument is made that some necessary conditions for capitalist survival, unavailable from the market, must be provided by the state (Poulantzas 1973; Offe 1975; Block 1977, 1980). Yet this argument is attacked for some typically functionalist deficiencies. (Why "*necessary*"? Why "*must*"?) Has not the core "necessity" of a "planning state" been repudiated by business since the Thatcher ascendancy (Przeworski 1985)? Is not the necessary knowledge needed for a compliant elite of a guardian state disproved by the repeated failures of Great Depression reforms—from Roosevelt's quickly spurned National Recovery Administration (Finegold and Skocpol 1995) to Hitler's ultimately destructive war economy (Block 1980)? General control of states and ideological institutions, although claimed by Miliband (1973) and others is surely an overstatement (Skocpol 1981; Amenta 1998). A structural dependence that proscribes progressive income redistribution faced exceptions and refutations (see Ringen and Uustitalo 1992, on Scandinavia; Przeworki and Wallerstein 1988, on possible redistributions). State structures may express past working-class defeats, as a weak U.S. Department of Labor was shown to by DiTomaso (1979), but they may also express working-class victories, such as the franchise praised by Engels ([1890] 1960) or, although class-relevant, express much more than class (e.g., proportional representation, federalism). True, specific propositions do seem useful. For example, capitalist disinvestment can strike effectively at redistributive governments (e.g., Allende's Chilean one), and conservative state structures may reflect proprietor savvy, as with U.S. right-to-work laws. However, their power is limited. For example, the Second New Deal was *not* stymied by a hostile business community (Amenta 1998). Proportional representation tends to empower workers by promoting greater working-class representation (Huber et al. 1993). See Table 1.1, Panel E.

Polity-centered theory uses a focus on state power to order group (and class) processes that are rather loosely organized by others. It grants the state autonomous power, rooting it in such state resources as state monopolies over the legitimate use of violence and the direction and administration of certain collective functions (e.g., highways and sewage systems, national security, and international agreements). It also sees the state as framing citizen political actions through its institutional structures and policy legacies (Skocpol 1992, chap. 1). The former is a compelling argument for most except Marxists, who tend to narrowly relativize (i.e., limit) the autonomy of the state. The latter, "framing" argument is compelling even for neo-Marxist state theorists, insofar as they grant the state ad hoc mediating roles such as that of the franchise as prerequisite for Social Democratic electoral practices (Engles [1890] 1960; Stephens 1979; Przeworski 1985). The argument for policy legacies also seems compelling. Polices aimed at outcome Y facilitate subsequent politics aimed at achieving Y, even sometimes to aid in their proliferation elsewhere (Abbott and DeViney 1992). Differences in particular state administrative capacities help explain outcomes as divergent as the brief life of Roosevert's National Recovery Administration and the enduring success of the Agricultural Adjustment Administration (Finegold and Skocpol 1995).

I have already presented hypotheses conditioning working-class welfare innovations on state contingencies, suggesting sympathy with the polity-centered principle of state-mediated (or reshaped) class effects. Nonetheless, as anticipated earlier in this chapter, I expect that working-class origins, identities, organizations, and goals are so tied to distributional, security, and living standard questions addressed by social insurance programs that class politics will be a continuing theme—a persistent determinative force—in the history of welfare states. I also expect that state structures and policy legacies will so frame the possibilities and courses for class politics that they would be quite shapeless without them. However, many state structures and legacies, from degrees of centralization to tax-raising capacities, will be disparate and accidental in origins with respect to welfare state politics. Other political factors will be outcomes of earlier spells of welfare politics, including class politics. With political contingencies of such divergent—sometimes class—origins, the direction, continuity, and logic of the politics of social insurance appear more a function of class than state. Class is expected to be more like the traveler and the state to be more like the terrain—or highway system—traversed.

Theory selection has always been a function of the questions asked (Alford and Friedland 1985). For the question of social politics, I pick *a class-centered theory of state politics* that stresses state-framed but class-driven processes, although without regarding the state as inessential or the politics of nonclass groups as irrelevant ex ante. This class-centered state politics theory is much like those variants of the neo-Marxist theory of the state that grant prominence to state as well as class, but it does *not* assume that the aspects of the state that impinge importantly on class are in turn class derived. It is much like polity-centered theory in that it acknowledges the relevance of class processes, as in Weir and Skocpol (1985), but it reverses priorities from a focus on state determinants that entail subordinated class (as well as other group) processes, to a focus on class processes importantly contingent on the state (Figure 1.1, panel G). It creates expectations that one might trace the direction of welfare state development to the hands of a class driver, rather than to the contours of the state terrain. This seems especially likely for destinations sought across an ever-changing landscape.

The theoretical perspectives just discussed, especially the class politics theory, will guide period-specific analyses. For some periods, additional theoretical tools will be introduced as needed. In particular, political resource theory will aid with the post–World War II period and social movement theory with integration of all the analyses.

A Theoretical Domain

I focus my attention on the welfare states of affluent capitalist democracies. These practically motivate attention because they are the earliest, most developed, and most generous of welfare states across the whole history of the institution: They capture the origins and limits of the welfare state. Methodologically, they warrant selection because they constitute a coherent theoretical domain.

They make for a coherent object of study for several reasons. For one, I expect regularities in macroscopic social processes to largely mirror commonalities in social institutions, rather than some invariant and undifferentiated human nature (Lonergan 1957; Ruechemeyer et al. 1991). For example, I am more confident of a theory of electoral participation in democracies than I am in a "general" theory of political participation; and I would be hard-pressed even to identify common hypothetical causes in institutional systems that were extremely heterogeneous. Developed democratic capitalism has substantial institutional commonalities.

During roughly the 1880 to 1920 period, economic development appears to be coterminous with capitalist development, albeit a capitalist development variously embedded in residues of precapitalist social organization as well as in a range of political crystallizations (Mann 1993). At least a very high proportion of "developed nations" (however we demarcate them) are characterized by such institutional similarities as capitalist firms and markets. In addition, the bulk of the developed nations appear to be democracies or, at least, protodemocracies. That is, they all manifest some definitive features of political democracy as characterized by Dahl (1971), Therborn (1977), and Rueschemeyer et al. (1991): free and competitive elections of top governmental/legislative officials, extensive suffrage, ample legislative authority in the legislature, and rights of expression and association. True, some are exclusive democracies with competitively elected, authoritative, yet restricted franchises such as pre-1917 Holland (Therborn 1977). Further, Austria and Germany, two of our relatively developed nations, were less than democratic through World War I. Yet Austria and Germany contained substantially democratic institutional elements by the 1870s. They are nations marked by competitively and extensively elected legislatures, albeit ones marred by incomplete enfranchisement, property-weighted votes, and occasional imperial circumscriptions of authority (e.g., suddenly suspended laws and outlawed parties). Both of these nations, indeed all of the world's most developed nations, as we shall see, were characterized by extensive associational life and by some electoral/legislative activity during much of the 1880s to 1920s period studied here. (Recall my evocation in the opening to this chapter of Bismarck's extensive accommodations of his social insurance designs to an uncooperative legislature.) This combination of developed capitalist and democratic (and protodemo-cratic) traits goes some way toward grounding both an institutionally cohesive theoretical domain and a reasonable, "most similar nations" strategy for the study of program consolidation (Pzreworski and Teune 1970). In addition, my theoretical domain appears to have been insti-tutionally homogeneous beyond the simple similarities of capitalism and democracy, at least initially. Its elements are almost all initially European, whether via geographic location or the geographic origin of the majority of their populations.[7] All share such institutional details as the departmental firm, contract law, working-class movements, and the voluntary association. As shown in Appendix 1, all initially shared prosperity beyond a threshold of economic development necessary for substantial welfare state development.

In short, if we simultaneously put some value on theoretical generality and institutional specificity, relatively developed democratic capitalism would appear to be a good bet for a sufficiently homoge-neous world—capitalist, productive, democratic or protodemocratic, bureaucratic, literate, national, statist, and so on—to sustain important generalizations about the politics of social policy. True, political differences among members of the type of nation in question may well be ample enough to differentiate these processes (Mann, 1993, chaps. 17–21). However, overall, similarities are a good bet to ground some common, integrative patterns.

The nations first selected for the 1880 to 1920 analyses in chapter 2 are Australia, Austria, Belgium, Canada, Denmark, France, Germany, Italy, the Netherlands, New Zealand, Norway, Sweden, Switzerland, United Kingdom, and the United States. This population loses Austria, Germany, and Italy during their Fascist spells but regains them, along with newcomers Finland, Japan, and Ireland, after World War II.[8]

A Methodological Preview

I shall historically and comparatively analyze the appearance of programs (and sets of programs) in about fifteen nations from 1880

[7] This is true for such turn-of-the-century early developers as Argentina and Uruguay, which qualify for a time but lack the data to permit their analysis. It is also true for the marginally more economically advanced Australia, the United States, and Great Britain. It is true for Japan, once it is included here for the 1940s (in effect, her post–1945) analyses.
[8] Argentina, Spain, Uruguay, and Czechoslovakia are excluded early when "top devel-opers" for want of complete and reliable data. Until after World War II, Ireland is excluded for excessively mimicking British social policy, Finland for Russian depen-dence and later limited franchise, Japan for undevelopment (see Chapter 2).

to 1950 and statistically analyze year-to-year traits of programs from 1960 to 1990 in eighteen nations.

Ragin (1987) has famously distinguished between two approaches to comparative social research, and he has provocatively proposed an intermediate approach. One is a case-oriented approach that stresses a few wholistically characterized cases and logically analyses these characterizations for potentially explanatory patterns. Typically, emergent explanatory patterns stress conjunctions of characteristics inductively arrived at, such as that of state breakdowns and peasant insurrections found by Skocpol (1979) to explain social revolutions in such agrarian empires as Czarist Russia and Bourbon France. The other is a variable-oriented approach that stresses relations among variables analyzed statistically across numerous cases. Typically, (variable) outcomes emerge from such analyses as linear additive functions of explanatory variables. Ragin's (1987) intermediate approach is one that uses Boolean tools of logical computation to expedite the analyses of characterizations of intermediate numbers (e.g., 10 to 30) of cases. Typically, a number of alternative explanatory conjunctures emerge inductively from what Ragin has dubbed "qualitative comparative Analysis," or QCA. For example, he concludes that ethnic political mobilization (E) results either from a combination of large (S) and growing (G) "subnations" or from subnational literacy in a separate subnational language (L) and subnational wealth (W): $E = S$ and G or L and W. Appendix 2 introduces QCA to readers not familiar with it (Ragin 1987).

Lonergan (1957, 103–140) divides scientific investigations of concrete systems into his own duo: (a) studies of the emergence of things (such as carbon molecules, jackrabbits, and states, and varieties of these) and (b) studies of covariation among the attributes of these things.

In this light, it is predictable that the burgeoning explanatory literature on the social security state diverges into two strands. One, relatively qualitative, case-centered, and historically intensive, stresses the emergence and fundamental transformations of major social security programs (Wilensky and Lebeaux 1958; Rimlinger 1971; Heclo 1974; Orloff and Skocpol 1984; Quadagno 1988; Usui 1993; Baldwin 1990; Abbott and DeViney 1992; Skocpol 1992; Orloff 1993). The typical product of this research stream identifies particular, "idiographic" causal sequences on the basis of intensive historical scrutiny backed up by cross-national (or cross-period) comparison. The other, highly quantitative, multivariate, and generalizing, focuses on trends, fluctuations, and variations in dimensions of spending and benefit provisions for "welfare" programs within the well-structured domain provided by institutionalized welfare capitalism (Cutright 1965; Wilensky 1975; Castles 1982; Myles 1989; Korpi 1989; Pampel and Williamson 1985; Esping-Andersen 1990; Hicks and Swank 1992; Huber et al. 1993; Ragin 1993; Hicks and Misra 1993). Its characteristic products are mathematical functions claimed to map, if not capture, abstract social laws and real-system regularities.[9]

In short, through midcentury I analyze qualitative program changes quite inductively by using QCA, backed by simple cross-sectional regression analyses. What data are available before mid-century are too incomplete to ground any effort at comprehensive quantitative modeling. Moreover, through mid-century, my questions stress qualitative outcomes—program adoptions and consolidations of the programmatic foundations for subsequent welfare state develop-ment—and I view such qualitative outcomes as historical events too tied to societal contexts, too short on orderly institutionalization, and too prone to causal heterogeneity for the highly formulaic expecta-tions of typical multiple regression analysis to hold. QCA especially suits such data because of its sensitivity to alternative explanatory con-junctures. It does so as well because of its inductive humility: by means of QCA, data and logic prune and order lists of proposed explanatory characterizations of cases into often unforeseeable explanatory for-mulations. Regression analyses are appropriate where QCA counsels simple additive explanation in certain historical contexts (as it largely does in Chapter 3 for the 1930s and 1940s).

After midcentury, I statistically analyze quantitative program traits, such as program expenditures and benefit levels, across large, pooled arrays of national time series. I do this guided by rather general theoretical propositions and theory testing procedures.

Both relatively qualitative and relatively quantitative modes of analysis are nested in, and enriched by, historical accounts of relevant historical periods. When both sorts of analyses are done, I attempt to tell a brief story—or meta-story—of the history of the welfare state in advanced capitalism by drawing together the analyses and ac-companying historical accounts.

[9] True, the two genres overlap. For example, Usui (1993) and Ragin (1993b) bring formal techniques of multivariate analysis to bear upon the emergence of qualitative outcome, whereas Baldwin (1990) and Orloff (1993) bring systematic frameworks and comparisons to bear upon their fine-grained historical analyses. Moreover, each has dis-tinct variants. For example, Orloff (1993) studies successions of major program changes, but Baldwin (1990) emphasizes transformations of particularistic and means-tested policy regimes into universalistic and egalitarian policy regimes.

Now I turn, with the help of the theoretical and methodological guidelines described in this chapter, to the first of a set of comparative analyses. Again, for theoretical guidance I draw on class, statist, and pluralist theories alike, but most attentively on a class-centered, state-framed theory of politics. For methodological guidance, I draw on Boolean formalizations of comparative historical analysis: not-so-fancy aids to the scrutinizations of cross-tabulations of data for simple logical patterns. My analyses collapse into simple multiple regression analyses where reality seems too blurry for logical patterns or plain enough for simple regressions. These first analyses are about how advanced consolidations of major social insurance programs emerged around the close of World War I and were modified in subsequent decades.

A P P E N D I X 1

Development, Politics, and Welfare Consolidation

On Economic Development and Welfare State Development

A promising laboratory for examining relations between development and welfare states is provided by the period of welfare state emergence amid the great turn-of-the-century "first wave" of the Continental Industrial Revolution. One means of focusing on welfare state emergence is to examine the point at which nations have adopted variants of all or most types of social insurance programs—work accident, retirement, health, and unemployment social insurance programs (Gordon 1988). A broadly used accounting of such adoptions, reported in Table A1.1, shows dates of some early adoptions of these programs (U.S. Dept. of Health and Human Services 1990). The close of the wave of political reform after World War I seems a good time to assess early welfare state emergence, so dates are shown for programs as of 1920. Few nations were quick to adopt all of these programs, even as late as

Table AI.I. A Preliminary Look at National Social Insurance Program Adoption and Consolidation in 1920 for Nations Stressed in this Study: Adoption Dates in Columns

	Work Accident	Health	Pension	Unemployment
Austria	1887	1888	1906	1920
Denmark	1898	1892	1891	1907
Italy	1898	1919	1912	1919
Netherlands	1901	1913	1913	1916
United Kingdom	1897	1911	1908	1911
Belgium	1903	1894	—	1920
France	1898	—	1910	1905
Germany	1884	1883	1889	—
Norway	1895	1909	—	1906
Romania	1911	1911	1911	—
Sweden	1913	1891	1901	—
Australia	1902	—	1908	—
Finland	—	—	1895	1917
Spain	1919	—	1919	—
Switzerland	1901	1891	—	—

Note: Argentina, Brazil, Canada, Chile, Columbia, Cuba, Greece, Hungary, Japan, Luxembourg, Panama, Peru, Poland, Portugal, Russia, United States, and Uruguay are other sovereign nations that had adopted at least one program by 1920.

1920, so adoption of a variant of each type of social insurance program would be a stringent criterion for early welfare state development. However, ten nations had achieved adoption of three or more of the four program types by 1920. This level of adoption seems a good gauge of early adoption, a good indicator of the consolidation of a program based on which subsequent welfare states might build. I use this level of adoption—program "consolidation"—to assess the relevance of development—and a couple of political variables—on welfare state development.

In addition, Maddison (1991) offers good data on GDP per head circa 1913. These data allow us to examine the relation of economic development to welfare state development at a time when development was still transformative (except perhaps in the United Kingdom) and welfare innovations still seminal (except perhaps in Austria and Germany).

The trick is to treat development as a threshold. This is possible because Maddison's data, although available only for a population of relatively developed nations, extend far enough among poorer ones for a set of "developed" nations, more stringently defined than his, to be selected. This selection done, we may, by assuming that all nations not documented by Maddison fall below the new developmental threshold, code every nation for which social security data are available as either developed or not. Then relations between a threshold of economic development and thresholds of welfare state development—welfare state consolidation as I'll call it—can be observed and quantified. To do this, economic development was measured with the data from Maddison (1991, 6–25) on per capita GDP (in 1985 U.S. dollars) circa 1913 plus a listing of sovereign nations *circa* 1913 (Rand McNally 1991). Developed nations were defined as nations with at least $2000 GDP per capita income in 1913. This just captures Spain (see data in Table A1.2). As the less *un*developed nations of Table A1.3 are on Maddison's list, and as there surely are more developed than any nations left off the list (of developed nations), one may assume that all nations excluded from his list are undeveloped.

The Yule's Q (or "phi") correlation coefficients (which specialize in associations between pairs of dichotomous variables) between development and consolidation is 0.650 (Table A1.3). Only one undeveloped nation—Romania—had adopted three or more by 1920. The pattern is instructive. Had *zero* undeveloped nations adopted them, we would have been able to precisely interpret the findings for the thresh-

Table A1.2. Indicators of Economic Development, Working-Class Mobilization and Social Security Development (c. 1910–1920)

	Real GDP per Capita[a] (1913)	Socialist/Labor Vote (percent)[b] (1906–1920)	Union Density[c] (percent) (1913–20[a])	Three-Program Consolidation (1920)
Australia	4523	45.9	27.5	0
Austria	2667	22.0	21.0	1
Belgium	3266	30.8	17.5	1
Canada	3560	0.0	9.0	0
Denmark	3037	28.0	20.0	1
France	2734	17.3	6.0	0
Germany	2606	32.9	20.5	1
Italy	2087	23.2	6.0	1
Netherlands	3178	16.2	18.1	1
Norway	2079	12.5	10.0	0
Sweden	2450	24.4	9.0	1
Switzerland	3086	17.5	6.5	0
U.K.	4024	7.8	32.5	1
U.S.	4854	3.7	9.0	0

[a] Data from Maddison 1991, Table 1.1; in $1980.
[b] Socialist/labor vote (as percent of total vote) in fifteen nations; cross-election average for 1906–1920. Figures from Mackie and Rose 1982.
[c] Union Density (membership as percent of nonagricultural employment) averaged across 1913–1914 and 1920; data from Stephens 1979, Table 4.8.
[d] See Chapter 2, Appendix 2A

Table A1.3. Correlations between Socioeconomic Development and Consolidation

Panel A   Correlations between Development[a] and 1920 Program Consolidation[b] for 49 1920 Sovereign Nation-States[c]

	Consolidation	
	Numbers of Major Program Types Adopted	
	<3	3+
Developed (High GDP)	8	10
Undeveloped (Low GDP)	32	1 (Romania)

Q (phi) = .650

Panel B   Correlations between Development (>$3000 equals high) and 1920 Program Consolidation in Eighteen Developed Nations of the 49 1920 Sovereign Nation-States

	Consolidation	
	Numbers of Major Program Types Adopted	
	<3	3+
Developed (GDP >3000)	5 Aust'l, Canada NZ, Switz, US	4 Belgium Denmark Netherlands UK
Undeveloped (GDP <3000)	4 France, Norway	5 Austria, Germany, Italy, Sweden

Q (phi) = .000

[a] 1913 GDP per head in $1984 U.S., where >$2000 equals high.
[b] Three-plus adoptions of social insurance programs. Data for 1920 program adoptions from U.S. Department of Health and Social Services 1990.
[c] Afghanistan, Albania, Argentina, Australia, Austria, Belgium, Bolivia, Brazil, Bulgaria, Canada, Chile, China, Colombia, Costa Rica, Cuba, Denmark, Dominican Republic, Ecuador, El Salvador, Ethiopia, France, Germany, Guatemala, Guyana, Haiti, Iceland, Italy, Japan, Liberia, the Netherlands, Nicaragua, Norway, New Zealand, Panama, Peru, Paraguay, Portugal, Romania, Russia, Republic of South Africa, Siam/Thailand, Spain, Sweden, Switzerland, Turkey, United Kingdom, United States, Uruguay, Venezuela.

olds as follows: development is a *necessary* condition for consolidation ("no development, then no consolidation"). Clearly, our findings support an approximation of this conclusion because there is but a single exception to the empirical pattern denoting a strict necessary condition—and as some will doubt, as I do, the substantiality of Romania's three programs. For development to constitute a sufficient condition for consolidation ("development, then consolidation"), we need to see zero cases of nonconsolidation for the developed subset of nations. This fails to occur.

In short, economic development qualifies, in effect, as a necessary condition for welfare consolidation, but hardly as a sufficient condition. But can a continuous measure of development distinguish among the welfare-consolidation levels of the set of categorically "developed" nations?

To answer this question, correlational evidence for the 18 "developed" nations just discussed was examined. For these eighteen nations alone, development and consolidation were again analyzed. First, development (defined as at least a $3000 per capita real income in this already quite developed new context) was cross-tabulated with a modified 1920 measure of consolidation. Second, the continuous measure of development and this new measure of consolidation were correlated. The new measure—the 1920 consolidation measure of the next chapter (see Table 2.1)—uses a somewhat more stringent datings of adoptions possible for a small set of eighteen affluent, data-rich nations. (This is the "principal" measure of Chapter 2.)

The cross-tabulation of Table A1.3, Panel B, reveals a singular lack of interdependence between development and consolidation among consolidators. If development is measured continuously, the correlation is trivially small.

Overall, except for Romania, no undeveloped nation was a notable welfare program adopter. We can say that economic development is a necessary but not a sufficient condition for consolidation. We can say that economic development differentiates among thresholds of welfare state development if a global population and a full range of levels of development are considered. However, for nations at least as developed as Spain, further development fails to differentiate welfare state development. This is, development appears to go no further toward explaining welfare state policy differences among affluent democracies—the present focus—around 1920 than around 1980 (see, e.g., Pampel and Williamson 1988, 1989). More explanation is needed.

Politics and Welfare States. The availability of people for mobilization and opportunities for effective concerted action jumped ahead with the second wave of development that swept the world in the decades bordering 1900. Despite the range of social actors—cultural, occupational, associational, and class—two actors stand out. They are the intellectual advocates of social reform from outside the neediest classes (Marwick 1967; Zollner 1982; Hofmeister 1982; Skocpol 1992; Williamson and Pampel 1993; Steinmetz 1993), including organized workers, artisans, and poor-person and other broadly defined working-class groups (Stephens 1979; Korpi 1983; Esping-Andersen 1985;

Ebbinhaus 1992; Steinmetz 1993). Of these, the latter are perhaps the more essential, as middle- (and upper-) class articulators and advocates of lower class interests often acted most decisively as agents for others—state bureaus, bourgeois and worker parties, and unions (Rimlinger 1971; Pampel and Williamson 1989). Among class actors, two types of lower class actors are both broadly affirmed as important and relatively well documented for early social policy reforms: labor unions and Socialist/labor (i.e., social democratic, socialist, communist and labor) parties (Stephens 1979; Rimlinger 1971; Korpi 1983; Zollner 1982; Hofmeister 1982; Esping-Andersen 1985; Ebbinhaus 1992; Steinmetz 1993; Mann 1993).

Table A1.2 displays data on working class mobilization (as well as economic development and program consolidation) for 15 nations in the period around the second decade of this century. (Data for Argentina, Spain, and Uruguay, the three other "developed" cases of Table A1.3, were not available.) It shows that (circa 1920) social democratic parties were popular enough to capture 20 percent of the vote or unions extensive enough to enroll 20 percent of the labor force in eight of these fifteen nations. To check on this possibility that differences in consolidation/nonconsolidation among relatively developed nations are poorly correlated with political ones, I compute some correlations between measures of early working-class mobilization and consolidation. I choose early working-class consolidation for several reasons. For one, this appears to be an especially prominent candidate for contributions to social insurance consolidation if the speculations of the preceding paragraph are in the ballpark. Second, working-class mobilization is a variable that we shall come to see as even more prominent by the next chapter. Finally, if others balk, as I do, at the possibility that development is not linked to social policy among advanced developers, a direct relation between worker mobilization and consolidation can help illustrate the possibilities for indirect relation between degrees of advanced development and consolidation. Early working-class mobilization (here early worker unionization and voter mobilization) is clearly rooted in such aspects of development as industrialization and democratization. (In, fact, the Yule's Q for development and mobilization among the eighteen most developed nations is 0.33.) Direct relations of such mobilization to program consolidation indicate more subtle, mediated, indirect relations of consolidation back to development.

Here I simply measure working-class mobilization in terms of a series of dichotomies. One dichotomy distinguishes between nations that do and do not average rates of union density (membership as a

Table AI.4. Correlations between Early Working-Class Mobilization and Program Consolidation in the Industrialized World (c. 1920)

Panel A   Q Correlations between Union Density (>20%) and 1920 Consolidation

	1920 Consolidation[a]	
	No	Yes
High density	I	5
Low density	6	3
	Q (phi) = .491	

Panel B   Q Correlations between Social Democratic Vote (>20%) and 1920 Consolidation

	1920 Consolidation[a]	
	No	Yes
High Left vote	I	6
Low Left vote	6	2
	Q (phi) = .606	

Panel C   Phi Correlations between Summary Worker Mobilization (Density *or* Social Democratic Vote >20%) for 1920 Consolidation

	1920 Consolidation[a]	
	No	Yes
High Mobilization	I	7
Low Mobilization	6	I
	Q (phi) = .764	

[a] See Table A 2A.1.

proportion of labor force size) exceeding 20 percent. A second distinguishes between nations that do and do not average rates of voting for socialist/labor parties of at least 20 percent. A third is defined by nations that exceed either of the 20 percent thresholds (on union density or socialist/labor parties). In each case the more mobilized nations are coded one (for high density or Left electoral support) and the less mobilized nations are coded 0. The nations studied are what we will come to know in Chapters 2 and 3 as the early democracies (and protodemocracies). These are Australia, Austria, Belgium, Canada, Denmark, France, Germany, Italy, Netherlands, Norway, New Zealand, Sweden, Switzerland, United Kingdom, and United States. (Argentina, Spain, and Uruguay, which might also have been included on political grounds, are excluded on grounds of data unavailability.) The 1920 measures of mobilization was correlated with the same 1920 measures of consolidation displayed in Table A1.2. Results are also displayed in Table A1.4.

The resulting correlations are consistent with the view that worker mobilization advanced consolidation (Table A1.4). Union density in 1920 correlates 0.491 with consolidation in 1920. Socialist/labor voting in 1920 correlates 0.606 with consolidation. Mobilization in 1920 measured in terms of either high density or socialist/Left voting correlates 0.764 with 1920 consolidation. In short, differences in the political development of socialistic working-class movements within advanced capitalism, appear strongly and directly linked to early welfare-state formation, whereas economic development (as measured in GDP per capita) does not. This counsels an emphasis on relatively political theories of welfare state.

CHAPTER TWO

The Programmatic Emergence of the Social Security State

. . . social demands which seem justified and which can be realized within the present order.
Otto von Bismarck (Zollner 1982, 13)

Class analytical, class mobilization, power resource, and social democratic theories of the welfare state, all centered on Left party reform, have risen to positions of preeminence in the literature on welfare state development (Stephens 1979; Korpi 1983, 1989; Shalev 1982; Esping-Andersen 1985; Hicks and Swank 1984a, 1992). Yet the relevance of these "left-power" approaches to any explanation of early welfare state formation is limited by the paucity of sustained left government before the Great Depression (Mackie and Rose 1982).

The relevance of these "left-power" approaches is thus open to strong competition from a variety of other theoretical perspectives, including Baldwin's (1990) neopluralist emphasis on a range of centrist and even conservative sources of universalistic pensions; Hage, Gargan, and Hanneman's (1989) statist focus on the social activism of centralized states, and Esping-Andersen's class analytical (1990) reprise of Rimlinger's (1971) patriarchal state.[1] Nevertheless, the

---

[1] More recently, they have encompassed Skocpol's (1992) revelations concerning the disparate, if polity-centered, sources of U.S. pre-Depression social policy in various elite strategies and reformist movements, and Williamson and Pampel's (1993) reassertion of (neo)industrialist and (neo)pluralist accounts of landmark pension policies as

absence of social democratic governments from the welfare state's formative years hardly precludes working-class influence on welfare reform during these years. On the contrary, each of the two most widely recounted episodes in the early history of income security policy involved a crucial role for working-class mobilization. This is so even though these roles are played out in concert with state forces as distinct as the social control strategies of autocratic governments and the electoral strategies of liberal parties (if held together by the common denominator of class). Indeed, we shall see that worker mobilization, in combination with autocracy as well as both Catholic and liberal parties, underlay early welfare states.

During the 1880s, Kaiser Wilhelm I and Chancellor Otto von Bismarck provided the world with its first national package of health, industrial-accident, and old age insurance. As assembled and enacted by Bismarck and the Kaiser, this legislation utilized a large and efficient bureaucracy of neo-absolutist origin and function to deflect a socialist challenge to Imperial rule (Rimlinger 1971; Zollner 1982; Alber 1986; Mann 1993). Bismarck and the Kaiser addressed, to use the former's own words once more, "those socialist demands which seem justified and which can be realized within the present order of society: (Zollner 1982, 13). To quote Wilhelm I's 1881 address to the opening session of the Reichstag, "The cure of social ills must not be sought exclusively in the repression of Social Democrats, but simultaneously in the positive advancement of the welfare of the working classes" (Kaiser Wilhelm I, in Rimlinger 1971, 114).

They indicate a Bismarckian route to the first welfare state (Rimlinger 1971). In the conventional account, this approach involved a strategic response of a patriarchal state to the growing strength of the socialist workers' movements (Rimlinger 1971; Zollner 1982; Williamson and Pampel 1993).

Two decades later in Britain, Anthony Asquith's Liberal Party and Ramsay MacDonald's Labour Representation Committee (LRC) reached agreement to accommodate each others' candidates in the parliamentary election of 1906. Specifically, the Liberals, eager to cut deadweight electoral losses to the Conservatives, arrived at a list of thirty constituencies in which they would "stand down," allowing the LRC free run against Conservatives in exchange for some sway over LRC campaign planks. Winning twenty-five of the thirty seats in ques-

---

outcomes of socioeconomic development and interest groups. Perhaps, most notable, if least direct, is Mann's synthetic (1993) account of working class incorporation into pre–World War I capitalism.

tion in the 1906 election, Labour went on to help Asquith's Liberals pass Britain's first national pension law in 1908 and, after extended collaboration in the election of 1910, landmark health and unemployment insurance bills in 1911. The Asquith government of 1906–1914 is a prominent example of the type of pre–World War I government engineered by liberals with labor union and labor party assistance that Mann (1993), among others, has termed *Lib-Lab*. Indeed, the Asquith government provides a paradigm of Lib-Lab reform. True, historians of ideas such as Kloppenberg (1986) and pluralists such as Williamson and Pampel (1993) have stressed the role of middle-class reformers and interest groups in Asquith's social-policy innovations. However, others have stressed the crucial role played by Liberal and Labour party politics in inducing, channeling, and ultimately realizing the efforts of social reformers (Marwick 1967; Ogus 1982; Mann 1993). From this vantage point, Great Britain appears to have taken a Lib-Lab path to the welfare state that resulted from the strategic responses of liberal government to growing labor strength.

Both Bismarckian and Lib-Lab paths to the early welfare state may again be generalized beyond single cases. They certainly warranted the core hypothesis of the class theory of state politics, namely, that working-class mobilization combined with state-centered contingencies was a pervasive source of early welfare-state formation.[2]

I examine welfare-state formation as exemplified in the early program consolidation of social programs in fifteen industrializing nations from the 1880s through the 1920s. Program consolidation refers to a state's adoption of most major types of social security programs extant during a given era. Early consolidation refers to the adoption of three of the four major programs by the 1920s—a hiatus between two eras of social reform.

Aided by a class theory of state politics, I specify hypothetical determinants of early program consolidation. Then, using systematic comparisons, (aided by QCA), I specify combinations of political institutional factors that predict consolidation. This method permits systematic comparisons that test the relevance of the hypothesized explanatory factors and advance theory-building by pruning hypothesized determinants and by refining the logical relations of robust determinants to outcomes (Ragin 1987; Hicks 1994).

[2] Although class analytical investigators have stressed post-Depression years (Stephens 1979; Korpi 1983), Mann's (1993, 597–793) 1815–1914 account of economic and political "entwining" in processes of working-class formation parallels our account of working-class "entwinings" with political institutions in pre-Depression welfare state formation. (See n. 23 on "entwining.")

Theory

My present focus is on social security program consolidation after World War I. An exclusive focus on the major social insurance programs—old age and disability insurance; sickness, health, and maternity insurance; workman's and unemployment compensation insurance programs—is justified by the relatively modern appearance, universality, generosity, and large budgets of these programs (as opposed to poor relief and veterans' programs of pre-modern lineage; see Gordon 1988, but also see Baldwin 1990 and Skocpol 1992).

Early program consolidation is important for several reasons. First, such consolidations shaped subsequent welfare policy by establishing statutory and bureaucratic precedents and resources (Cutright 1965; Wilensky 1975; and Hicks and Misra 1993).[3] Second, consolidation may provide a summary index of the income security achievements of relatively cohesive periods of welfare-state formation. The period from 1880 to 1920 was relatively cohesive: Extensive industrial expansion, mass enfranchisement, and social reform preceded the 1920s advent of rampant laissez-faire capitalism and the 1930s advent of world depression and extensive, durable, social democratic government (Alber 1982). Third, consolidations provide particularly useful handles on program innovations when, as for the 1880 to 1920 period, data are available only for coarse chunks of time and are too spotty to support systematic analyses of program adoptions year by year and program by program.

Explanations of welfare policy consolidation traverse orthodox theoretical boundaries (Pampel and Williamson 1989; Esping-Andersen 1990; Hicks and Misra 1993). Evidence has accumulated for aspects of each currently salient theoretical perspective (Pampel and Williamson 1989; Esping-Andersen 1990; Usui 1993; Hicks and Swank 1992; Hicks and Misra 1993; Ragin 1993b). Because this evidence argues against the sufficiency of any single theory, I draw on propositions from several perspectives, particularly class, pluralist, and statist.

Consistent with class-analytical traditions that date back to Engels ([1891] 1968a, 1968b) and Marx ([1890] 1969), working-class mobilization (class consciousness, union, party) advances welfare-state reforms. Affirmation of the reformist clout of labor and social democratic movements rings sharply throughout the empirical literature on the welfare state, although claims for working-class efficacy have seldom been made for pre-Depression years.[4]

---

[3] See Hicks, Misra, and Ng (1995, n. 3).

[4] Empirical support for structural and capitalist-rule theories of welfare-state reforms

Consistent with pluralist theory, centrist governments as well as leftist democratic governments have advanced welfare-state reform (Castles and McKinlay 1978; Pampel and Williamson 1985, 1989; Esping-Andersen 1990; Hicks and Misra 1993; Huber, Ragin, and Stephens 1993; Ragin 1993a). In particular, government by liberal and cross-class Catholic parties before World War II and by Christian democratic parties since then appears to have enacted substantial income security reform (Berghman, Peters, and Vranken 1987; Roebroek and Berben 1987; Baldwin 1990; Huber et al. 1993). Various interest groups and reform movements, nonpartisan as well as partisan, also have been important (Skocpol 1992; Williamson and Pampel 1993).

Consistent with statist, elitist, and managerial traditions dating back to Pareto (1935) and before, state autocracy and paternalism—most typically nondemocratic and having structural capabilities such as unitary state organization—have also been argued to advanced welfare-state reform. Diffuse operations of state elites have been recorded (Mosca 1939; Higley and Burton 1989), as have notable contributions by patriarchal elites and institutions to income security reform (Rimlinger 1971; Flora 1986b; Esping-Andersen 1990; Hicks and Swank 1992; Hicks and Misra 1993). For example, strategic social insurance initiatives by patriarchal Chancellor Bismarck were landmarks of early welfare-state formation. In addition, state centralization facilitates state responsiveness to demands for income security by reducing veto points for the potential obstruction of national reforms (Pampel, Williamson, and Stryker 1990; Hage et al. 1989; Hicks and Swank 1992; Hicks and Misra 1993; Huber et al. 1993). I expect to find that autocratic, paternalistic, and unitary states accelerated early welfare-state formation.

In summary, the principal causes that I have drawn from the literature are working-class mobilization, centrist governments (liberal and Catholic), autocratic and paternalistic states, and unitary state structure.

As already noted in Chapter 1, the accumulation of evidence across theories of the welfare state belies the sufficiency of any single theory, but systematic comparative-historical induction, concretized by the preceding sections' hypotheses, and framed by my politically alert class

---

sounds far less clearly (see Korpi 1978, 1983; Cameron 1978; Stephens 1979; Castles 1982; Esping-Andersen 1985, 1990; Flora 1986b; Hicks and Swank 1984, 1992; Myles 1989; Hicks and Misra 1993; Huber, Ragin and Stephens 1993; Ragin 1993b; and see Swank 1992, and Skocpol 1992, on capitalist and structural theories, respectively).

theory of state politics, can aid theoretical integration. This systematic inductive approach has the power to adduce relations among explanatory variables that refine and elaborate theoretical propositions. For example, I might simply hypothesize that unitary democracy, patriarchal statism, and working-class mobilization somehow furthered state social reformism, but comparisons might show that it was a combination of autocracy *and* worker mobilization, or of liberal government *and* worker mobilization, that generated welfare reform. Indeed, we expect these causes to operate in combinations. We expect the economic force of working-class mobilization to affect early welfare-state formation, but, pre-Depression worker mobilizations were seldom sufficient for working-class rule. Further, pre-Depression (indeed, pre-Cold War!) ruling institutions varied substantially among our advanced capitalist nation-states. Therefore, we expect working-class mobilization to operate in combination with various configurations of political institutions, prodded by reforms in patriarchal monarchies and liberal-led democracies (Mann 1993, chaps. 1, 20).

Data and Methods

Cases. To study early program consolidation around 1920 I focus on more than fifteen formally sovereign, relatively developed nations at the onset of World War I.[5]

I focus my theoretical and explanatory attention on nations at relatively high levels of development for two reasons: First, I assume that because the stage of economic development sets only broad limits on welfare-state formation, development will provide little explanatory leverage for a set of developed nations. Although some threshold of development is crucial for any substantial degree of welfare-state development, I assume that the degree of socioeconomic development is irrelevant to differential welfare-state formation, including program consolidation among developed nations.

Secondly, I assume that relatively homogeneous social processes require, indeed are constituted by, relatively homogeneous sets of institutions. In particular, I assume that advanced economic development around the turn of the century, being capitalist and Eurocentric, connotes a relatively homogeneous institutional world. Indeed, they constitute a world composed of those institutions—capitalist, indus-

---

[5] For more on nations analyzed, see "Theoretical Domain" in Chapter 1.

trial, statist, worker, and at least protodemocratic—that are most often evoked to explain early welfare-state formation (e.g., Rueschemeyer et al. 1992; Flora 1986b; Mann 1993). Thus, such a developed world (c. 1920) constitutes a reasonable domain for the explanation of early consolidation.[6]

This assumption that developed nations are institutionally homogeneous enough to plausibly conform to a relatively cohesive set of explanatory elements is supported by a number of factors. One is the preponderantly capitalist mode of economic organization in developed nations before 1918, considered here as a source of many likely institutional similarities from capitalist firms and markets to liberal and working class parties. A second factor is that all the developed nations considered may be regarded as protodemocracies; they all manifest some of the definitive features of political democracy as characterized by Dahl (1971), Therborn (1977), and Rueschemeyer et al. (1991): free and competitive elections of top governmental/legislative officials, extensive suffrage, ample legislative authority in the legislature, and rights of expression and association. True, some are exclusive democracies with competitively elected and authoritative legislatures but severely restricted franchises, as in pre-1917 Holland (Therborn 1977). Further, others are what I would call protodemocracies, marked like pre-1919 Germany by competitively and extensively elected legislatures whose final authority nevertheless is circumscribed by a higher autocratic authority (Rueschemeyer et al. 1992). All were characterized, however, by extensive associational life and by some electoral/legislative activity during much of the period from the 1880s through the 1920s studied here. This combination of developed capitalist and democratic (and protodemocratic) traits goes some way toward grounding both an institutionally cohesive theoretical domain and a reasonable, most-similar-nations strategy for the study of the program consolidation of the 1880s through the 1920s (Przeworski and Teune 1970).[7]

The core population of developed nations (with per capita gross domestic product of more than $2000 in c. 1913) consists of Australia, Austria, Belgium, Canada, Denmark, France, Germany, Italy, the

[6] For more on socioeconomic development, see Appendix 1.

[7] It does not preclude the protodemocracies from being autocracies: I conceive of protodemocracies as incipient democracies within still autocratic states but sufficiently like clear cut democracies for comparison. In devising protodemocracies, I was especially impressed by the fact that Bismarck's legislature continuously deprived him of reforms in anything like the form in which he presented his reform bills to them (Rimlinger 1971).

Netherlands, New Zealand, Norway, Sweden, Switzerland, the United Kingdom, and the United States.[8]

The population includes only capitalist democracies (and proto-democracies), and it includes all of the world's mass-franchise democracies with authoritative legislatures during the period, except states with severely limited effective franchises such as Chile (see Remmer 1984). Indeed, by 1917, the only protodemocracies are Austria and Germany. Finland is excluded because of its dependence upon Russia/USSR and Ireland because of its dependence on the United Kingdom, indeed its pre–World War II mimicry of British social policy.

Method. The method of systematic comparison, particularly Boolean logical comparison, is ideally suited to an analysis of program consolidation (see Przeworski and Teune 1970; Ragin 1987; Hicks 1994). Because "consolidations" are categorical thresholds that either have or have not been surpassed, they provide Boolean analysts with suitably qualitative or nominal (i.e., dichotomous) concepts. Moreover, not only does Boolean analysis serve to evaluate the explanatory usefulness of the repertoire of political institutions herein proposed as partial explanations of welfare program innovation and adoption, but it can provide inductive as well as deductive help with specification of the precise and often varied combinations of causal elements generating program outcomes, especially when empowered by the Boolean Program QCA. This implements successive approximation of a set of "leading" theoretical hypotheses to a body of data by means of a process of theoretically informed hypothesis formulation, testing, and revision reminiscent (despite an advance in technical sophistication) of what Rueschemeyer et al. (1992), following Znaniecki (1934), have termed *analytical induction* (see Hicks 1994). This process of theoretical refinement is especially advantageous for the analysis of as little theorized a question as the causes of "program consolidation." It opens theory construction to the sort of conjunctural or combinative formulation aptly illustrated by the Bismarckian fusion of state paternalism and working-class mobilization but largely lacking in the social scientific literatures on politics and change (see Ragin 1987, chap. 3; Ragin 1993b). It is appropriate to a small number of cases such as ours, far more so than, for example, the event-history technique for the

[8] This list excludes Czechoslovakia, a dependency of Austria until 1919, for which our 1880–1920 period is effectively reduced to a meaningless 1919–1920 period; Argentina and Spain, for which available information on social insurance programs is spotty; and the still undeveloped Japan (Maddison 1990).

analysis of qualitative outcomes (see Ragin 1993a; Usui 1993). QCA helps systematize comparisons of nations while it permits, indeed mandates, attention to historical and institutional detail and narrative life. The method of systematic comparison permits an attractive fusion of quantitative-formal and qualitative, comparative, and case study approaches (see Ragin 1987, chaps. 3–5; Hicks 1994; and Appendix 2B).

True, from the perspective of statistical analysis, QCA is (as claimed by Lieberson, 1991), insufficiently deterministic and excessively prone to model "underspecification" (i.e., the exclusion of "other" variables that, if excluded from analyses, may give rise to spuriousness). From the perspective of simple systematic, logical case comparsons in the manner of John Stuart Mill's methods of similarity and difference however (e.g., see Skocpol 1979, Rueschemeyer et al. 1992), QCA reduces problems of determinism and underspecification by elaborating models without eschewing the interpretative concreteness and subtlety of qualitative characterization, contextualization, and holistic comparison (Ragin, 1987; Hicks, 1994). I wield QCA here in this spirit of refined and empowered systematic (qualitative) comparison. Indeed, I do so by grounding discussion (after Table 2.1's presentation of raw data on program consolidations) in a cross-tabulation of cases by several qualitative distinctions (Table 2.2). This cross-tabulation is rather more complex than most foci of systematic comparisons, but that is the point of its use as a prelude to a Boolean (QCA) analysis. QCA makes the pattern in the table clear without reducing its dimensions or adstracting conclusions away from qualitative discussion of cases and sets of cases as "wholes."

In short, QCA is used here not as Lieberson's (1991) deterministic caricature of statistical analysis, but as a multivariate extention of the method of systematic comparison. This extention is one that retains respect for the historical, context-rich, finally irreducibly "holistic" character of cases seen close up and in intelligibly finite numbers.

Data. My measures of programmatic consolidations are based on refinements of the datings for program adoptions from the U.S. Department of Health and Human Services (1991) that were used in Tables A1.1 and A1.2.[9] These refinements, which go beyond the data source for

[9] For example, the SSPTW datings include the voluntary Belgian health insurance law of 1894, and this was, by our own criteria, neither legally binding nor seriously implemented. "Notable shares" are judged in sight of historical studies and standards, especially as expressed by the experts enumerated early in Appendix 2A (for W20C), however, "notable" typically means at least 15 percent of potential target group (e.g.,

Table 2.1. Programs Adoptions in Fifteen Capitalist Democracies by Two Datings

	Old Age, Disability and Survivors	Sickness and Maternity	Workers Compensation	Unemployment Compensation	Family Allowances
Australia					
Binding or extensive	1908	1944	1902	1944	1941
Binding & extensive	1908	1944	1902	1944	1941
Austria					
Binding or extensive	1927	1888	1887	1920	1948
Binding & extensive	1927	1888	1887	1920	1948
Belgium					
Binding or extensive	1924	1894	1903	1920	1930
Binding & extensive	1924	1945	1971	1945	1930
Canada					
Binding or extensive	1927	1971	1908	1940	1944
Binding & extensive	1927	1971	1908	1940	1944
Denmark					
Binding or extensive	1922	1892	1890	1907	1952
Binding & extensive	1922	1933	1916	1907	1952
France					
Binding or extensive	1946	1930	1946	1967	1938
Binding & extensive	1946	1930	1946	1967	1938
Germany					
Binding or extensive	1889	1883	1884	1927	1954
Binding & extensive	1889	1883	1884	1927	1954
Italy					
Binding or extensive	1919	1928	1898	1919	1943
Binding & extensive	1945	1946	1898	1919	1943
Netherlands					
Binding or extensive	1913	1930	1913	1916	1939
Binding & extensive	1913	1930	1913	1949	1939
Norway					
Binding or extensive	1936	1909	1895	1938	1946
Binding & extensive	1936	1909	1895	1938	1946
New Zealand					
Binding or extensive	1898	1938	1908	1930	1941
Binding & extensive	1898	1938	1908	1930	1941
Sweden					
Binding or extensive	1913	1891	1916	1934	1948
Binding or extensive	1913	1891	1916	1934	1948
Switzerland					
Binding or extensive	1946	1911	1911	1924	1960
Binding/extensive	1972	1911	1911	1976	1960
United Kingdom					
Binding or extensive	1908	1911	1897	1920	1945
Binding/extensive	1925	1911	1946	1920	1945
United States					
Binding or extensive	1935	NONE	1912	1935	NONE
Binding/extensive	1935	NONE	1912	1935	NONE

Sources for modifications of these dates from U.S. Department of Health and Human Services 1990 and Flora 1983 (Vol. I, p. 454) are documented in Appendix 2A.

The Programmatic Emergence of the Social Security State

Table 2.2. 1920 Program Consolidation by Four Explanatory Variables

	EARLY WORKER MOBILIZATION															
	NOT Mobilized								Mobilized							
	LIBERAL PARTY GOVT								LIBERAL PARTY GOVT							
	NO Lib Govt				Lib Govt				NO Lib Govt				Lib Govt			
	CATHOLIC GOVT		CATHOLIC GOVT		CATHOLIC GOVT		CATHOLIC GOVT		CATHOLIC GOVT		CATHOLIC GOVT		CATHOLIC GOVT		CATHOLIC GOVT	
	No		Yes		No		Yes		No		Yes		No		Yes	
	AUTOC		AUTOC		AUTOC		AUTOC		AUTOC		AUTOC		AUTOC		AUTOC	
	No	Yes	No	Yes	No	Yes	No	Yes	No	Yes	No	Yes	No	Yes	No	Yes
Consol			Neth							Ausr Germ		Belg [Neth]*		Denk Ital Swed U.K.			
No Consol	Cana Fran Norw Swit U.S. N.Z.								Ausl							

KEY TO NATION ABBREVIATIONS

Australia: Ausl
Austria: Ausr
Belgium: Belg
Canada: Cana
Denmark: Denk
France: Fran
Germany: Germ
Italy: Ital
Netherlands: Neth
New Zealand: N.Z.
Norway: Norw
Sweden: Swed
Switzerland: Swit
United Kingdom: U.K
United States: U.S.

KEY TO VARIABLES (see Appendix 2A for details)
1. Early worker mobilization—Strong unions or socialist vote.
2. Liberal Party government—Notable Liberal Party government.
3. Catholic Party government—Notable Catholic Party government.
4. Autocracy—Lack of polyarchy (i.e., mere "protodemocracy").
* Refers to possible recoding.

such earlier studies as Usui (1993) and Abbott and DeViney (1992), were made possible by a concentration on my core population of well-documented (OECD) Organization for Economic Cooperation and Development nations. The dating now requires that nations be (a)

retirees). Initial state or provincial adoption is allowed to count as national adoption for early cases of industrial accident insurance in federal systems through which workman's compensation adoptions quickly swept the state/provincial level of government, namely in Australia (for 1902–1918), Canada (1908–1918), and the United States (1911–1918).

binding or (b) extensive and funded, or, for the case of a backup measure, both.

Binding here refers to programs that are (a) legally compulsory for some set of national actors (citizens, firms, and so on) or (b) virtually binding, as in the case of Ghent unemployment programs, which include program participation rights among the requirements of voluntary, but plentifully rewarded, union membership.[10] *Extensive and funded* programs are programs that cover a notable share of potential target groups (i.e., labor force or demographic groups) and are adequately funded to begin provision of benefits within some short period of two or three years (after passage of legislation). My principal measure of programmatic consolidations is for 1920 and requires that programs be *either* binding *or* extensive and funded, but not both.[11] As a backup measure used in ancillary analyses to check on the robustness of results, a measure requiring both "binding" and extensive and funded programs by 1930 is used (Appendix 2A).

To qualify for the principal either/or variant of program consolidation (W20C), a nation must have adopted three of the four major pre–World War I programs—old age, sickness and maternity, industrial accident, and unemployment insurance—by 1920, a standard met by eight nations. For a nation to qualify for the second "both" variant, adopted programs must be *both* binding and extensive *and* funded. Because this backup "both" variant (W30C) is met only by three

[10] Without the caveat for "Ghent" systems of unemployment compensation, Belgium, Denmark, and Sweden's Ghent-style, union-administered unemployment compensation programs would be indistinguishable from other noncompulsory programs, despite these programs' extensive coverage, generous benefits, and ample state subsidies (Rothstein 1990). The ample pension coverage afforded by U.S. Civil War and "maternalist" pensions during the first three decades of this century might conceivably qualify the United States as a pension adopter before the 1935 Social Security Act—probably by about 1917, by which time thirty-five states had maternalist pensions while Civil War pensioners were a notable group. These long overlooked pensions would not, at best, add up to more than a second U.S. adoption, however, while at worst, they would not count at all (Skocpol 1992).

[11] Information on compulsory and binding programs is from Flora (1986a); information on insufficient coverage and funding from tables and figures of Flora (1986a), Palme (1990), Kangas (1991), and Wennemo (1991) is detailed in Appendix A2A. Possession of three programs out of four was chosen over possession of all four programs on the grounds that the four-program classification, which would confine us to Germany and the United Kingdom—plus Denmark in the longer period—would be too restrictive. A two-program classification, which would encompass all cases but Canada, France, and the United States—all but the last two in the longer period—would be too permissive. Because Denmark shares characteristics of Bismarckian and Lib-Lab consolidation, something like a Lib-Lab route to four-program consolidation appears to have obtained. What configurations of causes might suffice to explain more (and nearly general) two-program consolidation, I leave to others.

nations through 1920, qualification for it was extended beyond the immediate post–World War I period to 1930, and adoptions can include family allowances (first introduced in New Zealand in 1926). This allows the more stringent measure of consolidation to encompass six nations. The "or" and "and" datings of program innovations used for W20C and W30C, along with the benchmark datings used in Usui (1993) and Abbot and DeViney (1992), are shown in Table 2.1. (For details on all measures, see Appendix 2A.)

Working class mobilization (WORK, or W) is a measure of union and socialist party strength. It is coded as one for nations with (a) at least 20 percent of the labor force unionized (as averaged across union density figures for 1913 and 1919 and, for the longer 1880 to 1930 period, 1930), or (b) at least a 20-percent vote for the Left (Socialist, Social Democratic, Communist, and Labour parties) across all national elections to the lower, or sole, legislative house, 1906 to 1919 (1906–1930 for the longer period) (Mackie and Rose 1982). The measure is otherwise coded as zero.[12] Union density figures are from Stephens (1979, Table 4.8) and are normed on total rather than nonagricultural labor force because of the greater relevance of the former as a baseline for the measurement of political clout. Socialist votes are measured for Socialist, Social Democratic, Communist, and Labour parties across all national elections to the lower (or sole) house of the legislature for the period 1906 to 1919 (Mackie and Rose 1982).

Liberal (i.e., Democratic and secular Center party) government (LIB or L) is measured for both the periods from 1880 to 1920 and from 1880 to 1930, with ones for nations judged to have been characterized by Liberal party rule (i.e., Progressive Liberal, Free Trader, Radical, Center, or Farmers' party). These are the nations with Liberal-led government in at least 40 percent of democratic years. Catholic (Christian Democratic, Catholic Conservative, Catholic Republican, and Confessional) government (CATH or C) is measured analogously.[13]

[12] The 1913, 1919, and 1930 data points are used for lack of more extensive data. Twenty percent cut points are used for union and party measures because they tap thresholds of organizational strength paralleled in the literature (e.g., to differentiate stronger Australian unions from weaker New Zealander ones and stronger Austro-German Lefts from weaker, low country ones). Both union and party criteria are used because of a tendency for some nations to be notably strong on one criterion but not the other. For example, in Britain (32 percent on union density and 7.8 percent on Left vote), labor unions sufficed to be bulwarks of Liberal government during 1908–1814; in Italy electoral support for the Left (scored 22.5 percent) was strong enough to sustain Lib-Lab governments despite low union membership (7 percent).

[13] The strength of Liberal (and Catholic) government are coded for years in which nations are, at least, democracies of the exclusive ("partisal franchise") sort allowed by my Therbornian definition of democracy. Forty percent was chosen as a threshold

Autocracy (AUT or A) denotes nations that do not qualify as democracies in the Dahlian sense of polyarchies. Here, *polyarchy* is defined in terms of polities that select top executive and legislative elites by means of competitive elections by amply enfranchised populations. It is operationalized for 1920 as the possession of full or exclusivist democracy since, at latest, 1914, where full democracy requires legislative representation (with competitive parties) and extensive, if incomplete or unequally weighted, adult franchise (Therborn 1977). It is coded identically for the 1880 to 1920 and 1880 to 1930 measures, except for the deletion of Italy (authoritarian after 1922 as before 1900) from the Democratic ranks of the latter period (Appendix 2A).

Patriarchal statism (PAT or P), used only in the ancillary analysis, is rather complexly measured. This taps institutional and cultural legacies of traditional authoritarianism with its corollary traditions of paternalism, noblesse oblige, civil service privilege, and mass patronage, which has already been described at some length by Rimlinger (1971); Gosta Esping-Andersen (1990); Hicks and collaborators (Hicks and Swank 1992; Hicks and Misra 1993); and Huber et al. (1993). It was measured intially as the sum of 6-point (0-to-5) measures of (a) the extent of eighteenth and nineteenth century state absolutism (see Rokkan 1970, chap. 3); (b) resistance to universal enfranchisement (Rokkan (1970, chap. 3); (c) class rigidity, or the apparent precipitousness and impermeability of class and status gradations, as elaborated from the lead of Lipset (1983); and (d) Huber et al. (1993) measure of absolutism circa 1900. The measure then was dichotomized to code Austria, Belgium, Denmark, France, Germany, Italy, Japan, the Netherlands, and Sweden as 1 and all other nations as 0. It is invariant over all analyzed time periods (Appendix 2A). Unitary state (UNIT or U) is measured in terms of unitary, as opposed to federal, government. This stresses the subordination of intermediate and, by chain of command, local governments to the central state, as, for example, by means of prefectural systems of centralized appointment, financing, and authority (Blondel 1969; Lijphart 1984, 14).

Analyses and Findings

Formally, I engage in systematic comparison by means of Qualitative Comparative Analysis (QCA). This Boolean logical technique

---

because of permitted a substantial share of democratic rule without requiring it during most years. Liberal and Catholic government characterizations of a period are not mutually exclusive, but each type of rule tends to crowd out the other, and the two are negatively correlated.

identifies tables that describe, or fail to describe, categorical outcome variables as functions—ideally, logical expressions—of categorical explanatory variables. As we are all more familiar with tables than with Boolean algebra (or QCA), I begin with the examination of an instructive table. This cross-classifies the attainment or nonattainment of 1920 consolidation with the presence or absence of early worker mobilization and a few more especially promising variables for the explanation of 1920 consolidation (Table 2.2): Liberal Party Government, Catholic Party Government, and Autocracy. A sequence of tables, progressing from simpler to more complex, might be ideal here, but, one will do if we first consider that Table 2.2 principally cross-classifies 1920 consolidation and worker mobilization—my core class politics variable—and is merely complicated by a few additional variables. The table so considered, the association between mobilization and consolidation jumps out. (Indeed, unless we think that consolidation may have effects on early worker mobilization nearly as large as those of mobilization on consolidation, the explanatory power of mobilization stands out as very large.) Among "consolidators," only the Netherlands is not "mobilized." Among the mobilized, only Australia is not consolidated. Otherwise all early mobilizers are consolidators, and no nonconsolidator mobilizes its workers early.

There is no easy solution to these exceptions without further elaboration. What potential explanatory force or forces among the several considered in Table 2.2 (or any others) might overcome a lack of Dutch working class mobilization? Could *Catholic* government and democracy suffice for Dutch program adoptions and consolidations in the absence of working-class mobilization, when *Liberal* government and democracy never suffice without early worker mobilization? As for the Australian categorization as a nonconsolidator despite early working class consolidation, this is not too inscrutable. True, only the absence of autocracy distinguishes Australia from Austria and Germany, but this absence should suffice to exclude Australia from the Bismarckian scenario. In more democratic states socialists would have entered into the legislative alliances (or constituencies) of governing parties. However, a lack of extensive progressive liberal government precludes an Austrian Lib-Lab scenario, whereas a lack of Catholic government sets Austria off from the Belgian case. Let us proceed to a simple Boolean analysis restricted to consideration of 1920 welfare-state consolidation (W20C) as a function of early worker consolidation (W), Liberal and Catholic party government (L and C, respectively), and autocracy (A).

These proposed explanatory elements fit the data on 1920, post–World War I program consolidation. They do so elegantly, intel-

Table 2.3. Dichotomous Data for Analysis of Post–World War I Consolidation

Panel A Raw Data					
CONDITIONS				OUTCOMES	CASES
W	L	C	A	W20C	
I	I	0	0	I	Denmark, Sweden
I	I	0	0	I	United Kingdom
I	0	0	I	I	Austria, Germany
I	I	0	0	I	Italy
I	0	I	0	I	Belgium
0	0	I	0	I	Netherlands
I	0	0	0	0	Australia
0	I	0	0	0	Canada, Switzerland, U.S.
0	I	0	0	0	France
0	I	0	0	0	Norway, New Zealand

Panel B Solutions (to above data and Table 2.2)

Consolidation	=	WLca + WAcl + Cal (if the Netherlands coded "NOT Mobilized")
Consolidation	=	WLca + WAcl + WCal (if the Netherlands coded "Mobilized")
	=	W(Lca + Acl + Cal)

ligibly, and without contradiction: Panel A of Table 2.3 presents the distributions of the 15 core cases across the hypothesized preconditions and outcomes. As already seen in Table 2.2, Austria, Belgium, Denmark, Germany, Italy, Netherlands, New Zealand, Sweden, and the United Kingdom are consolidators, but no clear causal pattern was evident in that table. Application of the Occam's razor of Boolean reduction changes that. Worker mobilization, in conjunction with autocratic, liberal, or Catholic rule, proves to be a common cause of program consolidation.

Technically the raw data (or primitive terms) of Table 2.3, Panel A, solve for the outcome of 1882 to 1920 program consolidation. That is, no combination of the proposed preconditions for the outcome has contradictory outcome values; no combination of conditions has both outcomes W20C and w20c (or no-W20C). After Boolean reduction, expression for the outcome W20C is

(Eq. 1) $W20C = WLca + WAcl + Cal$ if the Netherlands coded "NOT Mobilized," that is
$$= \text{WORK} \times \text{LIB} \times \text{cath} \times \text{aut} + \text{WORK} \times \text{AUT} \times \text{cath} \times \text{lib} + \text{CATH} \times \text{aut} \times \text{lib}$$

(Note for technical clarification that variables are related by the logical *or* and *and* operators denoted by + and ×, respectively. Also, note that terms such as *WLca* are not joined by explicit *and* operators [just as the multiplication $A \times B$ may be rewritten, assuming an implicit $\times$ for adjacent variables, as AB]. Variable names in upper case letters express the presence of an attribute [e.g., *W* expresses the presence of working-class mobilization], whereas variable names in lower case letters express the absence of the state stressed in the upper case name [e.g., *c* expresses the absence of Catholic Party Government]. So, still rather technically, W20C *equals W* and *L* and *c* and *a or W* and *A* and *c* and *l or C* and *a* and *l*.)

In plain English, Equation (1) states that 1920 consolidation obtains if and only if (a) both working class mobilization and autocracy are present for the nation and both Catholic government and Liberal government are absent for it, or (b) working class mobilization and Liberal government obtain but Catholic government and autocracy do not obtain, or (c) Catholic government obtains and Liberal government and Autocracy do not.[14] In other words, three configurations of preconditions, suggesting three distinct routes to early welfare-state formation, emerge from our analyses: a Bismarckian one, a Lib-Lab one, and a Catholic one. (Plain English resumes by page 60.)

An element of arbitrariness is present in all dichotomizations of traits that are not, like life versus death, intrinsically dichotomous. One check on the robustness of findings is to redo analyses after small, plausible shifts in the dichotomizations of the explanatory variables to see whether findings remain stable in the face of such recodings. I did so by going through the 1920 model explanatory variable by explanatory variable. For each explanatory variable in each time period, I considered shifting codes twice: once including one *more* positive term (e.g., one more case with Liberal government = 1) than had previously been measured, and once including one less positive term (e.g., one less case with Liberal government = 1). I actually recoded variables wherever a recode was substantively plausible. For example, it was implausible to *reduce* the initial 1880 to 1920 repertoire of cases with positive values for Catholic government because no initial Catholic coding was uncertain. *Adding* Switzerland to the Catholic ranks for the 1882 to 1930 period was plausible, however. Whenever I switched a code (e.g., recoding Switzerland Catholic), I reanalyzed.

---

[14] In more precise Boolean detail, not only is the full right-hand side of the expression a necessary and sufficient condition for W20C. (Each of the configurations constituting the right-hand side of the expression [whether *a* or *b* or *c*] is itself a sufficient condition for W20C.) Moreover, each term in a configuration (e.g., "CATHG" in configuration "CATHG PATM UDEM libg") is a necessary condition for the sufficiency of the configuration for W20C.

Reanalysis yields only one change in the Boolean solution for W20C. This involves the recoding of early Dutch working-class mobilization from "weak" to "strong."[15] (Quantitatively, the Netherlands was, on the basis of its 18 percent unionization rate, next in line for a "strong" coding, whereas qualitatively such a coding was consistent with relevant literature [e.g., see Luebbert 1991].) This recoding changed the Catholic configuration for 1882 to 1920 from Cal to WCal: It added early working-class mobilization to the configuration (see Equation 1 and Table 2.3). This change suggests that our original Dutch coding of working-class mobilization may have been prejudiced against our hypothesis of pervasive (but variously conditioned, or "entwined") working class effects. (See discussions and Equation 3, which follow.)[16]

In fact, the Netherlands had just missed the threshold for a strong, pre-1920s working class: the Dutch union density score of 18 percent lies just below our 20 percent threshold for significant mobilization, and no score on either of the alternate (union membership or Left vote) criteria for mobilization is as high for any nation not already classified as a mobilizer. Allowing for the possibility that the classification of the Netherlands as low on working-class mobilization was an artifact of an excessively restrictive measure, reanalysis of the 1920 consolidation with Netherlands classified like Belgium yields the following variant of Equation 1:

(Eq. 2) W20C = $WLca + WAcl + WCal$, that is
WORK × LIB × cath × aut + WORK × AUT × cath × lib
+ WORK × CATH × aut × lib.

This, after rearrangement, yields:

[15] No cases straddle any other boundaries. No case remotely straddles the autocracy boundary or the Catholic boundary. Australia and the United States come closest to straddling the liberal boundary, but not very close. The United States straddles only if we both downplay the progressive characters of both Teddy Roosevelt's 1905–1909 Republican government and Woodrow Wilson's 1913–1921 government; Australia straddles only if we discount the sway of conservative landowners in the National Party government of 1919–1920. Italy and Austria come closest to straddling socialist boundary from above, but Italy's 23.2 percent socialist voting score is quite high (her more than 34 percent socialist vote in 1919 at the heart of post–World War I reconstruction period is very high for the pre-Depression world); and Austria, with two qualifying scores (22 percent for socialist vote and 21.1 percent for union density) is not much in doubt.
[16] *Entwining* means causes work "not like billiard balls, which follow their own trajectories, changing directions as they hit one another" (Mann 1993, 2).

(Eq. 3) $W20C = W(Lca + Acl + Cal)$
$$= \text{WORK}(\text{LIB} \times \text{cath} \times \text{aut} + \text{AUT} \times \text{cath} \times \text{lib}$$
$$+ \text{CATH} \times \text{aut} \times \text{lib}).$$

Here, in brief, early working-class mobilization emerges as a necessary component of all pathways to the 1920 program consolidation. This substantiates the introductory conjecture that working-class mobilization variously combined with other institutional conditions, was a pervasive and crucial source of early welfare-state formation. The question why early worker mobilization should figure in the generation of welfare program consolidation as a necessary accompaniment to Catholic government (when and where liberal government and autocracy are absent) ceases to be much of a puzzle: Belgian and Dutch Catholic parties were interclass parties representing notable worker constituencies within the context of weak socialist labor movements. Consistent with the similarity of the Dutch case to the Belgian one as regards strong working-class mobilization, Luebbert (1991) wrote as follows:

> It is clear that the Catholic party was a genuinely inter-class party. Its Christian democratic workers association, the Ligue Democratique Cretienne Belgigue, had 200,000 members by 1911. Catholic mutual help societies had 500,000 members by 1909. Although its Christian democratic wing, the agent of Catholic interests, never established supremacy within the party, it did play a decisive role in leading the party to accommodate workers. . . . The experience of the Netherlands . . . was little more than a variant of this (143).[17]

Thus, Equation 3 telegraphs the most cogent expression of post–World War I welfare state consolidation. A kind of proto–Christian Democratic, Catholic paternalist reformism emerges from Catholic parties in the crucible of Catholic-electoral competition for working class allegiance. This complements the autocratic, worker-prodded, preemptive reformism of the Bismarckian scenario and the reformism of Lib-Lab alliances.

Although current data alone are not far ranging enough to document a yet more elegant formulation, a little speculation may be instructive. The lack of Catholicism would seem more coincidental, and specific to the available history and actually occurring historical development, than essential to a Lib-Lab scenario. One can imagine a state

[17] In both nations, working-class mobilization, although notable around World War I, was largely separated from the socialist workers' movement—almost entirely so in Belgium—by strong Catholic worker movements and popular Catholic political associations under the auspices of Catholic Peoples' Parties (Fitzmaurice 1989; Jacobs 1989; Luebbert 1990, 139–144).

with the Catholic-worker dynamic of Belgium or the Netherlands in which liberal government was noteworthy. That is, one can reasonably suppose that a WLa— WORK and LIB and aut—term provides a theoretically sufficient expression of Lib-Lab. The cl component of the WAcl Bismarckian configuration may be intrinsic to an autocratic route welfare consolidation: No democratic partisan government, Catholic, Liberal, or anything else, is consistent with states such as Bismarck's and van Taafe's. Nonetheless, by the same logic, the "cl" component may be considered redundant and a WA (or WORK and AUT) configuration may suffice. Finally, the absence of any notable liberal government (l) may be regarded as incidental to a Catholic paternalism scenario as the absence of any notable Catholic government appears to a Lib-Lab scenario. In summary, Equation 2 might be simplified on theoretical grounds to W20C = WLa + WA + WCa and Equation 3 thus simplified to W20C = W(A + La + Ca). That is, early welfare state consolidation arose from the distinct reactions of autocratic, Catholic, or and liberal rule to early working-class mobilization. Consistent with my class-centered theory of state politics, this formula expresses the more general formulation that class mobilization, in interaction with a variety of political contingencies, is central to the emergence and development of welfare states.

Ancillary analyses of the 1930 measure of consolidation (W30C), although they specify somewhat distinct formulations, are also consistent with a focus on politically mediated class forces (Appendix 2C, Table A2C.1). Because these analyses add a decade of post-Hohenzollern and Hapsburg autocracy to the data, autocracy was dropped as an explanatory factor. In its stead, patriarchal statist legacies (PAT) and unitary government (UNIT) were added as crucial explanatory variables (see Appendix 2A). The Boolean analysis was framed as follows: The 1930 consolidation is (hypothetically) a function of worker mobilization (W), Liberal Party government (L), Catholic Government (C), P and U. The Boolean solution is as follows:

(Eq. 4)   W30C = PWCul + LUWc, which may be reexpressed to
                highlight class power as

(Eq. 5)   W30C = W(PCul + LUc), that is,
                WORK (PAT × CATH × unit × lib + LIB × UNIT
                × cath).

In other words, if working-class mobilization is combined with patriarchal statism and Catholic government is present in the absence of a unitary state and liberal government (as in Austria and Germany), or if working-class mobilization is combined with liberal government and a unitary state in the absence of Catholic government (as in Denmark, Sweden, United Kingdom, New Zealand), consolidation by 1930 obtains.[18] (the 1930s robustness checks altered no findings.)

Analysis for the more "binding and well-funded" 1930 measure of consolidation differs most dramatically in the deletion of Belgium and the Netherlands from the ranks of consolidators. Belgium and the Netherlands are not consolidators in the terms of 1930 consolidation, which requires both binding and well-funded programs. (A low-country tendency toward voluntary programs, for example, Belgian workman's compensation, suffices to explain the Belgian-Dutch absence from the ranks of stringently defined 1930 consolidation.) It is complicated by compounding of pre- and post-autocratic eras that join patriarchal legacies out of the Hohenzollern and Hapsburg eras to Catholic governments of the 1920s—important for 1927 Austrian and German adoptions of old age and unemployment programs, respectively. It is true both to the general principle of class-state synergy and to the specifics of Lib-Lab, however, so long as we allow for paternalistic routes to reform (Appendix 2C).

Empirical Patterns

Bismarckian paths to welfare-state consolidation emerge for both measures of consolidation. Only Austria and Germany travel this path to 1930 consolidation. For these nations, a federal, paternalistic state confronted with working-class mobilization in the form of socialist unionization and party formation and experiencing a notable degree of Catholic government led to welfare-state consolidations. My nations fit the model well: Narratives about Germany gave rise to my conception of a Bismarckian model in the first place. Moreover, Catholic parties were influential in the original Austro-German insurance innovations of the 1880s, and they were also crucial for 1920s enactment of unemployment insurance in Austria and Germany.[19]

Lib-Lab/unitary-democratic pathways to welfare-state consolidation emerged as well. A Lib-Lab pathway characterized by liberal

---

[18] For 1882–1930, it involved these additions/deletions: for liberal government, Australia/U.S.; for Catholic government, Switzerland/none; for paternalistic statism, Norway/both Belgium and the Netherlands; for unitary democracy, Italy/none; for working-class mobilization, France/Switzerland.

[19] For welfare program consolidation a decade later, it appears that Catholic parties become carriers of previously autocratic conservative legacies.

government and labor movement strength emerges for Denmark, Italy, Sweden, and the United Kingdom in the first two decades of the century. The cases are clear-cut matches to their Boolean pathways, although labor alliances were constituted more by unions and local association than by parties in turn-of-the-century Scandinavia and Sweden's 1916 accident insurance law issued from the formally nonpartisan but conservative-leaning government of Hjalmar Hammarskjold (Luebbert 1990; Lewin 1988).

Catholic paternalism emerges as a third way to early welfare state consolidation under the less stringent 1882 to 1920 measure, but low-country consolidation and the pathway to it dissolve if I require "binding" programs as the 1882 to 1930 measure does. Nations characterized by Catholic party government, patriarchal statism, and unitary democracy, but free from the complication of liberal government (e.g., Belgium and the Netherlands, the two WORK × CATH × aut × lib nations), achieve early consolidation only under the 1882 to 1920 model.

In Belgium, the Catholic Party has exercised virtual hegemony from the earliest days of exclusivist democracy (in the 1850s) until today, whereas Liberal and other parties, although often popular, were generally barred from government until after World War II. In the Netherlands, Catholic-led coalitions of Confessional parties typically held sway over parliament from the turn of the century until well after 1920, although Liberals did periodically govern during the last decades of the nineteenth century (Mackie and Rose 1982; Luebbert 1991). Despite Dutch Liberal governments in the last decades of the nineteenth century, the Dutch insurance adoptions of 1901 (accident), 1913 (old age and health), and 1916 (unemployment) were all implemented by Confessional governments. Although Belgian Lib-Lab alliances emerged in the early decades of the twentieth century as devices taken by *opposition* parties to shore up precarious electoral positions, the Belgian adoptions of 1894, 1903, and 1920 (for health, accident, and unemployment insurance, respectively) were all Catholic ones. Thus, Confessional hegemony in Belgium and the Netherlands effectively differentiates these nations from the liberal ones, indeed from all others, during the 1882 to 1920 period. As already noted, Belgian and Dutch Catholic parties were interclass parties representing notable worker constituencies within the context of weak socialist labor movements.

In summary, three routes emerge to the early consolidation of the welfare state. These are a Bismarckian route, a unitary-democratic Lib-Lab route, and a reformist Catholic route. Early working-class mobilization, differently conditioned and enacted in different contexts, seems pervasive. Thus all routes to program consolidation are cogently read as manifestations of working-class pressures for social amelioration (if not necessarily insurance) before the extensive 1930s entry of social democratic parties into government.

The routes to consolidation are rich in substantive and theoretical implications. Identification of each of the routes contributes to the literature on early welfare state formation. The general outline of a Bismarckian model—patriarchal state obviation of a burgeoning working-class movement's potential mass appeal by means of paternalistic social policy—is implicit in extant accounts of the German case (e.g., Rimlinger 1971; Esping-Andersen 1990). In fact, it is immediately recognizable in accounts of the Austrian case (e.g., Hofmeister 1982; Esping-Andersen 1990), but the model has neither been generalized nor abstracted before in anything like its present forms (see Equation 3). Moreover, no similar, comparably precise explanatory configuration of causal elements has been generalized as a sufficient condition for welfare-state formation (much less 1920 or 1930 program consolidation) or instantiated with Austria and the Italy of 1882 to 1920, as well as Wilhelmine Germany.[20]

Although the general outlines of the Lib-Lab model approximate various accounts of Asquith's landmark reforms of 1908 to 1911, no Lib-Lab model of social insurance reform (as opposed to government formation or democratic stabilization) has previously been extended beyond the case of the United Kingdom. Indeed, accounts of the Asquith reforms have sometimes pitted Liberal explanations against Labourite explanations, rather than joining Liberals and Labourite political agents together, as I do here (Williamson and Pampel 1993, but see also Marwick 1967).[21]

---

[20] Alber's (1982) general "authoritarian" model stresses the generalized responses of authoritarian states to the disruptions of industrialization but does not emphasize the working class, much less Catholic and Liberal parties. Esping-Andersen's (1990) general conservative model stresses state paternalism (or patriarchy) but does not emphasize class or center parties.

[21] For example, Williamson and Pampel (1993) provide a pluralistic, non-Labourite account compared to Marwick (1967) and Perry (1986); and Baldwin's (1990) stress on Liberal sponsorship of Sweden's 1913 pension reforms and on agrarian agitation for universalistic reforms downplays the decisiveness of Social Democratic support of the reforms and sidesteps the Liberal allegiance of Sweden's 1913 farm vote (Lewin 1988). Alber's (1982) Liberal model focuses on an early twentieth-century era of Liberal prominence in social reform without pinpointing the complementary role of Labor's political strategy, indeed the centrality of Liberal-Labor alliances.

Catholicism has been stressed in some treatments of early autocratic reforms and in others of post–World War II welfare legislation, but, researchers have not previously stressed the social policy innovativeness of nations combining Catholic governments with legacies of patriarchal statism. Instead, they have tended either to lump early Belgian and Dutch innovations inaccurately together with conservative or authoritarian ones, as in Esping-Andersen (1990) and Alber (1982), or simply to neglect them, as in Williamson and Pampel (1993). Moreover, explicit treatments of particular cases have refrained from generalization: general Christian democratic models have not reached back to the possibility of proto–Christian Democratic reformism in the pre– and immediately post–World-War II years (Kersbergen 1991; Huber et al. 1993).

Importantly, the three pathways taken together reveal much in common. In each, early working class mobilization, whether union-centered or party-centered (or both), combines with political conditions—e.g., liberal, Catholic, or patriarchal government—to constitute the particular causal configuration. To use Mann's (1993, 597–691) propitious term for relations among the several interdependent sources of working class identities within the major world powers circa 1900, class mobilization "entwined" with political institutions to bring forth early social insurance reforms (see n. 16).

These conclusions are not merely substantive; they are theoretical as well. Not only do they branch out from a simple theoretical stress on political institutions, but they reach out to any other cases of early protodemocratic industrializing states that have been (Argentina) or might have been (the first Czech Republic). That our conclusions stop short of contextless generalization seems to us for the better.[22]

Present findings shed light on other categorizations of advanced capitalist states. They bear directly on Esping-Andersen's (1990) categorization of conservative, social-democratic, and liberal welfare state regimes. Despite caveats about the impurity of his regime categories, Esping-Andersen (1990, 28–32) suggested that his regimes demarcate distinct, long-term causal paths to the modern welfare state. However, our paths go beyond Esping-Andersen's demarcations: Substantively, they suggest common Lib-Lab roots for some social democratic and liberal welfare states (e.g., the United Kingdom and Sweden); theoretically, they suggest that long, common,

[22] See n. 14 and Hicks, Misra, and Ng (1994).

homogeneous political histories cannot be inferred from common recent policy configurations, a basis for Esping-Andersen's typology of regimes.

Our configurations bear somewhat less directly on Mann's (1993) categorization of national modes of worker incorporation in terms of political crystallizations. Among Mann's crystallizations are a semiauthoritarian one encompassing Italy, Imperial Germany, and Austria (as well as Japan and Spain) and a liberal-representative crystallization encompassing this study's own British, Belgian, Dutch, Danish, and Swedish cases (along with Norway and France).[23]

Early social reform was a factor in Mann's analysis of worker incorporation (1993, 499–504, 651). Our combinations suggest that Mann's framework might profit from attention to degrees as well as modes (class, sectional, and so on) of worker organization, for the extent of unionization is crucial to the timing of incorporation (e.g., in Germany versus Japan). Our paths also indicate that Mann's (1993, 683) liberal-representative incorporation with its both British and Belgian exemplars, conflates distinctive liberal and Catholic modes of representative rule.

Routes to postwar welfare consolidation certainly are diverse and contingent enough to illustrate Mann's "entwining" and this work's class politics model. (They also make good use of Boolean aids to systematic comparison.) In the next chapter we encounter a pattern in welfare state development that requires no such subtleties. Analysis of early program consolidation indicates the pervasive, albeit state-contingent, operation of employee union and partisan organization and practice in the development of pre-Depression welfare states. Results of post-1936 analysis almost tempt belief in an increasingly unfashionable theoretical credo, monocausal explanation. It gives this wraith a form often evoked before now: This is, to recoin an old phrase from Seymour Martin Lipset (1983), the "*social* democratic class struggle."

---

[23] Mann (1993), who focused on world powers, does not deal with Canada, Australia, or New Zealand. Thus, he cannot be faulted for failure to deal with New Zealand as a Lib-Lab case or as a liberal-representative crystallization.

A P P E N D I X   2

A. Measures and Data

Post–World War I Welfare Program Consolidation (W20C). This refers
to consolidation by 1920 of the majority of principal extant types of
social insurance programs, namely, old age retirement (disabled
workers and survivor) insurance, worker accident and injury insurance,
sickness (including maternity leave) insurance, and unemployment
insurance. Coded 1, or consolidated, are nations with a funded, compulsory national law with ample coverage (i.e., coverage of at least 15
percent of target population) for at least three of these four major programs by end of 1920; and otherwise coded zero. (Compulsory restriction relaxed for cases of unemployment compensation following
Ghent system.) Baseline dates for first national programs in each functional area unqualified by the coverage/funding and "binding" character of programs are from U.S. Department of Health and Human
Services (1990) and Flora (1983, vol. I, 454). Modifications of these
dates for their binding character are from information on "compulsory" and Ghent programs from Flora (1983, vol. I, 454; 1986a, vol. IV),
and modifications to assure adequate funding (i.e., income replacement) and coverage (i.e., greater than 15 percent of maximum target
population) are based on information from Flora (1986a, vol. IV),
Palme (1990), Kangas (1991), Wennemo (1992), and unpublished
materials from the Stockholm Institute for Social Research. Further
information on dates regarding the binding programs and the implementation of funding/coverage was obtained from responses to
inquiries to national experts, namely, P. Baldwin (for France and
the United Kingdom); F. Castles (Australia, New Zealand); H.
Deleek (Belgium); G. Esping-Andersen (Denmark, Sweden); M.
Ferrera (Italy); O. Kangas (Denmark and Finland); J. Kohl (Austria,
Germany); S. Kuhnle (Norway, Sweden); R. Mishra (Canada); Luis
Moreno (Spain), J. Myles (Canada); G. Paz (Argentina); E. Huber
Stephens (Switzerland); W. Ultee (the Netherlands); and J. Vecernik
(Czechoslovakia). Dates for nations not listed, which are preponder-
antly from *Social Security Programs throughout the World*, are, moving
across programs as they are labeled in Table 2.1, Argentina (1934, 1944,
1915, NONE, and 1957); Czechoslovakia (1924, 1921, 1921, 1925, 1942);

Ireland (1925, 1911, 1945, 1920, 1945); Finland (1937, 1963, 1895, 1917, 1948); Japan (1941, 1922, 1911, 1947 and 1971); and Spain (1919, 1942, 1932, 1919, 1938).

1930 Welfare Program Consolidation (W30C). This refers to consolidation by 1930 of majority of principal extant types of social insurance programs, namely, old age retirement (disabled workers and survivor) insurance, worker accident and injury insurance, sickness (including maternity leave) insurance, unemployment insurance and family allowances. Coded 1, or consolidated, are nations with a funded, compulsory national law with ample coverage (i.e. coverage of at least 15 percent of target population) for at least three of these four major programs by end of 1930; otherwise they are coded 0. (Compulsory restriction was relaxed for cases of unemployment compensation following Ghent system.) See W20C for further details.

Early Working-Class Mobilization (WORK or W). Work is a measure of working-class mobilization coded as 1 for nations with (a) at least 20 percent of the labor force unionized, as averaged across union density figures for 1913 and 1919 (and, for the longer 1880–1930 period, 1930) from Stephens (1979, Table 4.8), or (b) at least 20 percent vote for Left (Socialist, Social Democratic, Communist, and Labour) parties across all national elections to lower or sole house of legislature, 1906 to 1919 (1906–1930 for longer period) (Mackie and Rose 1982). The measure is otherwise coded 0.

Autocracy (AUT or A). An autocracy is regarded, for analyses of 1920 program consolidation, as a polity without full or exclusivist democracy as late as 1918. Coded 1 for Austria and Germany; otherwise 0.

Liberal Government (LIB or L). Liberal (Democratic and non-Catholic Center party) leadership of government is measured for both 1880 to 1920 and 1880 to 1930 and coded 1 for a nation with at least 40 percent years of government by a liberal party (i.e., Liberal, Free Trader, Radical, Center, or Farmer's) or Liberal party–led coalition of parties in years since democracy. (Data from Flora 1983, 155–190; Mackie and Rose 1983; and Jacobs 1989.)

Catholic Government (CATH or C). Catholic (Christian Democratic, Catholic Conservative, Catholic Republican, and Confessional) party leadership of government is measured for both 1880 to 1920 and 1880 to 1930 and coded 1 for a nation with at least 40 percent years of government by a Catholic party or Catholic-led coalition of parties in relevant years since democracy; any other nation is coded 0.

Patriarchal Statist Legacy (PATS or P). Patriarchal statest legacy is measured by the sum of the following 5-point measures: (a) absolutist legacies or the extent of eighteenth and nineteenth century state absolutism, as inspired by Esping-Andersen (1990) and coded from materials in Rokkan (1970, chap. 3, Table 1); (b) resisted enfranchisement, as inspired by Esping Andersen (1990) and coded from materials in Rokkan (1970, chap. 3, Table 2); (c) class rigidity or the strength and precision of vertical status differentiation, an elaboration of Lipset (1983); and (d) Huber, Stephens and Ragin measure of absolutism (1993). Nations at least as paternalistic as Sweden are coded 1.

Unitary State (UNIT or U). Unitary, as opposed to federal, structure of government reflect constitutional and de facto national subordination of subnational governmental jurisdictions by means of appointment powers, chains of command, and control of revenues (e.g., Blondel 1969; Lijphart 1984; Hage et al. 1989).

B. Qualitative Comparative Analysis (QCA) and Analytical Induction

This appendix provides a succinct introduction to the Boolean method employed in the 1920s analyses of Chapter 2 and the 1930s and 1940s analyses of Chapter 3. Even methodologically schooled readers may want to have a go at Chapter 2 before deciding whether to read this appendix. (Comprehension of Chapter 3 hardly requires mastery of the materials of this appendix.)

The Boolean procedure that I use here has been elaborated by Charles Ragin (1987) as Qualitative Comparative Analysis. QCA is a logical/inductive analytical method, centered on Boolean logical techniques, with the ability to adduce precisely specified deterministic relations between a set (or subset) of hypothesized causes and an outcome, at least where data will support such relations. Indeed, it has the power to adduce relations among explanatory variables that refine and elaborate theoretical propositions.

Very briefly described, QCA's Boolean techniques analyze

dichotomous data on specified outcomes (O) and hypothesized pre-conditions (C) for them. Initially, these data are arrayed in the form of a *truth table*, which consists of combinations of Cs and (following a comma) corresponding values of Os (e.g., 10101,1 or 01111,1). Ideally, all theoretically possible combinations of Cs are included.

Note that it is best to reduce only a table that contains all possible logical combinations of conditions. Otherwise the logical structure of our theory will be limited by its grounding in a restricted range of observed cases. For example, incomplete coverage of all possible combinations of conditions might yield a Boolean expression (of outcomes in terms of conditions) that is inaccurate or unnecessarily complicated (or both) relative to the expression computed from a full table. There are three main ways of completing a truth table for a set of conditions whose combinations are not empirically exhausted—namely, by (a) setting outcomes for all unobserved combinations equal to zero; (b) specifying that all outcomes are "don't knows" free for assignment during the process of Boolean minimization of just those values that yield the simplest solution; or (c) theoretically specifying outcomes for certain empirically unobserved prime implicants.

Next, the data are simplified into rows of *primitive terms*. Then, if these primitive terms are solvable (i.e., without contradiction so that no identical combination of Cs conjoins with both O and "not-O"), the terms are reduced, via the application of Boolean algorithms, into the most parsimonious logical expression (purged of all redundancies) that equals O. Here the O for a data table without contradiction can always be expressed as equivalent to some expression of the C that consists of the C joined by logical *or* and *and* statements. In addition, *or* operators are denoted by "+", whereas *and* operators are denoted by "×". In logical terms, statements of the "equivalence of O to an expression of Cs" are, importantly, equal to statements that "the expression of Cs is a necessary and sufficient condition for O." For illustration, suppose that there is a causal relation of unitary democracy (U), patriarchal statism (P), and worker mobilization (W) to early welfare program consolidation (E). For the purpose of this illustration, I now stipulate that this relation boils down to the following formulation: $E = UW + PW$. More detailed exposition of the technique is available in Ragin (1987, 1993b).

Application of Boolean logic to the analysis of categorical data is ideally suited to an analysis of program adoptions and consolidations. For example, consolidations are categorical thresholds that either have or have not been surpassed; the Boolean method is suitable to their analysis. It can serve to evaluate the explanatory usefulness of the repertoire of political institution factors that I have proposed as causes of welfare program innovation and adoption, i.e., it can provide inductive as well as deductive help with specification of the precise and often varied combinations of causal elements that may be crucial for generating program outcomes. That is, QCA helps implement a successive approximation of a set of "working" theoretical hypotheses to a body of data by means of a process of theoretically informed hypothesis formulation, testing, and revision reminiscent (despite an advance in technical sophistication) to what Znaniecki (1934) and Rueschemeyer et al. (1991) have termed analytical induction (see Hicks 1994). This process of theoretical refinement is especially advantageous for the analysis of as under-theorized a question as what causes program consolidation. In particular, QCA opens theory construction to the sort of conjunctural, or combinative, formulation illustrated by the Bismarckian fusion of state paternalism and working class mobilization, even though such formulizations are largely lacking in the social scientific literatures on politics and change (Ragin 1987, chap. 3; Ragin 1993b). In addition, QCA is especially congenial to studies of small numbers of cases such as the present study, far more so than, for example, the event-history technique for the analysis of qualitative outcomes (Ragin 1993a; Usui 1993). It systematizes comparisons of nations while it permits, indeed mandates, attention to historical and institutional detail. It permits an attractive fusion of quantitative and qualitative comparative and case study approaches (see Ragin 1987, chaps. 3–5; Ragin 1993b).

The Boolean approach analyzes matrices of binary, 0–1 qualitative data describing the absence or presence (occurrence or nonoccurrence) of traits for a population of nations such as the German-speaking nations of Austria, Germany, the Netherlands, and Switzerland around 1980. Suppose that we wish to test two theses (Table A2B.1.). One is a variant of the Bismarckian thesis that proposes that a state will have developed social insurance laws early, that is, by 1890, if it has both a legacy of strong national state paternalism and a notable working-class threat to that legacy. The second is a fanciful neo-Weberian formulation attributing welfare program adoptions to Catholic majorities in national population. For the foregoing conditions of state paternalism, notable working-class mobilization, and a Catholic majority, we get a truth table like that of Table A2B.1, Panel A. This tells us what traits—proposed preconditions or outcomes—do or not obtain for each case. It specifically tells us that one case, the Netherlands, is characterized by the presence of a paternalistic heritage, but the absence of a Catholic majority, of notable working-class mobilization,

Table A2B.1. An Illustrative Boolean Model of Program Innovation in Catholic Nations

PANEL A. Truth Table of Observed, Primitive Terms*

P	C	W	Outcomes	No. of Cases	Cases
1	0	0	0	1	Netherlands
1	1	1	1	1	Austria
1	0	1	1	1	Germany
0	0	0	0	1	Switzerland

PANEL B. Truth Table of All Logically Possible Primitive Terms*

P	C	W	O	No. of Cases	Cases
1	0	0	0	1	Netherlands
1	1	1	1	1	Austria
1	0	1	1	1	Germany
0	0	0	0	1	Switzerland
1	1	0	0	0	
1	0	0	0	0	
0	1	1	0	0	
0	1	0	0	0	

PANEL C. Prime Implicated Variables

For positive outcomes
  1 — 1
For negative outcomes
  — — 0
  0 — —

PANEL D. Reduced Equations

For positive outcomes, $O = PW$
For negative outcomes, $O = p + w$

* P, Patriarchal statism: equal to 1 if true, otherwise equal to 0.
C, Catholic majority: equal to 1 if true, otherwise equal to 0.
W, Working-class movement: equal to 1 if true, otherwise equal to 0.
O, Program innovation: equal to 1 if true, otherwise equal to 0.

and of a national social insurance program (all as of 1890). It also tells us that a second one, Germany, is characterized by the presence of a paternalistic heritage, of notable working class mobilization, and of a national social insurance program, but lacks a Catholic majority; and that Switzerland is characterized by the absence of all three traits, whereas Austria is characterized by the presence of all three (see

Ragin, 1987, chaps. 6–7; Ragin 1993b). Particular combinations of conditions, such as 101 and 111, are called *primitive terms*.

Once we have written our truth table, we group conditions into distinct combinations of preconditions or primitive terms. Then we reduce the table into the simplest, least redundant possible set of primitive terms.

Panel B of Table A2B.1 adds all of the possible but empirically unobserved counter-factual primitives, completing our truth table. This done, we can proceed unhesitantly to the reduction of our truth table. We can go on to the elimination from it of any and all redundant primitive terms. For example, we can, by means of a sequence of comparisons by pairs of implicants, eliminate all prime implicants that, differing by only one term, yield the same outcome: We can delete the differing, redundant term (see Ragin, 1987, for more detailed terminology and procedures). For example, we can reduce 111 and 101 to 1-1 (where "-" means "anything"), yielding a single prime implicated variable for Austria and Germany. The set of all combinations of conditions for positive ("present") or negative ("absent") outcomes is the set of prime implicated variables for the outcome. Thus, for our innovative, positive program outcome, 1-1 exhausts our set of prime implicanted (variables Panel C and D), and the equation for presence of program innovation equals paternalistic statism and working-class mobilization, or

(Eq. A2B1) $O = PW$

The equation for absence of program innovation equals paternalistic statism or working-class mobilization, or

(Eq. A2B2) $o = p + w.$

According to our exemplary analysis, in Germanic nations around 1890, the joint presence of state paternalism and working-class mobilization was a sufficient and necessary condition for the existence of an early social insurance program; indeed both paternalism and mobilization were necessary for social insurance, whereas the combination of the two was sufficient for it. Similarly, the absence of either state paternalism or working class mobilization was sufficient for the absence of any early social insurance program in Germanic nations *c.* 1890; indeed, the absence of both was a necessary as well as a sufficient condition for lack of a social security innovation in the nation. (Catholicism was irrelevant to the outcomes.)

C. Analysis of 1930 Welfare Consolidation

Again, as a backup measure used in ancillary analyses as a check on the robustness of results, a measure requiring both binding *and* extensive and funded programs by 1930 is used (see Appendix 2A.2). Here, as for 1920 analyses, only cases that are fully observed on all analyzed variables are used. No unobserved configurations are analyzed, either with theoretically specified values for outcomes or with outcomes assumed equal to 0 for nonoccurrence. For instances of analyses with completely (but nonempirically) specified data, readers are referred to Hicks, Misra, and Ng (1995). Using data on only the fully observed cases of Table A2C.1, we set the equation for the 1930 measure of program consolidation as

$$W30c = WORK \times PAT \times CATH \times unit \times lib + WORK \times LIB \times UNIT \times cath, \text{ that is,}$$
$$W30c = WORK \,(PAT \times CATH \times unit \times lib + LIB \times UNIT \times cath).$$

Table A2C.1. 1930 Consolidation with Core 15 Cases

CONDITIONS					OUTCOMES	CASES
L	C	P	U	W	O	
I	0	I	I	I	I	Denmark, Sweden
I	0	0	I	I	I	United Kingdom, New Zealand
0	I	I	0	I	I	Austria, Germany
I	0	I	0	0	0	Italy
0	0	0	0	I	0	Australia
0	I	I	I	I	0	Belgium, Netherlands
I	0	0	0	0	0	Canada, United States
I	I	I	I	0	0	France
I	0	0	I	0	0	Norway
I	0	0	0	I	0	Switzerland

Panel B: Solutions to Data in Panel A

W30C = PWCul + LUWc
W30C = W(PCul + LUc)

L, liberal party government (LIB);
C, Catholic party government (CATH);
P, patriarchal statism (PATM);
U, unitary state (UNIT);
W, working-class movement (WORK);
O, Early 1930 welfare program consolidation (W30C).
Full operational definitions in Appendix 2A.

In other terms, if working-class mobilization is combined with patriar-chal statism and Catholic government is present in the absence of a unitary state and liberal government, *or* if working-class mobilization is combined with liberal government and a unitary state sans Catholic government, 1930 consolidation obtains. As reported in n. 18, reanaly-ses implemented for the purpose of checking on the robustness of findings yielded no changes in final solutions.

CHAPTER THREE

The Ascendance of Social Democracy

In every modern democracy conflict among different groups is expressed through political parties which basically represent a "democratic translation of the class struggle."

(Lipset 1983 [1959], 231)

Economic depression and World War I set the stage for a complete consolidation of welfare programs in the most industrialized countries. Before the stock market crash of 1929, no nation had adopted all five of the major social security programs that I have discussed in the preceding chapters, but with the 1930 to 1933 deepening of the Great Depression, politics polarized. Except where fascist dictatorships supplanted democracy—as in Austria, Italy, Germany and Spain, governments generally shifted toward the democratic socialist left. Where no such alternative existed, secular centrist parties electorally overwhelmed the Right. Emboldened by new theoretical justifications for deficit spending as well as by unprecedented legislative majorities social democratic, labor and socialist parties, such as the U.S. Democrats and the Canadian Liberals, became for a time reformist as never before or since.[1]

---

[1] Where does one begin an account of Great Depression reform? By a few years after the 1929 stock market crash, nations had begun a run of political experiments and reconstructions that economic depression, war, and war-time planning would sustain for two decades. By 1931–1939, nations turned from deflation to inflation of their currencies (e.g., Gourevitch 1986, 127–140). After two years of ineffectual tacking between Marxian and liberal economic orthodoxies, British Labour Party founder James Ramsay MacDonald jumped ship in late 1931 to head a conservative-dominated

In the surviving democracies of Europe, North America, and the Antipodes, politics polarized and shifted toward the Left, where a commitment to social security became part of the new Keynesian-welfarist orthodoxy. Democratic socialist parties, hitherto confined to a year or two of occasional rule, had inaugurated extended left government with Dane Thorvald Stauning's formation of a left-dominated, Socialist-Radical (worker-farmer) government in 1929. Then, in the early 1930s Danish and Swedish Social Democrats devised an exemplary formula for socialist-farmer alliances—price subsidies in exchange for unemployment insurance, agricultural-cooperative rights in exchange for union ones. This released reformist energies throughout Scandinavia; indeed, it inaugurated forty-four years of social democratic government in Sweden and inspired an initially parallel (but less prolonged) era of reform in New Zealand.

In entering governments during this period, working-class parties faced great pressures and opportunities for social amelioration, electoral popularity, and nonrevolutionary reform. As Przeworski (1985) has definitively argued, working class parties lacked the degree of secure, independent electoral power to even hazard any lingering commitment to the nationalization of the means of production, but their traditional socialist platforms called for "... public credit ... legislation concerning work conditions, old age, sickness and accident insurance, legal equality and freedom of organization, assembly, speech and press" (1985, 30). They provided an opportunity for "mitigating the effects of capitalism," if not so clearly for "transforming it piece by piece" into socialism (Przeworski, 1985, 131). This ameliorative capability often was backed up by the credibility provided by the new "demand side" ideas of Wicksell and Wigfross, French Front Populair, and Franklin Delano Roosevelt, ideas epitomized in the theoretical writings of John Maynard Keynes (Przeworski 1985, 36–38). By reconciling economic recovery with high and deficit spending, these ideas

---

National Labour government (see Skildelsy 1967). In 1933, Hitler and Dollfuss initiated dictatorships and antisocialist repression in Germany and Austria, while socialists rose to power in Sweden, Norway, New Zealand, Finland, and France (Gourevitch 1986, 131–147). By mid-decade Sweden and Germany had both turned from orthodox pro-cyclical fiscal austerity to counter-cyclical deficitory experiments that the United States and France would soon emulate (Gourevitch 1986, 124–146). Although the Great Depression conditions had arrived by late 1930, it would be some time before they were recognized, and so I begin in 1931. As it would take full-fledged war production to end the Great Depression and more reaction lags before the World War II era displaced economic depression concerns, I end the Great Depression era in 1940 (Maddison, 1991).

reversed economic orthodoxy with regard to the feasibility of sustained material improvements through governmental "nationalization of consumption" (Przeworski 1985, 36–38, 171–196). By reconciling government subsidization of the less fortunate with the general economic interest in enhanced aggregate productivity and income expansion, Keynesian ideas helped to legitimate (and often also to implement) social democratic social and economic policies that had conflicted with that pre-Keynesian panacea for depressions, the balanced budget. Before the 1930s social democratic parties had seldom led durable governments and had been torn between the politically elusive goals of revolutionary transformation and the economically discredited goals of redistributive spending. Thus, before the innovations in alliance and policy making of the 1930's, social democratic–led governments bred new types of national social security programs only in Austria in 1920. Now, as we can glean from Table 3.1, half a dozen social democratic, which is to say Social Democratic, Socialist, Labor, and/or Communist governments, initiated such programs during the 1930s. Moreover, social democratic governments would establish similar programs during the 1940s. Social democratic parties would participate in 88 percent of those governments that passed income security reforms (Table 3.1).

True, works as distinguished and diverse as Heclo (1974), Baldwin (1990), and Williamson and Pampel (1993) have stressed the role of centrist and conservative parties in the enactment of social security innovations, even for this 1931 to 1950 period. After all, these parties have ample constituents in the great "risk class" of potential beneficiaries of national income security schemes, a substantially middle-class grouping that crosscuts most conventionally defined classes; however, as we shall see, secular-centrist parties led the way to 1930s and 1940s income security reforms only in the United States, Canada and, arguably, Finland. Non-Catholic Conservative governments never participated in any of the basic income security program adoptions at issue here.

After the Great Depression, both mobilization for the armed resolution of World War II and preparations for the establishment of an enduring postwar peace galvanized much will and some means to avert the recurrence of economic depression. In particular, governments employed preventive macroeconomic stimuli and ameliorative social safety nets.

For example, Canada's 1940 passage of unemployment insurance reflected preparatory activity in Ottawa for the postwar reconstruction (Granatstein, 1975, 252). Canada's 1944 introduction of family

Table 3.1. Income Security Adoptions in Seventeen Affluent Democracies, 1931–1950*

	Types of Governments Enacting Adoptions			Government Participation
Adoptions	Social Democratic[†] (1)	Liberal-Centrist (2)	Catholic (3)	SDP Participation[a] (4)
1933	Denmark			Denmark
1934	Sweden			Sweden
1935		United States		
1936	Norway			Norway
1937	New Zealand			New Zealand
1938	Belgium,[¶] Norway	[Finland[††]]	France[§]	Belgium,[¶] France [Finland[††]]
1939			Belgium	Belgium
1940		Canada[b]		
1941	Australia			Australia
1944	Australia (2)	Canada		Australia[b]
1945	Belgium (2),[∥] United Kingdom		Italy Belgium (2)[∥]	Belgium,[b] Italy, United Kingdom
1946	Norway, France		Italy Neth.	Norway, France Italy, Neth.
1947	Japan			Japan
1948	Sweden		Austria	Sweden, Austria
1949	Finland			Finland
No. adoptions (total = 26)	17	3 [Finland?]	6	23
Percent of total adoptions	65.4%	11.5%	23.1%	88.5%

* Adoptions dated by using stringent criterion of Chapter 3.
[†] Includes Social Democrat, Socialist, Labor, and Communist parties.
[††] Finland's centrist-Left government confronted weak Right under protodemocratic conditions (outlawed Communist Party).
[§] Ideologically diffuse centrist government with radical leadership and important ideological influence of Partie Democrate (Cretien) Populaire.
[¶] Belgian adoption of family allowances is described by Wennemo (1993) as extending over two years and two governments.
[∥] A Socialist PM and Catholic majority (seventy-three Catholics, sixty-four socialists judged social democratic).
[a] Includes all adopting governments with social democratic participation (columns 1–3).
[b] Conservative-led passage of unemployment compensation followed by nullification by Canadian judiciary.

allowances dated back to Prime Minister Mackenzie King's 1941 formation of a Committee on Reconstruction, inspired in particular by committee member Leonard C. Marsh, a former L.S.E. assistant of British welfare reformer William C. Beveridge and therefore someone who was privy to Beveridge's famed wartime rethinking of British social policy (Granatstein 1975, 255–258). As Principal James wrote in a May, 1941, referendum outlining the role and purposes of the Committee on Reconstruction: "If for any reason, reconstruction should not proceed smoothly during the postwar recession the country would inevitably be confronted by rapidly mounting unemployment and widespread dissatisfaction" (quoted in Granatstein, 1975, 256). These words telegraph a portion of the governmental attitude, empowered by the massive mobilization and direction of resources in sustained wartime efforts, that steered the great 1940s reconstruction (Gourevitch 1986) and that was further empowered by Liberal Party parliamentary majorities of over 70 percent. As Gourevitch (1986) generalizes about the of core capitalist states, recently Axis as well as Allied, "the cataclysm of World War II," delivered a seemingly final blow to pre-Depression verities. It shook them

> ... to their roots. Arrangements were reconsidered and another round of debate and resolution became possible.... a historical compromise took hold in Western Europe and North America based on a system of market stabilization in economic and constitutional democracy in politics.
>
> In substantive policy terms, this stabilization sought to contain the chaos to which capitalism was vulnerable. It flattened the amplitude of business cycle swings by combining market forces with demand management, built in regulators, and an extensive social security system. (166–167)
>
> The pressures of war and depression pushed for extensive change in the proper mix between structuration and the market.... By the early 1950s the pattern was set, albeit to different degrees in each country. (179)

Thus, in World War II and postwar reconstruction periods, social democratic governments, unusually dominant liberal or Catholic-Left/Christian democratic coalitions, consolidated new programmatic foundations for the welfare states (Esping-Andersen 1990, 166–172). By the mid-1950s, Australia, Austria, Canada, Denmark, Germany, Italy, the Netherlands, Norway, New Zealand, Sweden, the United Kingdom, and Belgium (if an almost universally adopted program of voluntary workman compensation qualifies) had consolidated programs in each of the five major areas of income security policy (Table 3.1).

As we see from Table 3.2, programs developed rapidly during this period. The pace of adoption, accelerated during the second decade of the twentieth century, accelerated again during the 1930s and 1940s. Moreover, as we shall see, publications and working papers of the Stockholm Institute for Social Research indicate that income-security programs made major strides during the 1930s and 1940s toward placing a safety net under average households (Palme 1990, Kangas 1991, Wennemo 1992, Carroll 1994; and Table 3.3).

Table 3.2. Pace of Program Adoption, 1880–1950

	1881–1890	1891–1900	1901–1910	1911–1920	1921–1930	1931–1940	1941–1950
Australia			2				3
Austria	2			1	1		1
Belgium					1	1	2
Canada			1		1	1*	2
Denmark			1	1	1	1	
Finland		1		1		1	1
France						2	2
Germany	3				1		
Italy				1		1	3
Japan				1	1		2
Netherlands				2		2	1
New Zealand		1	1			2	1
Norway		1	1			2	1
Sweden		1		2		1	1
Switzerland				2			1
United Kingdom				2	1		2
United States				1		2	
TOTALS	5	4	6	14	7	17	23

Note: For data sources, see Table 2.1 and Appendix 2A, data are for "both" datings of Table 2.1.
Unemployment compensation bill passed by Conservatives in 1935, judicially revoked that same year; passed endur-gly by Liberal government in 1940.

Table 3.3. Zero-Order Pearsonian Correlations among Program Adoptions (Present or Absent for a Decade) and Program Changes in Coverage and Income-Replacement during a Decade for Pooled Data on the 1931–1940 and 1941–1950 Periods

	Decennial Change in Coverage*	Decennial Change in Income Replacement Rate[†]
Decennial Program Adoptions	0.529[††]	0.526[††]

* Averaged across old-age, health care, family allowance, and unemployment compensation programs from sources in Palme (1990), Kangas (1992), Wennemo (1993), and Carroll (1994), respectively.
[†] Averaged across old-age, family allowance, and unemployment compensation programs from sources in Palme (1990), Wennemo (1993) and Carroll (1994), respectively.
[††] Statistically significant at the 0.01 test level.

Routes to Innovations

Examination of the historical record for the 1931 to 1950 period suggests that the entry of social democratic parties into government, rare before the Great Depression years, is strikingly associated with welfare policy reform during the Depression and World-War decades. From 1931 through 1950, social democratic parties led 65 percent of all governments in introducing first (compulsory, well-funded) national income security program for the elderly, ill, unemployed, industrially injured, or child-bearing (see Table 3.1). Indeed, social democratic parties participated in 88 percent of such reformist governments. This suggests, in fact it virtually compels, one to believe, that social democratic governments were major sources of income security program adoption during the decades of the Great Depression and World War II.

Examination of the historical record for the period also suggests that, where social democratic (and kindred) parties are lacking, most remaining adoptions have direct explanations in the activities of *extremely strong* secular-centrist parties (e.g., U.S. Democrats and Canadian Liberals) or of Catholic parties (e.g., the Belgian *Parti Chretien*). Preliminary impressions of the record suggested that virtually all of the several program adoptions by Catholic-led governments emerged from Catholic-Left coalition governments. With this in mind, I hypothesize that *social democratic (i.e., Social Democratic, Socialist, Labor, and Communist) participation in government, supplemented by instances of extremely dominant secular-centrist government, generated most income security program adoption during the 1931 to 1950 period.* I write "most" because extraordinarily strong liberal governments appear to have made independent contributions to 1931 to 1950 program innovation whereas, in Catholic nations, Catholic parties appear to have collaborated with social democratic ones to bring about income security reform. Throughout the era no secular conservative party, except the Canadian Conservatives of R. B. Bennett, introduced a new, well-funded, social insurance or family allowance measure; and the Conservative innovation was quickly revoked by the Canadian judiciary.

In summary, it appears that social democratic and Catholic-socialist governments, complemented by secular-center (e.g., liberal) governments with massive legislative majorities, drove income security program adoption during the decades of the Great Depression and World War II. Furthermore, unusually strong liberal governments filled the reformist breach where nationally notable Left parties were absent, in Scandinavian and Catholic Europe, small farmers and large Catholic parties provided junior and senior governmental partners, respectively, for social democratic social reformers.

In light of my reading of the historical record, I begin analyses of the 1930s and 1940s with a rather narrow focus on partisan government, social democratic government in particular. Analyses of the above composite hypothesis of social democratic and secular-liberal reform prove this focus so fruitful that I find no cause for moving on to any other. But what precisely do data analyses, and complementary historical materials, tell us?

Routes to Depression-Era Innovations: Inducing an Interpretive Formula

Empirical support for the preceding hypotheses turns out to be emphatic for the twelve relevant Great Depression democracies. These include the fifteen core cases of Chapter 2, minus Austrian, German, and Italian defectors from the capitalist-democratic domain. In other words, they include Australia, Belgium, Canada, Denmark, France, the Netherlands, New Zealand, Norway, Sweden, Switzerland, the United Kingdom, and the United States.

Boolean analyses of data on the presence of (a) social democratic participation in government, (b) extremely strong secular-centrist government (or liberal governmental strength), and (c) 1930s welfare adoption (W30I) fully affirm expectations for the 1930s. (As we shall see, analyses go far toward affirming 1940s expectations as well.)

For analyses, a nation is coded 1 for 1930s welfare program adoption (W30I) if it enacted at least one introduction of a compulsory, well-funded national program in the areas of old-age and disability, industrial accident, illness, unemployment, or child-rearing during the 1931 to 1940 period. (See Chapter 2 on this stringent dating of income security programs adoptions.) Socialist governmental participation is coded 1 to include governments with social democratic prime ministers or with more than 30 percent of legislative support from social democratic parties, or both; (otherwise it is coded 0). Liberal governmental strength is coded 1 for liberal parties who occupy at least 60 percent of the seats in each relevant legislative house by having acquired at least 55 percent of the popular vote (and in presidential systems, by possession of the presidency). Social democratic governmental *control* (socialist government)—as opposed to participation—and Catholic Party governmental control (Catholic government) are also coded. Socialist government was set equal to 1 where social democratic parties (again, broadly construed) held all governing seats and heads of government or, in cases of coalition government, either (a)

40 percent of coalition seats *and* prime ministry or (b) 60 percent of the coalition seats in lieu of the Prime Ministry.[2]

Our cases for the period are a subset of the same early industrializers considered by Hicks, Misra, and Ng (1995) for the 1880 to 1930 period. For the 1931 to 1940 period, unlike the earlier period, some cases are so decisively nondemocratic, unlike such cases as turn-of-the-century Wilhelmine Germany, that they indicate radically distinct institutional contexts for politics and, hence, distinct domains for political theorizing: Britain, Belgium, Sweden, and the United States are reasonable cases for comparison, whereas Dolfuss and Hitler's Austria, Mussolini's Italy, and the Third Reich are not.[3]

Analyses consist of a combination of Boolean analyses and conventional ordinary least squares (OLS) regression analyses[4]; however,

[2] The 1931–1950 data on innovations (and party rule) are drawn from the datings of Table 2.1 (and Table 3.1). Data on party rule come from Flora (1983) and Mackie and Rose (1982), augmented by data from Jacobs (1989) and Lewis and Sagar (1992). Dates of stringent adoptions for nations not in Table 2.1 follow. For Finland, for pension, health, workman's and unemployment insurance, and family-allowance programs, they are 1937, 1963, 1895, 1917, and 1948, respectively; for Japan, 1941, 1922, 1911, 1947, and 1971, respectively; and for Ireland, 1925, 1911, 1945, 1920, and 1945, respectively.

[3] Czechoslovakia, Finland, and Spain arguably qualify for analysis according to all of my criteria of data quality except information on welfare adoptions themselves: For datings of such adoptions, I am dependent upon the single, sometimes indiscriminate U.S. Department of Health and Social Service (1990). Czechoslovakia and Spain are affluent by the standard of the 1913 data (per capita GDP in $1980 > $2000) (Maddison 1991, still the best data source available), but Finland is not. All three are arguably political democracies: Czechoslovakia despite a few years of national socialist influence even preceding the German occupation of 1938; Finland, if one makes light of her outlaw status for the Finnish Communists; Spain, at least through Franco's invasion from Algiers of July 18, 1936, and possibly through 1938. In Czechoslovakia, conservative rule, consistent with the results of present 1930s analyses, yields no reforms. Finland in 1937 was too poor and too equivocally democratic to qualify for my 1930s population of affluent capitalist democracies; the government, the first of a long series of "Red-Green" worker-farmer coalitions, was dominated by 83 (out of 143) legislators from the Finnish Socialist Democratic party (although headed by Progressive Prime Minister A. K. Cajander), and it commenced and quickly enacted national sickness insurance. In Spain the Center-Left government of Manuel Azana and the Left-Center government of Largo Caballero (respectively) introduced work accident insurance in 1932 and family allowances in 1938. Finnish and Spanish cases accord with the "socialist-participation" findings (e.g., Table 3.1) which their inclusion alongside Czechoslovakia only strengthens.

[4] To optimally implement the Boolean procedures, it was useful to decide on an outcome for the one empirically unobserved set of explanatory combinations for the basic model positing *social governmental participation* and *liberal governmental strength* as causes of W30I. This is the combination *social governmental participation* and *liberal governmental strength*. Here I decided that the combination of both governmental conditions, although unlikely, is plausible over the course of a period as long as a decade and might safely be assumed conducive to welfare program innovation. (In the symbolism of Chapter 3, I assumed "11,1.")

fit is so errorless for the 1931 to 1940 period that the latter, statistical analysis seems redundant.

Boolean analyses for the 1931 to 1940 period yielded the following simple pattern for outcomes on 1930s welfare adoption, or W30A:

(Eq. 1) W30A = *socialist governmental participation*
              + liberal governmental strength

That is, adoptions occurred if there was socialist participation in government or if there was a liberal government that overwhelmed its opposition (liberal governmental strength). Indeed, it should be clear that the composite condition, *Socialist governmental participation + liberal governmental strength* (the presence of socialist governmental participation or the presence of extremely strong secular-centrist government) is itself a necessary and sufficient condition for W30I. As uncompromised Boolean analysis requires, *socialist governmental participation + liberal governmental strength* fits all cases. Only one qualification of this strongly deterministic outcome need be made. France, despite Blum's Socialist governments, in fact passed its Depression-era adoption, a family allowance law, under a centrist government of strong Catholic coloration (Wennemo 1992; Misra 1994).

Multiple regression analyses of the same data are at once powerful and trivial. They provide a function that predicts the W30A perfectly, yielding the following nonstochastic equation:

(Eq. 2) W30A = 1.0 × *socialist governmental participation*
              + 1.0 × *liberal governmental strength*

This has infinitely large t-statistics and a R^2 of 1.00, which is to say that it predicts—or more accurately "postdicts"—W30A perfectly.[5]

Now, let us look at the cases that travel each of the routes to adoption, particularly a few cases that seem especially representative or, like the United States and Canada, close to home.

Routes to Depression-Era Program Adoptions

For the decade of the Great Depression, social democratic government, broadly construed to include even minority participation

---

[5] Because my number of observations is too small for maximum likelihood estimation models such as logit and probit and the skew in outcomes is not so large as to assure notable departures from linearity in predicting outcomes, I use ordinary least squares (OLS) estimation with simple, untransformed, dummy-dependent variables (see Wonnacott and Wonnacott 1985).

in Parliamentary governments, deserves detailed consideration as one route to income security policy reform. Secular, centrist governments, which seem to have had similar policy consequences in nations without notable socialist Lefts and eras without governmentally influential Rights, seem to merit similar consideration.

Social Democratic Route
In 1928, the Swedish Social Democratic Party (*Sveriges Socialdemokratiska Arbetarparti* or SAP), campaigning in the name of a socialization of wealth, suffered a severe setback at the polls. Although the Conservative-Agrarian government that emerged from the election was a minority one, SAP found itself with only 37 percent of the vote and isolated from all other parties. Under these circumstance, SAP entered into an intense internal debate over the future direction of the party. Although all participants in the debate concurred on the need to make socialism "current," one faction led by such SAP notables as Gustav Moller, Rickard Sandler, and Ernst Wigfross stressed a program of action centered about the concept of "socialization." Another faction, composed of such pragmatists as Per Edvin Skold and Per Albin Hansson, stressed more immediate provisions to limit and ameliorate the "personal insecurity, social dislocation and stultifying labor" brought on by capitalism (Tingsten 1973, 246–335; Tilton 1990, 271–272). Despite some discord, true dialogue ensued in an unusual context where the doctrinaire proved flexible and the dogmatic principled. On the one hand, the more systematically socialistic wielded a supple, usable brand of theory. For example, Sandler (Tilton, 1990) asserted the overriding importance of the *functions* and *uses* (rather than the simple legal ownership) of capital: capital need not be nationalized in order to be substantially socialized. Wigfross advocated deficitory public spending to buoy otherwise deficient consumption well before the 1936 publication of Keynes's general theory (Tilton 1990, 41–50, 271; Wigforss 1932 [in Tilton, 46]). On the other hand, the relatively pragmatic and populistic, such as Hansson, with his emphasis on the extensive employee character of the working class and the democratic essence of socialism, were struggling to realize rather than replace socialist ideals (Tilton 1990, 126–140). Whatever the final consequences of his ideas for decisive transition to socialism, it was for such a transition that Hansson announced his call for a "people's home." In one classic statement of this to the Swedish Rigstag, Per Alben proclaimed that

The good home . . . knows no favorites or step children. . . . there no one tries to gain advantage at another's expense, and the stronger do not oppress and plunder the weaker. In the good home equality, consideration, co-operation and helpfulness prevail. . . . The poor feel anxieties for the coming day with its potential for illness, unemployment, and other hazards. If Swedish society is going to be a good citizens' home, class differences must be eliminated, social services developed, economic equalization achieved, workers provided with a role in economic management and democracy carried through and applied both socially and economically. (Hansson in Berkling 1982, 227)

By the election of 1932, Hansson's broadly welfarist route to this conception of socialism as a "peoples' home" created by an innovative exercise of social and economic as well as political democracy had been laid out in some detail (Tingsten 1973, 246–335). Hansson's vision had been fitted by SAP intellectuals with an impressive set of tools, Wigforss's counter-cyclical spending policies among them. Swept to victory by public attribution of a deepening recession to four years of Right and Centrist rulers, SAP, led by now Prime Minister Per Albin Hansson, transformed its 45 percent plurality into a forty-four year rule by means of a remarkable ensemble of programs and deals. These included the unemployment insurance law of 1934. Social democratic legislative achievements, not surprisingly, included social democratic government, an accomplishment that the SAP could not have achieved on its own. A majority SAP-led government was negotiated with the Agrarian party by exchanging promises of statutory support for each other's most pressing demands. For the labor party, these included programs of deficit-financed public works, unemployment compensation, legal support for union organizational rights, the administration of unemployment benefits a la Ghent, representation, collective bargaining, and the like. For the farmers' party, these demands included deficit-financed price subsidies, rights for farm organizations to levy dues, a share in the administration of farm subsidies, and the right to represent and negotiate their interests on goods markets (see Esping-Andersen 1985, 86–87 on programs; and Rothstein 1994, on interest organization).

The unemployment insurance law of 1934 was central to the engineering of this social democratic route to welfare capitalism. Moreover, besides figuring in the preelection platforms and postelections compacts that sealed a SAP-led government, it was part of a seemingly effective social democratic response to the Great Depression. However much this effectiveness may have been aided by a rearming Germany's infamous demand for Swedish steel, SAP's perceived reversal of the Great Depression propelled SAP toward yet larger electoral showings and more robust governments in 1936 and 1940 (Esping-Andersen 1985, 87).

SAP's route to welfare capitalism was not unique, even if it was most remarkable for the forty-four year social democratic rule that it helped chart. In 1929, the Danish Social Democratic party recovered from its defeat in the election of 1926 by means of strategies like those which brought SAP to power in 1933. Whereas in 1926 it had run on a platform still pursuing nationalized production, in 1929 it ran with its sights set on the delivery of economic relief. This it promised in the face of prevailing economic doctrines prescribing balanced, even decimated, budgets during slumps on the basis of new claims for the stimulative capability of deficit spending in bad times. This it realized by forging a governing coalition with Danish agrarians that was made possible by the promise of farm subsidies. (In fact, it was the Danes who pioneered the first Scandinavian Red-Green alliance of socialist workers and agrarian liberals and populists.) This included the National Insurance Act, a pathbreaking organization of both old and new income security programs into a unprecedentedly universalistic package of benefits. The new addition to the package, crucial for our accounting, was the Health Insurance Law of 1933.

Norwegian Prime Minister Johan Nygaardsvold consolidated government in 1935 at the helm of a third labor-agrarian coalition. Nygaardsvold's coalition was also cemented by a major social insurance innovation. Here, a pension program, made especially attractive to farmers by broad coverage and partial financing out of general revenues, helped underwrite the socialist-led coalition.

In 1935, New Zealand's Labour Party was helped into office by means of extensive repudiation of its Right-Center predecessors and by means of a strong rural vote that was at least partially indebted to advocacy of counter-cyclical economic doctrines, much like those of Canadian Social Credit agrarian Major Douglas (Castles 1985, 26–29; Brown 1987, 450). With the Social Security Act of 1938, this Labour government passed legislation containing New Zealand's first national superannuation benefit. These Red-Green reforms secured Keynesian-welfarist policy regimes whose influences extended to other Depression-era governments and subsequent decades.

The French Exception

France's Popular Front governments of July, 1936, through April, 1938, are the only governments in any of our 1930s nations that, although marked by social democratic—here socialist and communist—participation, and even socialist leadership, did not enact any new income security programs during the Great Depression.

In part, this failure to generate income security adoptions can be attributed to the larger failure of the Front Populair to attain its first priority, a political as well as economic resolution of the problems of French unionism and industrial relations. These included Socialist-Communist tensions within the Confederation Generale du Travail (or CGT), which has reassimilated the 1922 Communist breakaway CGT-Unitaire in 1936—as well as between the CGT and the Catholic Confederation Francais des Travailleurs Chretiens (or CFTC); problems of inefficacy in both strikes and collective bargaining coinciding with high levels of industrial militancy; problems of low wages, poor benefits, poor working conditions, and high unemployment; and problems of stagnant union membership. These were all addressed by Leon Blum's first Front government of August, 1936, through August, 1937, mostly under the terms of the Matignon agreement on industrial workers.

The problem of internal divisions was specifically addressed by a merger of the Communist CGTU into the CGT and a focus on shared problems of all unionists. The problems related to ineffective collective bargaining were addressed with legal affirmations of the rights of wage workers to collective bargaining and union representation, plus a strengthening of state involvement in labor arbitration. Immediate material problems were addressed through provisions of the Matignon agreement between the CGT and the CGPF (*Confederation Generale de la Production Française*) guaranteeing two weeks annual paid vacation, election of shop stewards, and 12 percent average wage increases. They were further addressed by means of legislation mandating a forty-hour work week, collective bargaining, and an annual holiday, as well as by promises of public works, a revamping of the tax system, and much else. As a result of the heady atmosphere of reform cast by so many progressive measures, union membership soared from one to five million during the first year and a half of the Front, redressing the problem of union membership (Luebbert 1991, 219–223; Greene 1951).[6]

Nevertheless, the Front began to disintegrate. The first month of Front government had been devoted to resolving the situation of

[6] I use "*progressive*" in the general sense of *Progressive, new* or *reform* liberals, applicable to John Dewey as well as to Robert LaFollette, to T. H. Green, Lloyd George, and Leon Bourgeois, as well as to John Dewey. Indeed, I use it as a more universal sense of Kloppenberg's (1986) nonsocialist *via media*.

massive work stoppages amidst which Blum has been elected, but within a month of the state-arbitrated settlements of August, 1936, new waves of militancy had erupted. Compulsory arbitration was soon leveled by the Front government against workers who had recently celebrated unprecedented levels of governmental support. Action on public works and the general problem of unemployment were constrained by Socialist-Communist dependence upon its (petty bourgeois) Radical coalition partners. Amidst rapid economic deterioration, and intensified pressures from the economically orthodox for moderation of Front actions, governmental policy coherence and popular support waned. In February of 1937, Blum announced a pause in reform legislation, and in June the Blum government fell in the face of Radical opposition to an effort by Blum to obtain emergency economic powers to deal with the economic situation. Although Blum would have another hand at government leadership in 1938, the Radicals' August, 1937, ascent to Front leadership signaled the end of a radically reformist Front.

Unable to attain even its first labor- and macroeconomic-related priorities before unraveling as a reformist force, the *Front Populair* had little time to address social insurance and related income-security reforms low on its agenda. In this atmosphere, neglect of a major income security adoption was perhaps assured by the fact that France had at least modest voluntary programs in place in all major program areas, whereas family allowances was one area in which reform proposals had been a reserve of the Catholic Partie Democrate Populaire since the early 1930s on natalist and militaristic (i.e., population-for-conscription) grounds. Thus, despite general Depression-era democratic socialist commitments to improving income security policy, it should come as no surprise that the leftist government of the Front Populair enacted no notable income security adoption. It should also be no surprise that upon ascension to government, the new centrist government of Radical Front renegade Eduord Daladier moderated its substantial revision of Front legislation with passage of its own favored reform, the family allowance law of 1938 (Luebbert 1991, 222–223; Misra 1994).

The French combination of post–Popular Front, Catholic-led legislation of a family allowance law, and lack of any Popular Front income security adoption provides a substantive, if not formal, exception to the findings of Equation 1. Formally, the combination allows a solution for the Boolean model because of temporal aggregation bias: The Popular Front governments of 1936 to 1938 stand in for the reformist Catholic government of late 1938 that actually passed France's 1938 law. Substantively, we have an exception here to the ostensibly deterministic Boolean model.[7]

To summarize the wave of social democratic reform, by the mid-1930s Denmark, Norway and Sweden, the most governmentally robust of these Social democratic/labour governments, were on their way to what would retroactively be designated the socialist or "social democratic" model of welfare capitalism (Esping-Andersen 1990). New Zealand was engaged in a similar bundle of policy innovations, although without as strong a concentration on long-term working class mobilization or socialist universalism (Castles 1985). Belgium had turned from her early Catholic route to reform to a Catholic-Left route that would recur in many nations during the 1940s. With its family allowance law of 1938, the French parliament passed the last major income security adoption to issue from an entirely non-Socialist government in democratic, continental Europe until the 1950s. By that time income security programs had become well-institutionalized aspects of all affluent capitalist democracies.

Secular Centrist Routes

As I noted earlier, governments marked by social democratic leadership (or, at least, participation) did not entirely dominate 1930s (and 1940s) income security reforms. Wherever secular-centrist parties—namely, U.S. Democrats and Canadian Liberals—held such undisputed control of government as to render conservative oppositions politically impotent they also enacted major programs. Such strong liberal reformers arose only where nationally notable social democratic parties were lacking.

"We advocate unemployment and old-age insurance under state law" read the Democratic platform under which Franklin Delano Roosevelt was elected in 1932 (Schlesinger 1959, 301); however, that platform was broad-ranging in content and appeal. The Roosevelt

[7] In sum, social democratic government is not, strictly speaking, a sufficient condition for 1930s income security reform because the 1938 French reform was principally forged and championed by the Catholic *Partie Democrate Populaire* in the face of Socialist opposition (Quexteaux and Fournier 1978). The French case calls attention to possible problems of spuriousness in Boolean analysis and to the occurrence of a reformist government beyond our theoretical and inductive generalization. Fortunately, in all of the cases analyzed here other than France, it was a government marked by, at least, socialist participation that passed the reform or reforms in question. What is more, all of the reforms attributed to secular-centrist governments by the Boolean results were once that these governments passed. Thus, the results of our deterministic Boolean model closely describe the not quite deterministic reality of 1930 income security reform as measured here.

administration initially applied itself to its planks for fomenting a business-led recovery stimulated by governmental industrial reorganization and agricultural subsidy while providing temporary relief and public works. After all, "broad capitalist support for the 'first' New Deal" of 1932 to 1934 was not sensibly risked by pressing for labor, tax, or welfare reforms singularly unpopular with business (Schlesinger 1958, 1959; Amenta 1998.) Then, in June of 1934, President Roosevelt, affirming his faith in social insurance with a message to congress, sent a planning referral to the cabinet-level Committee on Economic Security that deferred action until after the congressional election of November, 1934.

With this election, the Democrats attained unprecedented majorities in the House (74 percent) and Senate (63 percent). In the theoretical terms of Amenta (1998), the 1934 election gave a "pro-spender" congressional coalition drawn from two-party, competitive, non-machine, Progressive, and Left party districts a near majority, enough of one, given a strong, progressively minded president, for major social policy reform. In simpler terms, Roosevelt, backed by rare, non–Southern Democrat majorities—270 non–Southern Democrat representatives and 71 non–Southern Democrat senators—spelled Second New Deal reform. In Amenta's statist-tilted terms, near legislative majorities from institutional contexts conducive to reform were key for reform. In my more class-analytical terms, release of the Democratic party (labor-allied since the Al Smith nomination of 1928) from its reactionary Southern Democratic bride of convenience fully galvanized the proto–social democratic, non–Southern Democrats of the next few decades, at least through the Democts' late-1960s alienation of labor (Quadagno 1994).[8] Indeed, the emergence in 1962 to 1966 of the *next* great advance of social reform (Great Society) off the *next* high plateau of non–Southern Democrat strength reinforces my proto–social democratic rereading of Amenta's "pro-spenders."[9] See Figure 3.1 for some illustration of "pro-spender" history.

Canada was the site of a second major Great depression-era income security reform. There, a Conservative government nearly succeeded in enacting a major social security adoption and violating the other-

---

[8] That populist and labor mobilizations played some part in the assembly and impact of this proto-Social Democratic ascendance seems clear (Schlesinger, 1958, 1959; Williams 1969).

[9] The brevity and moderate Presidential leadership of the 1934–1938 non–Southern Democrat plateau poses little threat to the view that approximate non-Southern congressional majorities and strong, Left-leaning presidential leadership have spelled proto–social democracy in the United States since 1934.

Figure 3.1. Non–Southern senate: Non-Southern seats as percentage of all (NONSSEN).

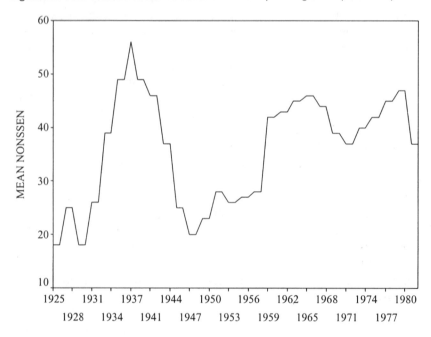

wise perfect Great Depression record of exclusively nonconservative party welfare adoption. R. B. Bennett, confronted with the unemployment of nearly a quarter of all Canadians and the burgeoning of radical and populist parties in the form of the Cooperative Commonwealth Confederation and Social Credit, moved for an eleventh-hour "new deal" just before constitutionally inevitable 1935 elections (Brown 1987, 452). An unemployment insurance bill was included among the hurriedly prepared bills the Parliament passed on the eve of the election; however, inexorable electoral defeat by the Liberals ensued. At once, Liberal Prime Minister Mackenzie King, guarding the Liberal flank against provincial objections to Federal encroachment, quickly referred the "new deal" legislation to the Canadian Supreme Court. The Court quickly declared most major provisions of the Conservative legislation, including the unemployment insurance law, unconstitutional (Brown 1987, 343; Granatstein 1975, 252–253).

Reformulation of an unemployment insurance law commenced soon, but it proceeded hesitantly because of antifederal objections from Alberta, New Brunswick, and Quebec (Granatstein 1975, 252). Only with the 1938 to 1940 ascendence of Keynesian counter-cyclical thinking among public service economists, onset of war, waning of unemployment, and provincial need for wartime federal grants did King's cautious return to federal economic interventionism extend to action on unemployment insurance (Granatstein 1975, Ch. 7; Brown, 1987, 453). On January 16, 1940, King wrote to the provincial premiers, "Authorities in the field of unemployment insurance are generally agreed that the most favourable time for its establishment is a period of rising employment during which a fund can be built up out of which benefits can subsequently be paid" (Granatstein 1975, 253). He completed this case for federal social action with an additional note to Alberta Premier William Aberhart counseling federal macroeconomic intervention. In this, King informed Aberhart that New Brunswick and Quebec "advised me that they realized the great importance of having immediate steps taken to meet post-war conditions of unemployment" (Granatstein 1975, 253). Shortly after, provincial approval for a constitutional amendment giving Ottawa the power to enact unemployment legislation was won. The Unemployment Insurance Act was finally passed in the late summer of 1940. A nearly three-quarters parliamentary majority was in place for six years after the 1940 election, permitting a measure of Canadian proto–Social Democracy. Indeed, by the spring of 1941, Principal March's Committee on Reconstruction had begun designing a Keynesian-welfarist peace. Social reform seemed ascendant.

Nonadopters

It is easy to imagine how the United Kingdom might have added major welfare reforms to the Depression era. Unemployment, stubbornly above 10 percent in Britain throughout the 1920s, was the main campaign issue in the election of 1929 that brought Labour, aided by Liberal coalition partners, to power. Prime Minister Asquith's pioneering social insurance bills of 1908 and 1911 had been sustained and developed Great Britain into a global welfare leader. Theories of deficitory, counter-cyclical fiscal policies gauged to counter unemployment were abundant by the close of the 1920s. Indeed, before Prime Minister Ramsay MacDonald's arrival at White Hall, Keynes had assisted the Liberal party in the composition of its economic platform with the 1929 campaign piece, *We Can Conquer Unemployment*, and defended the Liberal platform under his own name with the tendentiously titled 1929 pamphlet *Can Lloyd George Do It?* Although the formulae of Keynes' *General Theory* were at least a half-dozen years from completion, Labour had an ally uniquely suited for the inauguration of the Keynesian welfare state (Skidelsky 1967).

Nevertheless, the 1920s had brought an economic catastrophe upon economic unorthodoxy in the form of a deflationary debacle (following quick postwar return to convertibility at a high exchange rate for sterling). Moreover, they had provided a political and economic catastrophe for Labour in the form of the ineffectual General Strike of 1926. As a result, Labour was gun-shy in the face of orthodox economic opinion, then centered with the banking economists of the City of London. Moreover, if Labour patriarchs Ramsay MacDonald and Philip Snowden weighed in for the economic orthodoxy of the City, other strands of Labour's economic opinion favored the stress on industrial organization and socialization that would drive Oswald Mosly to emulate Benito Mussolini's prescription for the public anarchy and state paralysis of democratic class struggle. Thus, Labour squandered 1929 in a combination of squabbling and anti-Keynesian orthodoxy. Labour thereby achieved nothing but the alienation of its Liberal allies, its own fragmentation, and abject defeat in the 1931 election (Sidelsky 1967). By the time that Per Albin Hansson was entering government on the heels of Conservative-Liberal rejection in Sweden, Ramsay MacDonald was lending his name and that of National Labour to help inaugurate a new Conservative dynasty that was both fiscally conservative and antiwelfarist.

In Australia, Labour and its conservative (Country and Nationalist) oppositions followed a similar course. Labour, also in power at the onset of the world economic depression, was soon jettisoned, triggering the decades-long Nationalist/Country coalition government.

In Switzerland, Radical and Conservative Catholic pluralities were sufficient to sustain Social Democratic exclusion from the Federal Council until 1943 and to preclude any major Lib-Lab, Christian-Left, or other variant of welfare reform for almost another decade.

Routes to Program Adoption in a Era of War and Reconstruction

Examination of the historical record for 1931 to 1940 shows that the entry of social democratic parties into government, rare earlier, was a major impetus to that decade's income security reforms. The same holds for the 1941 to 1950 period, indeed for the whole 1931 to 1950 era of Great Depression, World War II, and postwar recovery.

Examination of the historical record for the full 1931 to 1950 era also suggests that, where social democratic (and kindred) parties are lacking, most remaining adoptions have direct explanations in the activities of extremely strong secular-centrist parties or of Catholic parties. Indeed, on closer examination, it appears that virtually all program adoptions by Catholic-led governments emerged from Catholic-*Left* coalition governments. Thus, Left-party government seems to have been essential to 1940s welfare reform even when Left governmental participation falls short of governmental leadership. With this in mind, I hypothesize that social democratic participation in government, supplemented by the rule of extremely strong (effectively unopposed) secular-centrist parties, generated most, if not all, income security program adoptions during the 1941 to 1950 period. In this decade, however, the number of Catholic-Left coalition governments passing reforms increased from one in the 1930s (Paul-Henri Spaak's Belgian government of late 1938 and early 1939) to six governments: Austrian, Belgian, Dutch, French, and, on two occasions (1945 and 1946), Italian. Christian democracy appears to have been shaped in the crucible of Left-Catholic political cooperation/ competition.

Routes to 1940s Adoptions: Second Formulae

Boolean analysis of 1940s data stresses the presence of (a) social democratic participation in government (*socialist governmental participation*), (b) extremely strong centrist government (*liberal governmental strength*), and (c) decennial introductions of any of the five major types of income security programs (W40I). Data confirm expectations. *Socialist governmental participation* was coded 1 to include governments with social democratic *prime ministers* or more than 30 percent of legislative support from social democratic parties, or both; and it was otherwise coded 0. *Liberal governmental strength* was coded 1 for liberal parties with at least 60 percent of the seats in each relevant legislative house and, in presidential systems, possession of the presidency by acquisition of at least 55 percent of the popular vote. Social democratic governmental control (*socialist government*) and Catholic control (*Catholic government*) were also coded. The former was set equal to 1 when social democratic parties (again, broadly construed) held all governing seats and ministries of government or, in cases of coalition government, either (a) 40 percent of coalition seats and the prime ministry or (b) 60 percent of coalition seats in lieu of the prime ministry. The latter was coded analogously. Again, nations marked by both *socialist governmental participation* and *liberal governmental strength* were assumed to be conducive to welfare program adoption. Cases are the twelve of the 1930s analysis plus Austria, Italy,

Germany, Japan, and Finland, all of which had joined the ranks of the industrialized democracies by the postwar years.[10]

A satisfactory Boolean analysis by strict QCA standards was impossible for the 1940s because the Danish case was inconsistent with a solution: Denmark, despite extensive, strong social democratic government passed no major new programs in our five program areas. (It did not legislate family allowances until 1952.) However, with Denmark excluded, the hypothesized two-factor explanation for which I found support in the 1930s, reasserts itself for the 1940s. That is,

(Eq. 3)   W40A = *socialist governmental participation*
                 + liberal governmental strength

The resistance of just one case, Denmark, to a Boolean solution despite only two explanatory variables documents strong statistical support for a partisan government model centered around socialist governance.[11] The simple multiple regression for the same variables that figure in the Boolean analyses follows (with unstandardized slope coefficient estimates and *t*-statistics in parentheses):

(Eq. 4)   W40A = 0.00 + 0.917 *socialist governmental participation*
                 (0.00) (9.95)
                 + 1.00 *liberal governmental strength* for 1931 – 1940.
                 (3.26)

This simple OLS equation has an R^2 (corrected for degrees of freedom) equal to 0.647. In standardized terms, where regression coefficients resemble partial correlation coefficients, we get the following:

(Eq. 5)   W40A = 0.917 *socialist governmental participation*
                 + .559 *liberal governmental strength*

[10] Nations included now are our core fifteen cases (Australia, Austria, Belgium, Canada, Denmark, Finland, France, Germany, Italy, the Netherlands, New Zealand, Norway, Sweden, Switzerland, the United Kingdom. and the United States; the Euro-Fascist Austria, Germany, and Italy (returned to democracy); and Finland (now clearly politically democratic and comparable to our other cases in affluence according to Maddison's [1991] 1950 tally) and Japan (now also clearly politically democratic and comparably affluent) (see Therborn 1977; and Maddison 1991).

[11] The "adoptionless" cases—Germany, Switzerland, and Denmark (the former consistent with predictions, the latter inconsistent)—are all "influential" cases in regressions; however, ancillary regressions "6" through "11" indicate robust conclusions about social (and Christian) democratic causal potency during the 1930s and 1940s. On OLS estimation procedures, see n. 5; on further regression equations 6–11.

Social Democratic Route

Equations 4 and 5 show once again social democracy's preeminent role as governmental participant in 1940s adoptions of income-security programs. The social democratic route taken up by Denmark, Sweden, Norway, and New Zealand during the Great Depression was continued by Sweden and Norway. (New Zealand exhausted possibilities for program adoption, as they are defined here, with its 1938 passage of a Social Security Act, whereas Denmark delayed passage of family allowances until 1952.) This route also was taken up by three severe pre-1940 welfare laggards, Australia, Finland, and Japan, along with one nation that had been in reformist hibernation since 1920, the United Kingdom. Joint socialist/Catholic reform from within Catholic-led governments in Austria, Italy, and the Netherlands, as well as from within socialist-led ones in Belgium, characterized further social policy innovations. All these cases, plus Canada's maverick liberal one, merit more detailed attention.

In Norway, and Sweden, the programmatic foundations of welfare capitalism that had been extended by socialist-led governments in the 1930s were further extended under socialist auspices by the passage of family allowance legislation in 1946 to 1948. These nations' adoptions of child-and-family support systems completed the programmatic foundations of these emerging paragons of welfare capitalism. They did so with notable help from women activists in the tradition of Ellen Key and natalist advocates of population growth via family support in the tradition of the Myrdals. Indeed, women's movement and natalist activists (the latter intent on increasing France's population of potential conscripts by increasing the birth rate) provided important allies for social democratic movements throughout the developed world (Misra 1994).

In Australia, program consolidation was realized in a flurry of pent-up reform. Across the length of the first four decades of the century (and sixteen federal, parliamentary elections) the Australian Labour Party (ALP) was far and away the most electorally well-supported socialist or labor party in the world, averaging over 43 percent of the vote in 16 elections. Moreover, it was supported by a relatively powerful labor movement that had typically mobilized a third of Australian workers—never as little as a fifth—since the turn of the century. Yet liberal (free trade) and conservative opposition, crystallizing into a right-of-center federal block by the close of World War I, had excluded the ALP from government, except for its disastrous 1929 to 1931 exposure to voter wrath caused by early World-depression economic disarray. This electoral anger led to prompt voter rejection. In a 1941 to 1949 repossession of government, however, ALP enacted overdue reforms. First, the ALP led government passed an amendment to the federal constitution to make welfare legislation a commonwealth rather than state responsibility (Castles 1985, 21–25). Previously, federal powers had been arguably restricted to invalidity and old-age pension, although not decisively enough to bar federal legislation: "... the achievement of the Federal Labour administration of the 1940s may be seen as the completion of the process of setting up the basic range of social security programs" (Castles 1985, 23). This process of somewhat tardy but very accelerated program consolidation proceeded through the passage of a federal law of child endowments in 1941 and of federal unemployment and health insurance laws in 1944. Before victory in the Pacific had been celebrated in 1945, the programmatic foundations for Australian welfare capitalism had been laid.

Finland merits 1940s inclusion in our population of industrialized democracies: In this decade its per capita GDP began to approach that of the other nations studied here (Maddison 1991, Table 1.1). Legalization of the Communist People's Democratic Union (PDU) lifted Finland out of the categorical limbo of ostensibly competitive polities marred by illegalizations of important aspiring electoral opposition (see n. 3). Yet more to the point for this study, Finland entered into the ranks of income security adoptors with the passage of a public pension law by Social Democrat Karl August Fagerholm's PDU- (or Communist-) supported government of 1948 to 1950.

In Japan, leftist parties were catapulted into a unique period of national leadership when the Japan Socialist Party attained 26 percent of the vote and nearly a third of parliamentary seats in Japan's second democratic general election in April of 1947: "Overnight, the Socialists became Japan's largest party in the lower house. ... A three party coalition materialized in June 1947 among the JSP, the Democratic Party, and the National Cooperative Party with Katayama serving as Japan's first Socialist Prime Minister" (Stockwin 1992, 527–528). Crisis-torn from the outset because of an economy beset by accelerating prices and food shortages, the government of Katayama Tetsu was soon fissured by conflicts over a vast array of problems: nationalization (of coal mines); divergent constituencies (worker and peasant, anti-Communist, and "fellow traveler"); labor relations; transit fees; and so on (Stockwin 1992, 528–529). Yet Katayama was able to spearhead passage of an unemployment compensation law before the March, 1948, collapse of his government.

In France, Gouin's Socialist-Center government of early 1946 passed

France's first compulsory, amply funded retirement and workman's compensation laws as part of a flurry of reforms enacted while the immediate postwar (i.e., post–Liberation Front) popularity of the Left was still high. In Belgium, Socialist Dan von Acker's Left-Center government (with sixty-four Socialist, nine Communist, sixty-three Catholic, and thirty-three Liberal seats) passed its first compulsory health insurance law.

Last but not least, the 1940s witnessed the historical high point of Labour Party power in the United Kingdom. Attlee's Labour government of 1945 to 1950 is perhaps best known for its 1946 inauguration of the National Health Service, a quantum leap in the national provision of health care and fundamental overhaul of the series of public health insurance policies initiated in 1911 by Prime Minister Herbert Asquith (and Treasury Minister David Lloyd George). Less famously, shortly after its ascent to power in July 1945, Clement Attlee's Labour government, exceeding all British predecessors in reformist vigor, passed Britain's first family allowance law. With the 1945 to 1946 passage of the National Health Service Act and National Insurance Act, health, pension, unemployment, and workman's compensation laws were dramatically upgraded. Indeed, at mid-century, Britain, whose welfare system has recently come to be viewed as a liberal, residual, laggard one, began a reign as welfare leader in the European march toward the legislation of social rights (Esping-Andersen 1990, chap. 3; Amenta 1998, chap. 7).

Secular Centrist (or Liberal) Route

In September of 1943, the "Report on Social Security for Canada" of Principal James's Committee for Reconstruction was sent to Prime Minister King (Granatstein 1975, 257). Intentionally or not, the report echoed the 1942 endorsement of a program of family allowances by the increasingly popular and influential Cooperative Commonwealth Federation (Granatstein 1975, 279). In addition, its stress on regular monthly payments to families with children "as part of the direct attack on poverty where it is bound up with the strain imposed by a large family on a small income" raised questions about federal favoritism and pandering to Quebec, where families were unusually large (Granatstein 1975, 286–287).

These factors added some inducements to the Liberal drive for a family allowance policy. For one thing, family allowances could drive a wedge between agrarians and the Canadian Commonwealth Federation (CCF), which had turned against such allowances on the grounds that they undercut the focus on higher wages urged by trade unionist supporters (Granatstein 1975, 281–283). For another, the Liberal party faced serious challenge in Quebec from the Bloc Populaire of Maurice Duplessis (Granatstein, 1975, 286–287). Moreover, the Liberal development of family allowance legislation preceded the 1942 and 1943 triumphs of the CCF (a foothold in Ontario and government control in Saskatchewan), whereas the Quebec factor weighed a measure of Francophone and anti-federalist cost against uncertain Quebec advantages. As clearly as it was an outgrowth of political pragmatism, Canada's 1944 passage of a family allowance law was the outgrowth of liberal Ottawa's consolidating, wartime Keynesian-welfarist bent (Granatstein 1975, 63, 270–289; Brown 1987, 453, 491).

A Catholic Route?

Signs of a sustained Catholic contribution to income security adoptions emerge with Spaak's Belgian Left-Catholic government of 1938, and they become prominent with the Austrian, Belgian, Italian, and Dutch Catholic-Left governments of the postwar years.

Catholic Church encouragement of personal responsibility for the poor—charities—is as old as the Church. According to the traditional Catholic interpretation of justice, however, "duties have no corresponding rights": the duty of the secure to help the poor comes unaccompanied by any right whereby the poor may enforce charity from the well-to-do (Kersbergen 1991, 111, 74–80).

Nonetheless, the Church came to pronounce it judicious that "wage-earners, since they mostly belong in the mass of the needy, should be specially protected and cared for by government" (*Rerum Novarum* in Gilson 1954, 225–226). True, "the law must not undertake more, or proceed further, than is required for the remedy of the evil or the removal of the mischief" at hand (*Rerum Novarum*, in Gilson 1954, 225). This, according to Kersbergen (1995, 188) presages the doctrine of welfare state "subsidiarity," clearly defined in the 1931 *Quadragesimo Anno*: "Just as it is wrong to withdraw from the individual and commit to a group what private enterprise and industry can accomplish, so too is it an injustice . . . for a larger association to abrogate to itself functions that can be performed efficiently by smaller and lower societies" (McOustra 1990, 45–46). As Kersbergen (1991, 115–117) details, wages ought to be sufficient to support the life and virtue of a frugal wage earner and his family. Indeed, Kersbergen (1991, 1995) suggests a crystallization of Catholic social doctrine and political practice into a Christian democratic theory of "social capitalism" comprising five elementary principles: (a) capitalism's tendency to pay an unjust wage; (b) need for the state, subsidiary to the market, to promote a just wage; (c) advocacy of the interests of society as a whole over divisive interests; (d) repudiation of revolution; and (e) promotion of family savings and proprietorship.

These evolving doctrines influenced the antisocialist reforms of Bismarck and Eduard von Taafe (Zollner 1982; Hofmeister 1982), not to mention low country "early consolidations." Then, during the 1930s, proto–Christian democratic governments systematically committed to movement toward "social capitalism" appeared in Belgium and the Netherlands. Belgium's important 1930s political pioneering of the social gospel of 1931's *Quadragesimo Anno*, via her family allowance law of 1938 to 1939, was propelled from within the Peoples Party's heavily unionized constituency (Boswell 1990, 171–172). This contrasts with France's family allowance law of 1938, which appears to have been more inspired by natalist population reformers seeking national security through augmentation of the pool of military conscripts than it was inspired by progressive social reformers seeking social justice and amelioration (Misra 1994).

Austria's 1948 passage of a family allowance law marked a resumption in Austria's progress toward a complete set of elementary social security programs, interrupted by the authoritarian and fascist turns in 1933 and 1938. Indeed, they capped the successive Absolutist-Socialist reforms of 1883 to 1920 with a more cooperative Catholic-socialist reprise. Leopold Figl's government, which passed it, was the first of the Grand ("Red-Black") Coalitions, which governed this new, highly consensual Austria through 1966. Formation of a fusion of corporatist, consensual, socialist, and Christian democratic elements placed a strong social democratic heart within an equally strong social Christian organism. In fact, Christian democratic metamorphoses of early Catholic parties and Christian democratic entrees into income security reform emerged concurrently during the 1940s. Moreover, the first Christian democratic parentings of social insurance in Austria, Italy, and the Netherlands occurred in the context of Christian democratic coalitional governments with socialist, social democratic, labor, and/or communist partners. Where Christian democrats ruled alone, as in postwar Germany, we find more restrained, delayed welfare reforms.

Again, the pervasiveness of broadly defined social democratic partners to Christian Democratic–led governments in the passage of income-security reforms is suggestive. Catholic parties seem to have picked up the reformist thrusts of social democratic partners in governmental coalitions. (Perhaps this first greased coalitions and later aided competition for working class votes.) In any case, a review of

Red-Black coalitions suggests the following intriguing hypothesis for future study: The postwar Christian Democrat commitment to social safety nets emerged as a reaction to some combination of competition and coalition with social democracy.

In nations short on "Red-Black" coalitions, the just-described Christian democratic route to welfare (or "social") capitalism was foreclosed or atrophied. The French, Dutch, and Italian governments of the Catholic Left and Left Catholic coalitions of Georges Bidault, Louis Beel, and Alcide de Gasperi that marked this era now had major programs to pioneer where social security was concerned. In France, Bidault's Left-Center government, dependent upon the Catholic Mouvement Republicaine Populaire, passed important pension and workman's compensation laws in 1946. In the Netherlands, Beel's coalition launched a decade of Christian-socialist government. Equally important, the early Christian-Left coalitions under de Gasperi set precedents for the next half century of Italian politics. Their pervasive inclusion of il Partito Socialista legitimated the reformist tendencies of Democrazia Cristiana's internal labor movement. This, in turn, kept them open to influences from the Left and from their own union movement that may have buttressed the Democrazia Christian Italiana's (DCI) interclass facet and Christian democratic (as opposed to simply conservative Catholic) character (Kersbergen 1991, 1995). (On the other hand, their 1946–1947 inclusion but 1947 ejection of the Partito Communista set up the PCI's elusive thirty-plus-year pursuit of *il compromiso istorico* between the Church and Communism.)

Nonadopters

Germany, Switzerland, the United States, and Denmark were nonadopters. The absence of adoptions in Germany and Switzerland, although consistent with my predictions for nations lacking socialist participation in government or extremely strong secular-centrist leadership, appears to reflect more reformist foot dragging than reaction. Germany and Switzerland would both pass national family allowance programs within a few years: Germany in 1954 and Switzerland in 1962. The Swiss potpourri of socialist and liberal, as well as conservative, forces within the ruling, seven-person Federal Council contained a complex Catholic component. This encompassed Christian democratic as well as conservative and laissez-faire ideas within the Conservative Catholic Party, ideas that would eventually help promote social reform. Similarly, worker and centrist tendencies within the German CU would soon join forces with conservative neonatalists to press through German family allowances.

Returned in the early 1940s to non–Southern Democrat pluralities of only 35 to 45 percent, the United States reverted to its nonreformist ways. During the 1940s, the U.S. social policy is most notable for its postwar dilution of full-employment legislation, the passage of Taft-Hartley restriction on labor unions, and rejection of national health insurance, (Orloff 1993; Goldfield 1989, 1991; Amenta 1998).

The most interesting nonadopter is Denmark, with no 1940s policy adoptions, despite social democratic–led (minority) governments during the summer/fall of 1945 and throughout most of 1947 to 1950. As already noted, Denmark did pass a family allowance law in 1952 under a Liberal Party–led government.

What can be said about Denmark's delayed 1952 adoption of family allowances? The Danish "delay" may in part reflect the incompleteness of basic-program adoptions as indicators of reform, although Esping-Andersen (1985 205–208) stresses the vapidity of postwar Danish economic policy through 1957. This delay can also be attributed to the general disarray of Danish politics after Prime Ministers Thorvald Stauning, Vilhelm Buhl, and Erik Scavenius's 1939 to 1943 collaboration with Denmark's Nazi conquerors. Although the pattern of social democratic acquiescence to Nazi occupation ended with the refusal of the Scavenius government to impose the death sentence on saboteurs, the name of the Danish Social Democrats was already tarnished. In particular, Nazi demands for the imprisonment of all communists had been implemented with some success, thereby creating a strongly motivated accuser of social democratic war crimes. The damage was done. At the same time Danish communists, both because of their key role in the anti-Fascist resistance and because of extensive popular enthusiasm for the accomplishments of the Red Army, gained popularity and influence after World War II. Indeed, they gained roughly 12 percent of the popular vote and of parliamentary seats in the 1945 general election. The inability of the Social Democrats to overcome continued communist bitterness, despite some conspicuous courting, left the Social Democrats out of government throughout 1946 and 1947 and deprived them of a majority government in 1947 to 1950—indeed, helped deprive them of this until 1957. Moreover, the debilitation of the Social Democrats left a vacuum that no other party could fill: an unbroken succession of minority governments, Liberal as well as Social Democrat, from the end of World War II until 1957. In this atmosphere, the passage of important legislation was generally stymied. (For example, Esping-Andersen [1985] reduces the Social Democrats to one important piece of legislation for the entire 1945–1957 period, the "much delayed" universal, flat-rate pension of 1956 [p.91]. I attribute the failure of a Danish Social Democratic income security reform during the 1945 to 1950 period (effectively, due to the Nazi Occupation, the 1945 to 1950 period) to this temporary Social Democratic political emasculation. Indeed, I impute the absence of any income security reform during the period to a general political disarray and incapacity rooted in Social Democrat–Nazi wartime collaboration. I attribute the eventual Liberal's passage in 1952 of a Danish family allowance law to the inevitable adoption of a broadly legitimate and popular policy by one of the other left-of-center parties before too many years had passed.

Rounding out Welfare Reform in Hard Times

Overall, a simple partisan rule model goes a long way toward explaining welfare program adoption during the 1930s and 1940s. But how important are these adoptions?

In Chapter 1, I provide some sense of the impact of cumulative program adoptions c. 1920 on subsequent program development. In particular, I showed that early adoptions and consolidations are related to program performance around 1980. However, shorter term assessment of the relation between program adoption and performance can help further assess the importance of adoptions. Such assessment is possible with data on social rights generously provided by the investigators Professors Walter Korpi and Joakim Palme and associates at the Stockholm Institute for Social Research.

Monographs and papers by Palme (1990), Kangas (1991), Wennemo (1992), and Carroll (1994) of the Stockholm Institute for Social Research provide preliminary data on old-age, health care, family allowance, and unemployment compensation policies, respectively.[12] That is to say, they offer information on all of the policies of direct concern to us except workman's compensation policy. These data provide information on coverage (of maximum potential target populations) for each of these programs. They also document income replacement features of each of the programs. Income replacement figures document the extent to which income is sustained at

---

[12] These data were obtained from graphs as well as tables in Palme (1990), Kangas (1991), Wennemo (1994), and Carroll (1994), and they are elaborated on in n. 13. These are preliminary data because fully revised, updated, and publicly available data from the Stockholm Institute Social Research (SISR) project await Korpi (forthcoming). The data used here in analyses, though not yet available for display, were graciously provided for use by Korpi and his SISR colleague.

pre-coverage levels, such as pre-retirement or pre-unemployment levels, by program benefits; or they measure the extent to which, in the case of family allowances, subsidies give a percentage boost to pre-allowance income.[13] Table 3.3 on page 81 displays correlations between program adoptions (present or absent for a decade) and program changes in coverage and income replacement during a decade (for pooled data on the 1931 to 1940 and 1941 to 1950 periods). Very simply, the correlation between the presence (versus the absence) of adoption during a decade and changing coverage and income replacement during a decade are substantial: 0.529 for program adoption and increasing coverage during the same decade, 0.526 for program adoption and increasing income replacement during a decade.

Returning to the explanation of 1930s and 1940s adoptions, the simple model of socialist participation in government, augmented by strong secular-centrist government, fits the two decades very well. Using OLS regression for the pooled data for the 1930s and 1940s, I obtain the following strong results:

[13] The underlying measures of program coverage are averages of coverage figures for several programs for 1930, 1939, and 1950. These figures are then converted into change figures for the 1930s (1930–1939) and the 1940s (1939–1940). This is done with data on coverage figures from scholars of the Stockholm Institute for Social Research, often in the form of figures extracted from graphs (i.e., Palme 1990 for pension programs; Kangas 1991 for health care programs; Wennemo 1992 for family allowances; and Carroll 1994 for unemployment compensation). In somewhat more concrete terms, coverage is measured as benefit recipients as a proportion of retirees in the case of old-age pensions; as the portion of the population publicly insured against illness in the case of health care; and as the insured public (entitled to make claims in case of unemployment) as a proportion of labor force participants for the case of unemployment compensation. It is measured somewhat more idiosyncratically for the case of family allowances, that is, as a set of "guesstimates" of proportions of children covered. These estimates are 0.1, 0.2 and 0.3 for nations with means-tested coverage for third (and up), second (and up), and first (and up) children, respectively; and, in the case of non–means-tested systems, as 0.5 for third children, (and up), 0.75 for second children, and up, and 1.0 for first children (on up).

Income replacement is similarly measured in terms of decennial changes in indexes of items for several programs. It is measured for the case of unemployment compensation in terms of the following underlying measure: unemployment compensation benefits for a four-person, two-child, one-earner household in which the earnings are those of an average industrial worker and benefits are expressed as a proportion of these earnings. (Carroll 1994). The underlying measure for health benefits is health benefits as a proportion of the income of the same four-person, two-child, one–industrial-worker-earner household (Kangas 1991). The underlying measure for family allowances measures benefits for the same household, again as a proportion of its income (see Wennemo 1994). No replacement rates are used for pensions due to the absence of available data on 1939 programs. Korpi and colleagues are thanked for permission to publish results of analyses done with these data before their full release into the public domain.

(Eq. 6)   W3 - 40I

$$= 0.00 + 0.944 \times \textit{socialist governmental participation}$$
$$(0.00) \quad (10.91)$$

$$+ 1.00 \times \textit{liberal governmental strength} \text{ for } 1931 - 1950,$$
$$(7.46)$$

$$R^2 = .822.$$

In standardized terms,

(Eq. 7) $W3\text{-}40I = 1.00 \times \textit{socialist governmental participation} + .684$
$\times \textit{liberal governmental strength}$

That is, the two variables, *socialist governmental participation* and *liberal governmental strength*, explain 82 percent of the variance in whether or not a nation passed one or more adoptions in either decade. Indeed, the increment to the probability of an adoption from a strong liberal government was about 1.00 (specifically 1.01), whereas that for the occurrence of socialist participation in a government was 0.944. In the virtually correlational terms of the standardized equations, the impact of *socialist governmental participation* seems larger, a perfect 1.00, whereas that of liberal government is still a very substantial 0.684. What if measures of social rights are further analyzed?

When I regress the pooled 1930s and 1940s measures of decennial change in coverage that were used in Table 3.2 on the regressors of Equation 6, neither slope is remotely significant (e.g., greater than its standard error). However, when I regress analogous income replacement rates on the same regressors, there is support for the partisan model:

(Eq. 8)   Income replacement$_{1930-1950}$

$$= .074 + .079 \times \textit{liberal governmental strength}$$
$$(0.94) \quad (1.61)$$

$$+ .093 \times \textit{socialist governmental participation}$$
$$(1.71)$$

The partisan effects are now marginally significant (at the .05 level for *socialist governmental participation* and at just below that for *liberal government strength*). Indeed, *socialist governmental participation* has a standardized regression coefficient of .301. Moreover, if we focus attention on *socialist governmental participation* alone and employ a continuous measure of socialist participation in government, namely, a measure of average of proportions of the legislative seats held by Left parties participating in government across all the years of a decade, we obtain significant results for program coverage as well as income replacement. The coverage equation in question is

(Eq. 9) $Coverage_{1930-1950}$

$$= .074 + .100 \times socialist\ governmental\ participation$$
$$(1.72)\ (2.03)$$

The analogous income replacement equation is:

(Eq. 10) $Replacement_{1930-1950}$

$$= .029 + .090\ socialist\ governmental\ participation$$
$$(1.68)\ (1.73)$$

Equation 9 has a standardized coefficient of .370 and a corrected R^2 of .104, whereas Equation 10 has a standardized coefficient of .321 and a corrected R^2 of .070. In brief, the socialist core of my partisan model tends to hold for measures of social rights as well as for program adoptions.

It bears repeating that Catholic, as well as liberal, parties play a role in providing socialist ones with coalitional partners. For example, if I extend the specification of the pooled 1930s and 1940s equation for adoptions (Equation 6) by separately specifying instances of socialist participation in government marked by Catholic leadership of government, this specification yields the following for 1931 to 1950:

(Eq. 11)   W3-40I

$$= 0.00 + 0.844\ socialist\ governmental\ participation$$
$$(0.00)\ (9.95)$$
$$+ .956\ liberal\ governmental\ strength$$
$$(6.34)$$
$$+ .355\ Catholic\ government$$
$$(4.50)$$

This equation has a corrected $R^2 = .849$. So switching from a focus on social democratic participation in government to one on separate Red- and Black-led governments, we see that both mattered for 1930s and 1940s welfare policy.

Conclusions and Discussion

The pervasiveness of social democratic–engineered social insurance reforms during the Great Depression and World War II years *wherever* social democratic parties were electorally notable is no truism. On the contrary, works as distinguished and diverse as Heclo (1974), Baldwin (1990), and Williamson and Pampel (1993) have stressed the role of centrist and conservative parties in the enactment of social security adoptions. In fact, for this 1931 to 1950 period, conservative reform is nonexistent except for Canadian (non-Catholic) Conservative R. B. Bennett's short-lived 1935 unemployment compensation reform. Enduring secular-centrist reforms are premised on the absence of legislatively consequential social democratic parties, as in Canada and the United States. Overinterpretation of such factors as civil servant William Beveridge's authorship of his famed report of 1942, *Social Insurance and Allied Services Under a Conservative Government*, is used to link conservative parties to legislative outputs, whereas no interpretation of actual legislative (e.g., parliamentary) activities would be corroborative.

Catholic reform is, except for France's 1938 Family Allowance Bill, always joint Red-Black (Socialist-Catholic) reform. The extensive role played by social democratic allies or competitors in Christian democrat–led reform has gone virtually uncommented on, even in the best of the works on Christian democracy (Kersbergen 1995). The extreme predominance of social democratic reform from Hansson's 1932 assumption of government to Attlee's 1951 replacement by Winston Churchill has also been missed. My work has unearthed a social democratic ascendance in income security reform shortly before and after World War II that had been lost amidst the fanfare for post-1950s social democratic reform (e.g., Korpi 1978, 1983; Stephens 1979; Baldwin 1990; Williamson and Pampel 1993).

Social democracy's predominance in 1930s and 1940s social reform points to a kind of Golden Age of social democracy, as well as to a Golden Age for so-called social democratic theories of the welfare state. As we shall see in forthcoming chapters of this work, the 1960s and 1970s, although widely highlighted as apogees of social democratic reformism, are less so than the 1930s and 1940s. This, as we shall see, at least is the case unless we consider neocorporatism to be little more than a euphemism for social democracy.[14]

---

[14] The participation of women political activists in the development of late-1930s and post–World War II family policies provides one important reminder that parties function as aggregators of various interests within themselves as well as out in society at large (Misra 1994); however, the presence of such activists does not seem to have been necessary for 1930s and 1940s adoptions of major new social programs. New Zealand Labourites implement reforms without female activism, as do European Christian Democrats generally.

Paradoxically, the Golden Age of social democracy is a kind of Golden Age of liberalism as well.[15] It provides the occasion for such reformist "secular centrist" parties as the "Second New Deal" Democrats and the "Mackenzie King" Canadian Liberals. Freed from both classically liberal and conservative factions and oppositions, from both laissez-faire and traditional caution, recently centrist liberals begin to implement the Progressive liberal agenda in force. However, as Przeworski (1985, postscript) suggests, these progressive liberal agendas of income maintenance, plus progressive taxation, macroeconomic regulation, and industrial regulation, were virtually identical to the agendas pursued by actually governing Social Democrats. Indeed, in the abstract, where matters of income and job security are concerned, the realized Social Democrat agenda is the textbook agenda of progressive liberalism (Musgrave and Musgrave 1985; see also Chapter 8 following). Thus, we should neither be surprised at the occurrence of proto–social democratic policy action by secular-centrist parties (e.g., the Democrats of the Second New Deal) nor by a substantial dovetailing of social democratic and liberal agendas and policies.

Still, it was social democratic and labor parties, aided by agrarian and Catholic allies, who typically provided the mass mobilization and collective action needed for realization of the progressive liberal policy agenda of stable markets and secure citizens. In developed capitalist democracies of Great Depression and immediate postwar years, the time of this provision truly entailed a measure of that democratic class struggle famously proclaimed by Lipset (1983, [1960]).

[15] Present reference to 1930s and 1940s "Golden Age" of social democracy may seem to conflict with claims for a trio of "golden" and "glorious" post-1950 decades (see Esping-Andersens 1999, and Scharpf 1999, respectively). The two historical dubbings are not irreconcilable. My pre-1950 golden "child may be father to man"—mature, then paunched—gilded by those stressing post-War welfare state achievements; my golden era may figure as foundation to the burgeoning (if increasingly indebted) coffers of 1950–1980 advanced welfare states.

CHAPTER FOUR

Midcentury Consolidation

> Labour organization followed closely on the heels of industrial development in Europe and by the last decade of the last century the labour movement was a social and political force to be reckoned with. . . . The crisis of the 1930s and the high employment levels of the war brought on a growth of labour organizing.   (Stephens 1980, 113–117)

By 1950, following two decades of social democratic reform, ten of the seventeen largest affluent capitalist democracies had implemented all five major types of income maintenance programs—those for the aged and retired, victims of work accidents, the sick, the unemployed, and child-rearing households—and had thereby consolidated firm programmatic foundations for subsequent welfare-state development.[1] Only Canada, Denmark, Finland, Germany, Japan, Switzerland, the United States, and, arguably, Belgium had not achieved such consolidation,[2] and even

[1] With a tally that includes Ireland, which will join the analyses of Chapter 5, eleven of eighteen nations were consolidators by 1950. However, Ireland has been deleted from qualitative analyses of programs because of her formal dependence on Britain through its first four adoptions (completed eight years before her 1919 independence) and her 1944 mimicry of Beveridge's (United Kingdom) family allowance proposals of 1943, a year before Attlee's formation of a Labour government and passage of a family allowance law in 1945.

[2] One might argue that Canada's Hospital Insurance and Diagnostic Service Act of 1957 warrants its inclusion among the postwar consolidators. However, Canada's wartime and postwar planning were precocious, not deferred by a need for protracted prior legal or even constitutional reform; and they were accompanied by a Liberal rather than a Conservative government. For Canada, unlike Germany, no license for an extended postwar period can be purchased for 1952, much less 1957. Indeed, the Hospital Insurance and Diagnostic Service Act of 1957 merely subsidized existing provincial programs that the Medical Care Act of 1966 would comprehensively reorganize and upgrade or arguably replace (Guest 1985, 147–163).

three of these would soon catch up by adopting family allowance programs: Denmark and Switzerland in 1952 and the Federal Republic of
Germany in 1954 (see Table 2.1).

What can we say, overall, about the long-term causes of this consolidation of the basic repertoire of social insurance programs? What patterns emerge from an examination of the welfare state's long-term
trajectory from Otto von Bismarck to Konrad Adenauer and Herbert
Asquith to Clement Attlee? Can any simple, underlying commonality
be discerned in the programmatic emergence of advanced capitalist
welfare states through midcentury? Whatever pattern might emerge,
how would it compare with the patterns proposed by Esping-
Andersen (1990), Castles and Mitchell (1991), Ragin (1993b), and
others? What movements and institutions underlie the adoption of
communitarian functions by states?

Patterns of Explanation in Review

When nations cross a certain threshold of economic "development," complete with its attendant dissolution of traditional familial,
communal, and other insitutional safeguards against destitution, they
subject themselves to new modes of social insecurity. Yet the new
insecurities generate demands for new social safety nets. Moreover,
development provides unprecedented material abundance and with
it, means to meet the new demands. In Chapter 1, I pinpointed this
threshold for early in this century at around $2000 in per capita
GDP (in $1980). Furthermore, an examination of data on about fifty
nations during the second decade of the century indicated that development, for all the maladies and capabilities that it brought forth, was
a merely necessary condition for the adoption of three or more social
security programs by 1920. Politics, broadly construed to encompass
major political institutions and movements as well as governance, are
needed to transform socioeconomic needs and capabilities into policy
reforms.

Do the political institutional sources of welfare reform uncovered
here reveal any simple root cause for income security policy around
midcentury? Seminal German and Austrian precedents seem to have
arisen from the strategic responses of patriarchal state elites to emergent socialist workers' movements. Other early waves of program
innovations and adoptions appear to have involved strategic adoptions
of more centrist Liberal and Catholic governing groups to the rise of
industrial workers' movements (all within the context of unitary

parliamentary democracies). Then, with the advent of the Great Depression, social democratic government became commonplace wherever social democratic parties were already on good electoral footing and wherever their formations of effective (and, thus, sustainable) government were facilitated by strong union allies and centralized state structures. Once social democratic parties had become commonplace participants in government, their reform efforts transformed income security policy. Typically, this occurred under social democratic–led governments, completed by secular centrist (most typically agrarian) junior coalitional partners. Often it transpired under the auspices of Catholic-socialist coalition governments, not infrequently Catholic-led ones.

As for possible root causes, one type of explanatory factor does seem to have figured persistently in the innovation, adoption, and consolidation of major classes of income security programs in the first half of the twentieth century. This is the labor movement. In either of its two principal organizational forms, the labor union and the social democratic (i.e., Social Democratic, Socialist, and Labor) party, the labor movement exerted strong pressures for enhanced social security. Sometimes, as in social democratic Scandinavia, labor movements intentionally steered development of income security policy. Sometimes, as in Bismarckian Germany, they did no more than unintentionally provoke policy development.

Through World War I and its immediate aftermath, labor movements situated outside government, as in Bismarckian Germany, or at the margins of government, as in prewar Britain, tended to provoke governments into cooptive reform measures, albeit at times inadvertently. During the inter–and post–World War II eras, governments with major social democratic participants implemented virtually every income security reform. Catholic party reforms, rare in the 1930s, became closely tied to Red-Black coalitions with working class parties by mid-1940s. Importantly, social democratic parties developed in tandem, indeed in mutual interdependence, with labor unions. Typically, these parties have served as political arms for labor unions; often they have been industrial offshoots of social democracy; commonly both (see Ebbinghaus 1992). Because of the pervasive relevance of labor unions for social democracy and because of social democracy's prevalent relevance to income security policy from Bismarck to Attlee, labor unions merit a close look as a possible long-term force behind the varieties of social democratic routes to welfare-state reforms.

The Union Movement

Average union density (i.e., membership as a percentage of the labor force) over the 1919 to 1950 period provides a straightforward index of the strength of union movement during the period. (Such union density measures have good face validity as first approximations of labor union strength; and data for such measures are available for 1919, 1930, 1939, and 1950.) I measure union density as the average of two figures. One, calculated to get at the long-to-intermediate-term history of labor, is average union density for 1919, 1930, and 1939. The second, used to single out strong post–World War II waves of unionization, which I conjecture to be important for concurrent waves of social democratic governmental and (in turn) income security reform, is union density in 1950. Averaging two measures yields the series of Table 4.1.

This composite 1919 to 1950 union density series is strongly related to 1950s welfare-program consolidation. Eight of the nine most unionized nations are the eight earliest consolidators (consolidated by 1952). Only Belgium, which had no compulsory program of workman's compensation until 1971, breaks the perfect match between most-unionized nations and earliest full consolidators; and the Belgian exception is not clear-cut. Contrary to its ostensibly laggard status, Belgium had a well-funded and extensively adopted program of state-subsidized workman's compensation protection by 1950, despite the program's voluntary status (Berghman, Peters, and Vranken 1987). The program's failure to qualify as a consolidator because of the voluntary character of its system of workman's compensation is largely formal. It does not indicate poor coverage or funding for Belgium voluntary system of industrial accident insurance. In fact, when Belgium's compulsory system of outlays for industrial accident and occupational illness insurance was finally introduced in 1971, expenditures for accident insurance only rose from 12,326 million Belgian francs in 1970, the year before the passage of the new compulsory law, to 16,309 million Belgian francs in 1972, the year after industrial insurance became compulsory for Belgian employees (Berghman, Peters, and Vranken 1987, 816).

If one corrects for Belgium's merely apparent 1950s nonconsolidation, the relation between union density and consolidation approaches perfection, at least if two sources of indeterminacies in our data are addressed. One of these indeterminacies involves the appropriate terminal date for qualification for midcentury consolidation; the other involves where the dividing line between nations with relatively strong

Table 4.1. Union Density and 1950s Welfare Consolidation

	1 Average union density for 1919, 1930, 1939	2 Union density* 1950	3 Average of Cols 1 and 2	4 Year of consolidation	5 Consolidation by 1952
Australia	33.3	50	41.7	1941	1
Sweden	21.3	51	36.2	1948	1
United Kingdom	28.7	40	34.4	1945	1
New Zealand	24.3	38	31.2	1938	1
Belgium	21.0	36	28.5	1971	0
Denmark	22.8	33	27.9	1952	1
Netherlands	20.0	31	25.5	1949	1
Norway	15.3	34	24.7	1946	1
Austria	15.3	40	22.7	1948	1
Switzerland	16.0	29	22.5	1976	0
Germany	12.7	29	20.9	1954	0
Japan	1.3	40	20.7	1971	0
Italy	2.5	37	19.8	1955	0
United States	10.7	22	16.4	not	0
France	10.3	22	16.2	1976	0
Finland	9.7	22	15.9	1963	0
Canada	8.5	19	13.8	1971	0

* Union density data from Stephens 1980 (Table 4.8); consolidation data from Chapter 2, especially Table 2.1.

labor movements and relatively weak labor movements is to be drawn. Here, I pick a 1952 final qualification year for consolidation, adjusting for Denmark's deferral of family allowance legislation until 1952. I also designate Austrian unions as the least strong (the least so of strong unions) because Austria's rate of unionization, although only marginally higher than Switzerland, is deflated by its zero rate during its 1934 to 1944 authoritarian interlude (Table 4.1 and Lueb-bert 1990). With these 1952 and Austrian outer limits to consolidation and union strength, we get a dichotomization into two mutually exclu-sive and exhaustive groups of nations: one of relatively unionized con-solidators and a second of relatively nonunionized nonconsolidators (Table 4.1). (Note the above Belgian adjustment.)

Now, as ranked on overall 1919 to 1950 union density, the nations of Table 4.1 are consolidators all the way down the ranking, from top-ranked Australia with its 41.7 percent long-term average density figure and its 50 percent 1950 density figures, to Austria with its 22.7 percent long-term average density figure and its 40 percent 1950 density figures. Below Austria, all nations are nonconsolidators, from Switzerland with its average union density of 22.5 percent (and 1950 density of 29 percent), through Canada with its average density of 13.8 percent (and its 19 percent rate for 1950).

True, the 1952 and Austrian cutoffs are somewhat arbitrary. Theoretically, I might just as well have picked 1950 or 1955, rather than 1952, as the deadline for consolidation; and I might reasonably have picked Norway or Germany, as opposed to Austria, as the last nation to make the cut as a strong-unions nation. But the designated cutoffs are appropriate. To make no accommodation for Denmark's delayed passage of family allowance legislation (due to the temporary weakening of her collaborationist wartime Left) would show a rigid disregard for historical contingency. To incorporate Austria into the ranks of strongly unionized nations because of the handicap imposed by her authoritarian interlude, despite the strong postwar recuperation of the Austrian labor movement, would misread the Austrian case (see Table 2.1). This is especially so given the irrelevance of Austria's 1934 to 1944 interlude of welfare reform and the quick postwar recuperation of Austrian reform. With the cut-off points selected, the set of top unionizers and the set of consolidators perfectly match. With Belgium dated for a 1950 consolidation instead of for a 1971 one, the correlation between *percentage* of union density and year of consolidation—continuous measures that do not rely on the 1952 and Austrian choices—is 0.869. Indeed, even if Belgium is judged a 1972 consolidator, the correlation between percentage union density and year of consolidation remains a high 0.697.

By any standard, the extent of unionization closely aligns with midcentury consolidation of all five major types of income security programs. Recall that in Chapter 1 we saw that 1920s measures of working-class mobilization and program consolidation correlate quite closely. In particular, working-class mobilization and 1920 consolidation correlate 0.762, and working-class mobilization and 1930 consolidation correlate 0.780. In Chapter 2, we saw that working-class mobilization, although variously operative in distinct contexts, was crucial to income security reform through about 1920. In Chapter 3, we saw that two decades of social democratic–led social reforms followed the onset of the Great Depression and continued through the aftermath of the World War II. Now, Table 4.1 demonstrates that a second, underlying facet of labor movements, the extent of unionization, dovetails with midcentury welfare consolidation. Unions are major societal foundations, allies and political arms of working class parties (Ebbinghaus 1992). As we have seen, they may prompt government policy action even when they are excluded from the corridors of governmental power (Rimlinger 1971). Joined to these aspects of labor movements, the close association between labor union strength and midcentury welfare consolidation indicates that labor did operate as an important underlying source of welfare-state formation. Unionization operates as a general background condition for long-term cumulative income security reform, Indeed, nations that succeeded in building up memberships (relative to potentially recruitable nonagricultural portions of the employed labor forces) strongly, perhaps invariably, tended to lead in the adoption of major welfare-state programs. Nations that lagged behind where union growth was concerned lagged behind in income security policy as well.[3]

I next examine the lessons learned here about the emergence of the welfare state from 1882 through 1952 in relation to those lessons offered by Gosta Esping-Andersen in his influential *Three Worlds of Welfare Capitalism* (1990). I return to the long-term development of welfare states in the chapters to follow, especially Chapter 8.

The Worlds of Welfare Capitalism?

Esping-Andersen (1990) delineates three types of welfare regimes as configurations of policy traits that match up with underlying political projects, particularly social democratic, conservative, and liberal policy regimes and political projects. Each regime is defined in terms of a number of program-related criteria. The social democratic regime denotes universalistic program coverage and low differentiation of program benefits across beneficiaries, similar to Baldwin's (1990) "universalistic" and "solidaristic" welfare state (although Baldwin would uncouple it from social democratic origins). The conservative regime is characterized by its fragmentation and stratification of pensioners, its privileging of civil servant pensioners, and its reinforcement of status differentiation more generally. The liberal regime is defined by the extent of its means testing of beneficiaries, deference to private insurance schemes, and more general deference to free-market mechanisms (Esping-Andersen 1990).

Although each regime is defined in terms of a number of program-related criteria, each is also associated with a political project crucial to its origins, development, and direction. In particular, the social democratic project is one of wage earner solidarity and extensive social

---

[3] Whether labor movements remain central to the development of basic income security programs—their spending levels, coverage rates, benefit characteristics, and so on—after midcentury is a major topic of chapters to come.

democratic electoral mobilization, which was advanced in Denmark, Finland, the Netherlands, Norway, and Sweden (Appendix 8).[4] The conservative one entails a preservation, indeed accentuation of status differences, and a reinforcement of traditional institutions, as advanced in Austria, Belgium, France, Germany, and Italy. The liberal project aspires to some minimal measure of income security whose upper bound is defined by the measure's limits of compatibility with the maintenance, if not the furtherence, of the free market. Australia, Canada, Japan, Switzerland, and the United States tread this political pathway toward a small measure of welfare capitalism.

Esping-Andersen (1990) also analyzes Ireland, New Zealand, and the United Kingdom, but he treats them, finally, as residual cases that fall close to but never squarely within any particular regime type. (Ireland is not quite conservative, New Zealand is not quite liberal, and the United Kingdom resembles both social democratic and liberal types.)

At first sight, Esping-Andersen's regimes show some striking parallels to my configurations (Table 4.2). In particular, his five conservative cases include all three of my Bismarckian early consolidators (Panel A); his five social democratic cases include the three Scandinavian adopters of the 1930s (Panel A); and his liberal cases closely approximate my early nonconsolidators (Panels A and B). Nevertheless, these parallels are quite partial. Although Esping-Andersen's conservative cases encompass my pre–Depression Bismarckian consolidators, they draw in the Catholic consolidator Belgium and the Catholic nonconsolidator France as well (Table 4.2, Panels A and B). What most of Esping-Andersen's conservative cases share, if we recall the Boolean formulas for Bismarckian and Catholic routes to the early consolidation of most major types of welfare programs, are paternal statist legacies plus, by the 1920s, organized Catholic participation in government. Yet so far as pre–Great Depression politics go, they differ on reformer strategies. In particular, they differ on how to deal with labor movements: the Bismarckian state attempted to estrange workers from the workers' movement by means of paternalistic favors, whereas Catholic governments tried to incorporate workers into their own Catholic union movements (Esping-Andersen 1990; Misra and Hicks 1992).

From my perspective, Esping-Andersen's social democratic cases draw on three distinct clusters of pre–Great Depression

[4] Nations are allocated to the regime for which they rank "strong" in Esping-Andersen (1990, Table 3.3). No nation ranks strongly on either less or more than one dimension, which assures a mutually exclusive categorization.

Table 4.2. Clusters of Welfare State Regimes and Routes

Panel A. Clusters of Welfare States According to Esping-Andersen's Welfare Regimes*

Conservative	Social Democratic	Liberal	Residual
Austria	Denmark	Australia	Ireland
Belgium	Finland	Canada	New Zealand
France	Netherlands	Japan	United Kingdom
Germany	Norway	Switzerland	
Italy	Sweden	United States	

Panel B. Welfare States Clustered by Routes to Early Consolidation (see Chapter 2)

Bismarckian	Catholic	Lib-Lab	NonConsolidating
Austria	Belgium	Denmark	Australia, Canada
Germany	Netherlands	Italy	France, Norway,
		New Zealand	Switzerland, United States
		Sweden	[Finland, Ireland,
		United Kingdom	Japan†]

Panel C. Welfare States Clustered by Routes to Program Adoptions in the 1930s or 1940s or both (see Chapter 3)

Social Democratic		Other Route		
Agrarian Alliance	Catholic Alliance	Secular Centrist	Catholic	Nonadopter
Australia	Austria	Canada	[Belgium 1930s]	Germany
Denmark	Belgium 1940s	United States	[France 1930s]	Switzerland
Finland	France 1940s		[Ireland 1940s]	
Norway	Netherlands			
New Zealand	Italy			
Sweden				

Panel D. Midcentury Labor Movement Consolidators and Nonconsolidators

Consolidators	Nonconsolidators
Australia	Canada
Austria	France
Belgium	Finland
Denmark	Germany
Netherlands	Italy
Norway	Japan
Sweden	Switzerland
United Kingdom	United States
New Zealand	

* Nations are allocated to all regimes on whose indicators they are ranked "strong" in Esping-Andersen's (1990) Table 3.3, except nations allocated to the "residual" category because of no strong rankings at all.
† Finland, Ireland, and Japan are excluded from core Chapter 2 analyses but clearly are nonconsolidators.

consolidators/nonconsolidators: Lib-Lab and Catholic consolidators and the nonconsolidating Norway and Finland (Table 4.2, Panels A and B). Here the consolidators among Esping-Andersen's social democratic regimes, the Lib-Lab Denmark and Sweden and the Catholic-governed Netherlands, share alliances between centrist parliamentary governments and labor movements; however, it is not clear what they share with Norway, where labor remained weak into the 1920s, or with Finland, barely protodemocratic during the 1920s and a czarist dependency before that. Moreover, unlike his conservative regimes, which encompass my Bismarckian configuration, Esping-Andersen's social democratric regimes never fully encompass any of my three routes to early consolidation. Indeed, they comprise cases—Australia, Norway—that cannot be said to have embraced social democratic projects until the Great Depression (Table 4.2, Panel C). Thus, if Esping-Andersen's conservative regimes show a degree of Catholic-centered homogeneity during the era of pre–Great Depression reform, social democratric regimes do not appear to cohere until the Great Depression and after. Yet by that time, each social democratic "regime" had already laid important programmatic foundations for later income security policy (Esping-Andersen, 1990).

In terms of my routes to consolidation and adoption, Esping-Andersen's liberal cases encompass not Lib-Lab welfare reformers but welfare laggards (Table 4.2, Panel A). All of Esping-Andersen's liberal regimes fail to achieve early consolidation in this work (Table 4.2, Panel B). Indeed, all of them but Australia fail to attain mid-century consolidation (Table 4.2, Panel D). In short, seen in light of the present study's configurations, particular policy regimes in particular nations are not usually outcomes of single hegemonic political projects—conservative, social democratic or liberal—in nations. Policy regimes are historical residues of shifting and conflicting projects, not single or decisively overriding ones, as indicated by Esping-Andersen (1990). Specifically, they are outcomes of Catholic projects that incorporate worker organizations (as a series of Catholic and Christian democratic projects did in Belgium throughout the first half of the century); of conservative projects such as Bismarck's that attempt to secure worker loyalties in the face of competing socialist overtures; and of secular centrist partisan projects that shift under coalitional opportunities and popular pressures into Lib-Lab projects such as Asquith's first governments and into proto–social democratic ones, such as FDR's short-lived Second New Deal. They are social democratic.

In summary, the welfare regimes that Esping-Andersen operationalized with 1980s-type data appears to result from accumulations of distinct political projects. Their differing political contents (universalistic, residual, and so on) reflect more than one political project or era. Esping-Andersen's conservative Austria in fact has a history rich with Christian and social democratic welfare reforms that helps account for its highly decommodified policy profile relative, for example, to Germany. The preeminently social democratic Sweden is a post–Great Depression labor movement construction built on Lib-Lab foundations. The residual New Zealand and United Kingdom cases are no mere North American laggards but descendants of Lib-Lab and social democratic (specifically, Labourite) pioneers that have regressed back down the slippery slope of their Tory-Liberal English heritage (Esping-Andersen 1990; Mann 1993).[5]

Examination of Tables 4.3 and 4.4 helps clarify this point. The former table checks off the types of political reform actors and projects that gave rise to particular reform outcomes, particularly Bismarckian early consolidation and Great Depression social democratic program adoptions. (Types of political projects, specified in terms of the routes to consolidation of Chapter 2 and partisan conditions for program adoption identified in Chapter 3 are noted in Table 4.3 because they are necessary for the second scoring of nations as potential reformers in Table 4.4).

Table 4.4 cross-tabulates a cumulative scoring of nations' structural and historical—organizational and reform-making—preconditions for mid-century consolidation on the one hand and program decommodification on the other hand.

Table 4.4 scores a nation high on worker reformism if (a) it engaged in two or more of the types of reforms outlined in Table 4.3, and if (b) it also had strong unions during the same period as designated in Table 4.1 Here, for example, Sweden and Norway qualify, as do all the midcentury consolidators of Table 4.1. However, Germany and Switzerland, bereft of social democratic or laborite reforms; the United States, a 1930s social democratic reformer with a weak labor base; and Finland, a 1940s social democratic reformer with a weak labor base, do not. Decommodification is dichotomized around Esping-Andersen's own

---

[5] If Esping-Andersen's (1990) "conservative/social democratic/liberal" classification is revised as the "corporativistic/social democratic/liberal" classification constructed by Ragin (1994), after an innovative cluster analysis of Esping-Andersen's data, little changes. In Ragin's (1994) reclassification, Finland, leaving the social democratic ranks, replaces Germany (now a residual or "spare" case) as a "conservative" regime. The Netherlands and Japan are yanked from "social democratic" and "liberal" regimes and placed in the "spare" grouping. These shifts in no way modify the general conclusion that each 1980-type regime derived from a heterogeneous historical past rather than from a single, overridingly important political project.

Table 4.3. Esping-Andersen's Regime Types and Historical Reform Periods and Projects Leading to Program Adop tions (1990)

	1920 Consolidation*				1930s/1940s			1920-19
	Bismarckian	Catholic	Lib-Lab	Socialist	Red-Green	Red-Black	Centrist	Laborit
Conservative								
3 Austria	x					x		x
3 Belgium		x				x		x
1 France						x		
1 Germany	x							
2 Italy			x			x		
Social Democrat								
3 Denmark			x		x			x
2 Finland					x			
3 Netherlands		x				x		x
2 Norway					x			x
3 Sweden			x		x			x
Liberal								
2 Australia					x			x
2 Canada							x	
1 Japan				x				
0 Switzerland								
1 United States							x	
Residual								
3 New Zealand			x		x			x
3 United Kingdom			x	x				x

* Attainment of either 1920 or 1930 consolidation suffices to classify a nation as an early consolidator.

threshold score of 30: it equals 1 if that scale equals at least 30 and oth-erwise equals 0 (1990, Table 2.2). The cross-tabulation of worker reformism with decommodification in Table 4.4 yields a strong associa-tion (Yule's $Q = 0.697$). If only six of nine frequent recent reformers are relatively decommodified, all eight infrequent recent reformers are not relatively strong decommodifiers. That is, no decommodifier was not both (a) a 1930s or 1940s adopter and (b) a longer run, midcentury program consolidator with several decades of strong labor movements. In fact, all decommodifiers were both 1930 to 1940 socialist adopters—in the sense of having adopted a program under at least one govern-ment marked by socialist participation—and strong-labor consolidators in the longer run. In propositional terms, if a nation has no strong post–World War I labor movement and no 1930s or 1940s socialist adoption, then it has no strong decommodification: a strong post–World War I labor movement emerges as a necessary condition for strong decommodification. The only nations that qualify for this necessary condition that do not turn out to be strong decommodifiers are Britain

Table 4.4. Association between Decommodification and a Composite Measure of Worker Reformism (Strong 1920–1950), "Interconsolidation" Labor Unions, and Past Social Democratic Reform

	Low Decommodification		High Decommodification
Strong worker reformism; strong 1920–1950 soc dem reform and labor unions	Australia New Zealand United Kingdom		Austria Belgium Denmark Netherlands Norway Sweden
Weak worker reformism; weak 1920–1950 soc dem reform and labor unions	France Germany Italy Finland	Canada Japan Switzerland United States	
Yule's Q = 0.697			

* Nations are judged high on decommodification that have decommodification scores over 30. See Table 1.4 and Esping-Anderson (1990, Table 2.2).

and two of its former settler colonies, Australia and New Zealand. For nations without dominant Anglo-Saxon origins, the *combination* of 1930s or 1940s socialist reform plus strong inter–/post–World War II labor movements ends up both a necessary and a sufficient condition for strong 1980 decommodification.

Interestingly, the three English-speaking socialist reformers with strong labor movements—Australia, New Zealand, and the U.K.—that fail to qualify as strong decommodifiers *c.* 1980 are all midcentury consolidators of major welfare programs. Unless British cultural and institutional legacies provide satisfactory explanation for this pattern, it presents a puzzle worth revisiting.[6]

[6] Castles and Mitchell (1991) have a "radical" hypothesis for distinguishing both social policy and the politics of social policy in Australia, New Zealand, and the United Kingdom from those in other strong-labor nations. They, too, single out these extensively unionized nations for, in their words, a post-1950 "failure to obtain the governmental status required to legislate more generous welfare benefits"; however, they link this failure back to a particular "radical" or liberal-laborite heritage. This is a heritage of union-centered politics anchored outside the socialist tradition of the First and Second Internationals (perhaps extending back to the pre-Marxian Chartists), with

The finding of Table 4.4—that the English-speaking portion of nations with strong social democratic and labor movement records around midcentury consolidators had a flatter developmental trajectory than the rest of the nations—restates the puzzle of Australian, British, and New Zealander backsliding from positions of leadership among income-security reformers—a puzzle I'll revisit.

In summary, decommodification around 1980 is rooted in the accumulated outcomes of heterogeneous political projects. No strong decommodifier is the result of a single conservative or social democratic project. Indeed, projects themselves are more diverse than Esping-Andersen's three regimes suggests. Liberal legacies bifurcate into those with and without Lib-Lab phases. Social democratic legacies subdivide into three principal subsets: One is an electoral socialist set, dependent in Protestant and multiparty (proportional representation) contexts like Sweden on secular centrist allies. One is a similarly social democratic set whose members are dependent on often more powerful Catholic allies in Catholic countries (with proportional representation systems, as in Austria and Belgium).[7] One is a laborite set situated within virtually two-party (majoritarian) political systems.[8] Strong, recent social democratic legacies may mask Lib-Lab episodes, as in Denmark. Conservative policy legacies may mingle with social democratic (and Bismarckian) ones as in the Austrian case. Currently liberal welfare regimes like Australia may have been social democratic pioneers not very long ago.

Midcentury Income Security Consolidation

A concise narrative of midcentury income security consolidation can now be written. Through the World War I, developed nations were the only ones to attain a notable degree of income security reform.

Among these nations, three broad routes to the extensive adoption of income security programs can be abstracted from the empirical

---

solidarities extending out to "the people" (before the populist turn of 1930s Social Democrats), with goals distinct from the establishment of a postliberal "socialist" society and with policy instruments that stress heavy, progressive taxation and high wages more than public transfers. A social democratic view is simpler.

[7] The democratic-Catholic path would evolve, where notable social democratic party strength temporarily imposed Red-Black alliances upon Catholic parties, into a Christian democratic path. However, welfarism would be muted where, as in Germany and Italy, Red-Black alliances were inhibited.

[8] Belgium emerged as a conservative "regime" in Esping-Andersen (1990).

record. One begins as an autocratic, mildly (proto)democratic, route energized by socialist threats that materialized in Germany and Austria (see Table 4.2, Panel B). A second is a Left-Catholic response to working-class mobilization that emerged in Belgium and the Netherlands. A third early pathway is the Lib-Lab one shaped by alliances between governing liberal parties and labor movement parties or voters (or both). This route fed into both enduring and transient social democratic cases of post-Great Depression income security reform (Table 4.2, Panels B, C, and D).

Where social democratic reforms were implemented on a foundation of a strong labor union movement and with the aid of secular-centrist, usually agrarian, allies, explicitly social democratic policy regimes emerged, developed, and endured (recall Table 4.2, Panel C). Where social democratic reforms were implemented in alliances with Catholic parties, as in Austria, Belgium and the Netherlands, Christian democractic–led regimes paralleled social democratic regimes, but without the help of Lib-Lab precedents and as only as a phase in the transition from paternalistic Christian to Christian-democratic Catholic welfarism (see Table 4.2, Panel C).[9] Again, British and Anglo-settler Labour parties gave rise to vanguard welfare states during the 1938 to 1948 period, as with the Attlee government's implementation of the Beveridge Report; however, such cases stagnated or unraveled during more settled subsequent decades, devolving into welfare laggards by 1980.

Legacies of social democratic reform also did not endure where they were simply weak as in Japan (Gordon 1998) or where, as in such English-speaking nations as Australia, Great Britain, and New Zealand, they proved . . . what? Why the English-speaking nations neither sustained the degree of welfare state development implied by mid-century consolidation, nor attained the degree of decommodification eventually attained by other midcentury consolidators, is a question worth returning to once we have examined the period following the 1950s.

In the end, six very strong decommodifying polities emerged, six nations that substantially secured household incomes against the vicissitudes of the market. Of these, three were the Red-Green reformers of 1930s and 1940s Scandinavia—Denmark, Norway and Sweden—all social democratic "regimes," in Esping-Andersen's terms (see Table 4.4, Panel B). Two of these (Denmark and Sweden) were rooted, in

---

[9] "Christian-democratic Catholic welfarism," I should add, in frequent partnership with social democracy.

turn, in the Lib-lab reformism of the three preceding decades, whereas the third (Norway) was a more purely bred child of Great Depression era reform (see Table 4.2). The three other cases—Austria, Belgium, and the Netherlands—drew nutrients from other mixes of historical soil. Preceding the Great Depression era, Austrian roots tapped both Bismarckian and democratic-Catholic sources of reform (see Table 4.2).[10] After World War II, Austria drew (despite its conservative status in Esping-Andersen) on social democratic as well as Red-Black legacies. The Netherlands and Belgium also drew on both social democratic and democratic-Catholic legacies (and upon both patriarchal and Christian democratic variants of the latter). Other large affluent capitalist democracies, ranked as "low" decommodifiers by Esping-Andersen, have diverse histories. These include backsliding Bismarckian and Lib-Lab consolidators such as Germany and Italy—the former a modest backslider—and backsliding Lib-lab/social democratic adoptors such as the United Kingdom, Australia, and New Zealand. Still others have been simple laggards (France, Finland, Japan, and Switzerland)—at least at midcentury (Esping-Andersen 1990).

Interestingly, the three strongest decommodifiers following the six strong ones highlighted above—Finland, Germany, and Japan—all developed notable neocorporatist institutions or economic coordination (Katzenstein 1985; Lijphart and Crepaz 1991; Crouch 1993). The Lib-Lab/social democratic backsliders—the United Kingdom, Australia, and New Zealand—did not. Neocorporatism seems to merit further attention.

[10] See Chapter 2, equations 1 and 3.

CHAPTER FIVE

The Rise of Neocorporatism

... social democrats trade off the abolition of private property in the means of production for cooperation of capitalists in increasing productivity and distributing its gains.

(Przeworski 1985, 430)

The era of social democratic governmental ascendance and social reform was more than a period of partisan pact making and social insurance innovation. It was also a time of neocorporatist institution building, an era of innovative coordination among major business and labor associations and states. For example, in Sweden, the 1936 Red-Green alliance between Social Democrat and Center parties was followed by the Saltjobaden agreement of 1938 whereby central organizations of business and labor secured labor market harmony in the wake of a tumultuous half-decade of strikes and lockouts. By midcentury, this neocorporatist era had extended beyond Scandinavia to the low countries and to those states that had experienced fascist interludes.

In Switzerland and the low countries, neocorporatist institutions developed similarly, although under Catholic as well as social democratic political auspices and on the basis of economic accords not always so explicit or so far reaching as Scandinavian ones (Katzenstein 1985). Within the nations that passed through fascist interludes, corporatist coordination of economic classes and sectors institutionalized state (and business) elite control of all working classes, strata, sectors, occupations, and organizations to an unprecedented degree. Moreover, after fascism's demise, strong degrees of economic coordination survived the return of organizational autonomy to labor (and business) associations (Maier 1984; Crouch 1993).

By the 1960s neocorporatism had matured into a central political economic institution in many of the more affluent democracies. Indeed, as we shall see, it had become a bridge from the working class and social insurance reformism of the first half of the twentieth century to the welfare state in the second half.

In the rest of this chapter, I shall more fully introduce neocorporatist institutions and their origins, systematically review hypotheses about these origins, present data for their investigation, and pursue this investigation and analyze these data. In this chapter, results of data analyses help me delineate a corporatist bridge spanning two eras: one the era of Great Depression and 1940s social democratic welfare-state reform and the other an era of more institutionalized, multipartisan welfare-state development extending from mid-century to today.

Neocorporatism

Corporatism is a mode of interest organization that obtains to the extent that members of the most important economic locations are incorporated, via their organization, into institutionalized networks of negotiation over key economic transactions (e.g., wage setting) and shared aspirations (e.g., income and job creation).[1]

By Schmitter's (1974, 1981) account, fully realized corporatist organization entails inclusive monopolies of major, functionally defined economic categories, hierarchically arranged. That is, organizational representation of economic actors would, in the extreme, be inclusive. Each organization would monopolize representation of its functional constituency. Each organization would have a defined ordinal relation (ties included) to the others. Inclusiveness and monopoly are especially important with regard to such neocorporatist performance criteria as low inflation because they allow for a representation of interests that is at once sufficiently comprehensive and sufficiently compact for viable, economy-wide concertation. Hierarchy is also important because it averts jurisdictional squabbling and representative proliferation subversive of viable, economy-wide policy concertation (Dahl 1982; Moe 1980; Lange and Garrett 1985; Scharpf 1987; Streeck, 1984). All three traits are also important because they help contrast neocor-

---

[1] "Important" here means important both in terms of union members' degree of effective organization and of unions' functional importance.

poratist interest organization with the fragmented, unmanageable, and upper-class accented interest configurations of "fractionated pluralism" (Dahl 1982; Lehmbruch 1984). They also help to contrast tripartite—labor-business-state—corporatism and such less comprehensive, *ex*clusive configurations as Lehmbruch's (1984) labor-exclusive, statist mode of corporatism.

To further follow Schmitter's (1974, 1981) formulation, neocorporatism may be voluntary or coerced; its interests or goals may be endogenous or given, either to organizational members or leaders; its representation may be delegated from below or articulated above; and its interest organizations may be relatively external to the state or constitutive of it. These traits seem less useful for defining corporatism in general, however, than for differentiating its postwar, democratic variant (relatively voluntary, interest-defining, and societal) from more statist and authoritarian variants, the classical fascist variant in particular. The fascist mode of corporatist organization was not merely one in which membership, functions, and interests were defined by state oligarchs. It was also an organizational form that gave additional meaning to the notion of hierarchy by arraying a proliferation of economic grouping (results, in part, of a strategy of *divide e impera*) into a state-headed hierarchy. It was characterized by the Nazi, Austro-Fascist, Italian Fascist, and 1936 to 1945 Japanese modes of interwar corporatism (Crouch 1993, 157–162; Garon 1987).

Here, neocorporatism is treated as a matter of degree, particularly the degree to which economic interests and their interrelations, including those with the state, are organized for the negotiated and harmonized making of economic policies that transcend simple firm-level adjustment to market forces. The model of such economic organization employed here assumes that with increasingly corporatist systems of economic-interest organization come (a) increasingly monopolistic and centralized organization, (b) increasing policy-making centrality for such organizations, and (c) increasing economy-wide economic bargaining, whether by formal centralization or informal arrangement.

Hypothesized Causes of Neocorporatism

The Swedish case is quite illustrative of democratic neocorporatist development. A tradition of business-labor accords began in 1932 with a social democratic entry into government. This coaxed a weakened business and a newly responsible labor to abandon a pattern of interrelations that had been previously marked by strikes and lockouts and to replace it with one increasingly made up of negotiations. By 1933 a tradition of business-labor accords had begun. This accelerated with a social democratic assumption of majority-government leadership in 1936 that culminated in the 1938 Saltjobaden signing of an agreement stipulating extensive labor-market regulations. In this landmark accord, principles set down in previous wage negotiations were codified, and statutes aimed at limiting industrial conflict were refined. Henceforth, business and labor participants in industrial relations would negotiate before resorting to such conflictual actions as a strike or lockout. They would do so first locally and, if local negotiations failed, then nationally. Unsettled disputes would be referred to labor courts where the law applied or otherwise to new forums for arbitration (Heclo and Madsen 1987). Parallel industrial "peace treaties" incorporating labor into a new political economic consensus arose at about the same time in Denmark, Norway, and Switzerland (Katzenstein 1985).

Such economic peace treaties were only beginnings. In Sweden, 1941 and 1951 statutory reforms reinforced the power of national union confederations to coordinate union locals and sectors in centralized bargains. Inflationary postwar booms pressured business and labor toward ever more centralized national wage bargains to dampen chains of wage and price inflation and resulting trade and payments imbalances (Heclo and Madsen 1987; Katzenstein 1985).

By the late 1950s, labor had been incorporated alongside Swedish business in fully elaborated corporatist institutions of collective bargaining and policy making, public as well as private, supply-side (as for labor training) as well as demand side (e.g., Keynesian). During the 1950s and 1960s, similar neocorporatist institutions developed in Denmark and Norway, in Austria and the Netherlands, and, somewhat later, in Belgium and Finland. They developed, albeit in less fully and formally national forms, in Germany and similarly but with more modest or informal incorporation of labor, in Switzerland and Japan. Variation in neocorporatist development across these and other nations have been variously "explained."

As we have seen, important enduring consequences have been claimed for 1930s "economic treaties." At least some appear to have been rooted in the developments of "organized business" consolidated around the turn of the century (Crouch 1993). Yet earlier constructions of consensual institutions such as nineteenth century establishments of proportional representation electoral systems may have also been claimed to advance neocorporatist evolution (Lijphart 1984, Katzenstein 1985). Fragmented bourgeois class and conservative political forces may have eased laborite corporatist initiatives in some nations (Katzenstein 1985; Kangas 1992). Economic openness to world market fluctuations may have entailed functional imperatives for ameliorative corporatist concertation, whereas smaller societies may have been better able to accomplish a degree of labor centralization conducive to corporatist development. Fascist interludes may also have contributed to postwar neocorporatism (Crouch 1993, 157–162; Garon 1987, 212–215).

Indeed, a rich literature discusses the origins of neocorporatist institutions. A more detailed review of this literature and its hypotheses is in order.

Propositional Inventory

The preconditions for neocorporatism that scholars have so far considered may be usefully divided in terms of a couple of distinctions. They split neatly into preconditions involving economic institutions (their structures, origins, transitions, and so on) on the one hand and institutional environments on the other. They also divide up nicely into relatively long-term causes that I shall call "legacies" and relatively short-term or "proximate" causes.

My definition of institutions includes not only their structural characterization (e.g., "organized business") but also their historical aspects (e.g., key events in institutional histories such as pact makings). What I call "legacies" consist not only of seminal institutional precedents for labor-business accords but also of simple societal precedents (e.g., "fascist legacies") at some historical distance from the neocorporatist entities under study.

In short, we have distal and proximate institutions and institutional events to examine; and we have more general circumstances, both distant and recent, to examine as well. I proceed by progressing through the cells of Table 5.1, column by column from top to bottom.

Institutional Legacies

Organized Business

According to Crouch (1993, 333), "Basic patterns of functional representation as they affected employers and industrial interests . . . were more or less fixed before the outset of the First World War." To be sure, historical fluctuations have occurred since then. In particular, Crouch continues,

Table 5.1. Hypothesized Determinants of Neocorporatism

Temporal Distance	Institutional Distance	
	Political-Economic	Environmental
	Organized business	Openness
	Early pacts (PR, class)	
		Nation size
	Fascist interludes	
Legacies	Fragmented bourgeoisie	
	Early social democratic government	
Proximate Forces	1950s social democratic government	Openness
	1950s Christian democratic government	Nation size

the fascist and Nazi upheavals that have been the main drastic regime shifts affecting western European countries during the twentieth century did not affect the long term approach of states to such interests. . . . The more indelible change wrought in the twentieth century has been the role of labor within functional representation in many countries. The period immediately after the Nazi defeat was, at least temporarily, of major importance in this process. But . . . it is the accommodation of labour to representative structures that comprises the thoroughly new element [in industrial relations] making itself felt in the twentieth century. . . . Where business representation has been fragmented and more geared to lobbying than to administration, labor had little incentive or opportunity to do otherwise. Where capital's organizations were strong and disciplined, labor had to adopt such a pattern if its organizations were to flourish. (p. 334)

Crouch also attributes importance to early state recognition of a place for organized labor and to the extension of guilds into the period of organized capitalism. And he notes that labor organization has been a prod to business organization. However, Crouch qualifies early state recognition and late guild presences as both leading to labor incorporation on a "narrower range of issues" than *fin de siecle* "organized capitalism." Moreover, he places impacts of labor organization upon business organization within a cycle of business-labor-business interrelations, and he stresses the importance of business organization outside industrial relations proper—capitalist organization for "trade representation, foreign trade, training arrangements, etc."—for ". . . subsequent industrial-relation's organization on both sides" of the business-labor divide (Crouch 1993, 334–335).

Crouch's account is an overtly "ironic story" in which "powerfully organized capitalism might ... exclude labor and break its organizations," but in which, "once heavily organized," capital, both "heavy" and "middle-sized," was likely to encounter a powerful and integrated labor movement that it could "integrate only by going the full distance to neocorporatism." It is a story in which, not without irony, "Scandinavia, which is where labour's role ended by being the most determinative, started with employer-led organizational drives" (Crouch 1993, 335–336).

To Crouch, the degree of "organized business" (or capitalist "articulation") around 1914 is close to a root cause of neocorporatism, eclipsing even social democratic government. Indeed, Crouch writes of social democracy that "the variable is a secondary one. Where capitalism was of an organized type, the rise of social democracy—once it had passed the crucial threshold of legitimacy—was likely to lead to a considerable intensification of such trends; where capitalism was more purely laissez-faire, social democracy did not make much difference." This, at least, is Crouch's view of the relative importance of organized capitalism and social democracy in the origins of neocorporatism (1993, 335).

Importantly, "organized capitalism" is a gauge of the collectivist orientation of business in political and economic arenas, labor markets most especially. As regards labor markets, it expresses a tendency on the part of business to establish institutionalized relations with labor as a collectivity (or set of these), relations that go beyond the relations among atomized firms and workers postulated by classical liberal (and "new classical") market theory. It does *not* refer to business's partisan organization within the formal political system, although it certainly may have implications for the tenor of business's partisan politics—its liberalism or illiberalism, its willingness to use the state, and so on. Business's partisan politics are, we shall see, addressed by discussion of its part in the making of certain "pacts."

Early Pacts on Proportional Representation and
Labor Market Regulation

Economic Treaties. Several authors attribute great importance to the kind of "economic treaty" or "peace" that business and labor organizations, confronting a dangerously volatile level of class conflict, cobbled out at Saltjobaden, Sweden, in 1938 (Przeworski 1985; Gourevitch 1986; Katzenstein 1985).

Distinctly economic pacts, in fact, began not with this most widely heralded pact but with the Danish pacts of 1933 to 1936. They run from the Kanslergade Left-Center "treaty" of 1933, which included Left-Center ventures into wage policy, to actual collective bargaining pacts of 1935 to 1936. The sequence of pacts continues, after Saltjobaden, with the Swiss national consensus of 1937, in which Swiss industrialists and unions agreed on a private-sector bargaining formula, including procedures for arbitration. This sequence runs out with the Norwegian basic agreement of 1940, which provided regulations for pay and labor bargaining in 300 trades, although it left precise wage determination to "routine rounds of collective bargaining" (Katzenstein 1985, 139–150).

Such agreements also shade into the Belgian and Dutch *Plan van den Arbeid* of the early 1930s, although despite economic contents they center more on social democratic incorporations into governments than into the structure of authoritative, national labor-markets policy making per se (Katzenstein 1985, 144). The set of economic treaties might conceivably be stretched to include Left-Right Austrian *Angstgemeinschaft* of 1945, which included a business-labor reconciliation, however, the *Arbeid* "class compromises" converged on two outcomes other than industrial regulation: systems of proportional representation (PR) and franchise extension (Katzenstein 1985, 189). Moreover, the *Angstgemeinschaft* encompassed far more than economic pacts, shading most specifically into *Arbeid*-like Left-Right reconciliations and more generally into very broad institutional reconsolidation (labor-markets included) that marked all transitions from fascism (Crouch 1993, 334).

Consensual Electoral Reforms. Katzenstein (1985, 151) writes of two phases in the adoption of systems of proportional representation (PR), as follows: "In the first phase before World War II, proportional representation aimed at protecting minorities. In the second phase, during or immediately after World War II, national representation sought to contain the threat that socialist parties appeared to pose throughout Europe to the established order." In both cases, PR was, according to Stein Rokkan (1970, 76–80), a kind of "saddle point" or compromise position in a societal game of conflict resolution. Indeed, both phases seem quite relevant, for, if the post-1914 cases involved "labor parties," they fell short of addressing industrial-labor relations, and if the earlier phase addressed overtly ethnic political conflict, the corporatist compromises might have been difficult without the earlier "electoral" ones (Katzenstein 1985, 150).

Proportional representation tended to advance the inclusion of labor parties within the political systems, whether by augmenting their likely shares of the vote or by merely granting them an additional measure of legitimacy. This tended to strengthen labor's power within extant systems of industrial-labor relations, most likely at the expenses of whatever hierarchical advantage business (or the state) might have within them. If organized capital advanced neocorporatism by strengthening its foundation in prior, relatively hierarchical, and labor-exclusive modes of "old fashioned" corporatism, PR strengthened labor's political position for advancing its interest in more labor-regarding, labor-centered, or even labor-driven modes of (neo)corporatism. In doing so, it tended to enact its general function as a resource for popular inclusion and, despite its tendency to proliferate partisan identities in Parliament, as a force for national political consensus (see Lijphart 1984; Tsebelis 1990). By making a degree of coalition—and thus consensus—a likely condition for the formation of effective governments and a virtual sine qua non of parliamentary effectiveness and legitimacy, systems of PR tend to foment consensus as well as inclusiveness.

In Denmark, the Conservatives, facing the prospect of legislative marginalization by increasingly successful social democratic candidates for parliamentary office, led the 1915 establishment of PR representation and a concurrent disestablishment of property qualifications for voting. In Norway, PR, used since 1896 in local elections, was extended to the national level in 1919 as a buffer against such extreme electoral volatility as might expedite the emergence of a Labor majority in Parliament. In Sweden, PR was adopted in 1907 to 1909, when it appeared to assure Left access to Parliament and Conservative legislative majorities. According to Lorwin (1966), the Belgians adopted PR in 1900 when the majority Catholic party employed it as a means for stabilizing the vote share received by its Liberal-Socialist opposition and as a means for averting the risk of a Catholic-Socialist parliamentary polarization; in the Netherlands between 1878 and 1917, however the Dutch progressively adopted PR as a means of reconciling parties in secular-religious, enfranchisement, and industrial relations conflicts. In Switzerland, PR was passed in 1919 as a parliamentary sop to an increasingly militant social democratic labor movement (Katzentein 1985, 150–156).

Further adoptions of PR may be adduced in France and Italy during World War I and in the nations reverting from fascism after World War II. However, PR was repudiated by Mussolini in 1922 and abandoned by France in 1928. In the former Axis states, PR was mixed with a single-district/winner-take-all system in Germany, embedded in virtual one-party systems in Italy and Japan, and tailored to two-party rule and extended into the allocation of bureaucratic positions in Austria (Lijphart 1984; Katzenstein, 1985).

PR compacts to extend parliamentary representation to small and moderate minorities generally signaled agreements to disperse power, agreements that required compromise among two or three substantial parties for subsequent successful government. At once mirroring, constituting, enforcing, and enabling consensus, they are reasonably hypothesized to have promoted neocorporatist systems of labor-market and more general economic policy-making cooperation.

Divided Rights and Fragmented Bourgeoisie Classes

Divisions within the ranks of the propertied and the conservative, especially their political organizations, and most especially their parties, have been argued to advantage outcomes favored by workers and their parties, neocorporatist outcomes among them. Although organized capitalism tended to advance corporatist arrangements, laying foundations (however initially pro-business, hierarchical, statist, labor-inclusive, and even labor-repressive) for more labor-friendly modes of neocorporatism, a politically fragmented bourgeoisie tended to be one hamstrung in its ability to apply the break to neocorporatist developments favorable to labor. Castles (1982) has argued that where the Right (in fact, nonsocialist parties or the non-Left) has been split up into many competing factions, the Left has been better able to advance its agenda. And Katzenstein (1985, 161–170) has singled out such circumstances as ones that offered the Left such opportunities as breathing room from the encroachments of a concentrated Right and varied coalitional prospects in the absence of such a strong Right. Others have similarly stressed the reformist opportunities offered by a "fragmented bourgeoisie" (Esping-Andersen and Fried-land, 1982). Such a hypothesis is at an unfair disadvantage against alternatives directly stressing Left strength, for these appropriate to themselves a good portion of the causal mechanisms by means of which any effects of Right fragmentation operate. Such inequity is not complete, however: A fragmented Right may aid reform at given levels of Left government, for example, by more means than aug-menting left strength, by averting a strong conservative ideological advantage. Moreover, potential effects of a fragmented Right on neo-corporatism cannot be suppressed in models that hold measures of Left strength temporarily aside, as my models will.

Fascist Interludes

As Rueschemeyer, Stephens, and Stephens (1991) have powerfully established, European democracy broke down, to be replaced by fascism in nations characterized by nationally powerful, landed upper classes. These upper classes were dependent on repressive labor practices that motivated them to vigorously support illiberal traditional views. Moreover, the limited Japanese democracy of the 1920s and early 1930s fell victim to equally illiberal state-bureaucratic and military forces. Thus, laissez-faire, competitive-market objections to neocorporatism were singularly weak in these societies. In fact, authoritarian variants of corporatism characterized the fascist regimes (Garon, 1987; Crouch 1993). Although fascist industrial-relations systems repressed autonomous labor organizations, they were highly organized and included a nominal place for labor (Garon 1987; Crouch 1993). Although these systems were repudiated after the war, these repudiations were not comprehensive. Instead they focused on deconstructing authoritarian aspects of industrial relations and on rehabilitating labor within the industrial relations systems. Thus, the actually occurring fascist interludes (with democratic aftermaths) may be regarded as legacies favoring postfascist democratic corporatism. This may even be the case after analytical adjustment for such other prior, related features of the nations in question as Crouch's "organized business."

Early Socialist Participation in Government

Many writers have suggested that neocorporatist institutions resulted from social democratic advocacy and guardianship of labor's interest in tripartite of neocorporatist institutions (Stephens 1979; Korpi 1983; Esping-Andersen 1985; Rothstein 1987; Western 1991; Hicks and Misra 1993). Indeed, Crouch's strong case for the importance of organized capitalism pits itself against a single social democratic alternative (Crouch 1993, 332–334).

The Great Depression was the first era of extensive social democratic governmental leadership (indeed, governmental participation) and occasioned initial attempts to construct, in the form of economic pacts, the kind of labor-inclusive neocorporatist institution favored by labor and its parties. Therefore, it should be a key period for any social democratic advancement of neocorporatism. Yet Crouch (1993, 333) stresses the "major importance" of the "period immediately following the Nazi defeat." Indeed, the crucial need for a postwar period of liberation from externally imposed and domestically evolved fascist regimes, not to speak of general postwar institutional reconsolidation, seems at least as compelling as any claim for the prominence of the Great Depression. In line with the seeming importance of the 1930s and 1940s in neocorporatist emergence, plus the view that particular historical periods may be seminal in institutional development, I propose this distinctly distal or long-term hypothesis: "Early" (1930s and 1940s) social democratic participation in government advanced neocorporatist development.

Proximate Institutional Causes

I distinguish proximate causes from distal ones to make room for a focus on longer term, more rudimentary, causes of neocorporatism. In particular, they are set apart to provide a simple shorthand for grouping variables in longer and shorter run statistical analyses. Separate long-term and short-term analyses are performed. The former permits assessment of the relevance of longer term causes that are not disadvantaged by controls for more recent variables that may act as conduits for longer term effects.

Certainly, a voting analyst would not want to preclude political attitudes of voters shortly preceding elections from being disqualified as analytically important causes of their votes just because the statistical effects of these variables are "controlled away" by measures of voting intention on election morning. Similarly, we would not want to preclude identification of long-term effects on neocorporatism just because they might be obscured by excessive attention to proximate ones.[2]

1950s Social Democratic Participation in Government

Social democratic participations in government in the 1950s is our principal proximate factor. For much the same reason that we hypothesize effects of 1930s and 1940s social democracy upon neocorporatism, we hypothesize effects of 1950s social democratic government as well. The former effects act (if at all) during a time of preliminary accords and early institution building and by means of the durability and eventual repercussions of such effects. Any 1950s social democratic effects would operate during a time of institutional evolution (or devolution) by means of institutional revisions

---

[2] As we shall see, measures of neocorporatism used in analyses are for the 1960 to 1990 period, centered somewhere in the 1970s.

and developments built on the programmatic foundations set by midcentury.[3]

1950s Christian Democratic Participation in Government

Christian Democrats in the 1950s may also have used government to advance neocorporatist institution building. After all, Christian Democrats were a notable political force. Indeed, they were often coalition partners in the post–World War II social democratic governments (substantial in Austria and the low countries, brief in France and Italy, but nonexistent in Germany); and this is the same postwar period that Crouch (1993, 333) has claimed to have been most crucial to neocorporatist development. Moreover, historically Catholic parties in Austria, Germany, and Switzerland were involved in state-led facsimiles of tripartite systems of labor market regulation during the 1920s (Crouch 1993, 129, 151). Indeed, philosophically, the Catholic social philosophy of respect for all classes and transcendence of class conflict in the interest of society as a whole was tailored to reconcile, if not utterly win over, Catholic parties to neocorporatist institutions (Kersbergen 1995); and politically, Christian democratic support for neocorporatism had been claimed (e.g., Wilensky 1981). Thus, some Christian democratic propensity as well as capacity for contributing to neocorporatist institution building seems quite likely, as Christian Democrats can, at least, be assumed to have been more supportive of (certainly less hostile toward) neocorporatist institutions than secular conservative and centrist parties. In short, I hypothesize that 1950s Christain democratic participation in government helped advance neocorporatist development.

Environmental Effects: Distal and Proximate

Economic Openness

Much attention has been given to possible effects of economic openness on neocorporatism. For Katzenstein (1985), open economies are particularly vulnerable. Economies are open to the extent that domestic consumers are dependent on imports, and domestic producers (and wage-earning consumers in turn) are highly dependent on exports (Cameron 1978, 1249; Katzenstein 1985, 81–87). When economies are open, cooperation is encouraged by the large and unpredictable impact of the international market on the domestic economy: key state and

---

[3] Some attention will also be given to Christian democratic governmental participation during the 1950s.

economic actors cooperate to ensure and buffer populations against "developments they can never fully control" (Katzenstein 1985, p 236; Wallerstein 1987; Western 1991). This argument is offered by Katzenstein (1985) as, what seems to me, his specification of the principal causal mechanism linking small states to cooperative institutions, neocorporatism in particular. It is economic vulnerability and openness, manifest correlates of small states and not size per se that centers Katzenstein's interpretation of relations between state smallness and neocorporatism.

National Size

The capability of states to engage in neocorporatism is affected by their size (in itself) in two ways. According to Olson (1965) large groups—insofar as they have more numerous actors, whether individual-like citizens or organization-like interests associations—find it more difficult to coordinate for action: Communication is complicated by the geometric relation of a number of actors to the number of potential interrelations among them, and incentives for particular actors to free ride increase with the number of potential actors. Costs of group mobilization by group leaders (e.g., of union recruitment or coordination of members by labor leaders) are higher in larger groups (Wallerstein 1987). For example, efforts to centralize Britain's large unionized force with its numerous craft unions met size-related obstacles that union centralization did not encounter in nations such as Norway, with fewer workers and unions (Crouch 1993). In short, I hypothesize that the smaller the nation the greater the degree of neocorporatist organization/coordination.

These openness and size hypotheses are equally posed for longer run and shorter run analyses, with measures timed differently for the two.

Data and Analyses

The hypotheses reviewed in the previous section are operationalized, catalogued, and statistically analyzed here. Analyses are simple regression analyses of linear, additive relations of explanatory variables to outcome variables. They begin with longer run models of neocorporatism that concentrate on the distal explanations proposed for neocorporatism. They continue with later explanatory factors, although not without regard for the continued relevance of earlier factors (crucial as "statistical controls" and as legacies with the power to reach forward past such more immediate forces as post-1950 social democratic strength and impact on neocorporatism). Analyses are performed for the set of long-standing, postwar, affluent, capitalist democracies: Australia, Austria, Belgium, Canada, Denmark, Finland, France, West Germany, Ireland, Italy, Japan, the Netherlands, New Zealand, Norway, Sweden, Switzerland, the United Kingdom, and the United States.

Neocorporatism is measured as a composite of two measures that themselves distill an extensive literature on the measurement of this institution. To do this, I draw upon two past efforts to measure neocorporatism. These are the factor analytically constructed scales of Lijphart and Crepaz (1991) and of Hicks and Swank (1992).

The former scale factor analyzed twelve "expert judgments" taken from Wilensky (1976, 1981), Schmitter (1981), Schmidt (1982, 1983), Czada (1983), Cameron (1984), Lehmbruch (1984), Bruno and Sachs (1985), Crouch (1985), Marks (1986), and Lehner (1988). A number of the items that Lijphart and Crepaz use (e.g., Bruno and Sachs's, Schmidt's) downplay the importance of labor union strength and inclusion within policy-making circles, ranking nations as highly corporatist that have weakly, subnationally, or equivocally centralized, incorporated unions—as in Switzerland, Germany, and Japan, respectively. Accordingly, I call the Lijphart and Crepaz index an index of "generalized" neocorporatism. The Hicks and Swank (1992) measure consisted of the factor scores for the first dimension extracted from a twelve-item dimensional (i.e., principal component) analysis that ended up identifying three dimensions of state structure. These consist of the Left Corporatism factor of immediate concern, plus State Centralization and Bureaucratic Patrimonialism factors. The Left Corporatism factor loaded high (>0.75) on items indexing union strength, union centralization, class mobilization, and cumulative Left-led government, besides loading nontrivially on measures of unitary/federal and revenue-centered state centralization (c. 0.300). Because this index emphasized the *union* pillar of tripartite corporatism and takes explicit account of social democratic political strength (as a bulwark for the union role), I call it "*Left* corporatism." Scores for both generalized and Left neocorporatist scales were rescaled so that they would vary tidily between 0 and 1 and then were averaged together into my final composite scale. I'll refer to this third composite scale as "*tripartite* neocorporatism," because it offsets the generalized scale's marginal disregard of labor's tripartite role by including the relatively labor-centered Left corporatism scale. Scores for this composite scale, its generalized and Left components, and a number of other neocorporatist scales are displayed in Table 5.2, Panel A.[4]

I prefer the tripartite measure to the generalized one because it ranks all of the incontrovertibly labor-inclusive cases—the first seven (Austria through the low countries) of Cameron's labor-centered ranking (Table 5.2, Panel A)—more highly than such equivocal sites of labor's neocorporatist incorporation as Switzerland and Germany. (Indeed, the generalized scale ranks such equivocal cases above such labor-inclusive stalwarts as Belgium and Finland.) I prefer the tripartite scale to the Left corporatism one because recent writings by Soskice (1990, 1998) suggest that the latter scale's idiosyncratic ranking of such cases as Australia and New Zealand above Germany, Switzerland, and Japan, however labor-exclusive the former cases are, is erroneous.

Organized business is measured with a scale constructed from a numerical coding of the information in Crouch (1993, Table 4.13), ("The Organization of Capital c. 1914"). This table displays information on three aspects of organization: (1) "the extent of organization of employer interests" ("Scope"); (2) "resources available to employer interests to co-ordinate action" ("Power"); and (3) "activity directed at trade rather than employer issues ("Other . . . "), which Crouch (1993, p. 335) regards as a crucial indicator of early business "organization" relevant to subsequent neocorporatist industrial-relations systems.[5] Scores vary from 0 to 3 with each nation coded 0, 0.5, or 1.0 for each aspect of organization (see Table 5.2, Panel B).

Early pacts are measured as the average of two highly collinear measures, one of Great Depression "economic treaties" and another of pre–World War II establishments of systems of PR for defining votes and translating them into parliamentary compositions. Each of these measures involves a simple nominal, or dummy variable, coding of ones or zeros. Economic treaties are coded, following accounts of them in Katzenstein (1985) and elsewhere in the literature, as 1 for Denmark, Norway, Sweden, and Switzerland, and 0 for the rest of our nations. PR pacts are coded as 1 for Belgium, Denmark, the

[4] National "scope" is coded 1 for descriptions of association growth and antiunion campaigns, 0.5 for descriptions of formations of an association (the Austrian HAOI in 1907 and Swizz Zsao in 1908), and otherwise 0. They are coded 1 for descriptions of power emphasizing authority and expansionist goals, 0 for descriptions emphasizing weakness, limitations, and lack of success. They are coded 1 for statements of their involvement in or importance for trade issues.

[5] Note that for some characterizations of business organization around 1914, Table 4.13 refers the reader back to Table 4.7 (Crouch 1993).

Table 5.2. Measures of Neocorporatism and its Hypothesized Preconditions

Panel A: Measures of Neocorporatism

Nation	Tripartite Neocorp. I	Lipjphart & Crepaz Neocorp. II	Hicks & Swank Neocorp. III	Union Centered IV	Cameron* Labor Unity V
Australia	.21 (14)	.11 (14)	.30 (11)	.18 (11)	0.3
Austria	.85 (3)	1.00 (1)	.70 (4)	.49 (3)	1.0
Belgium	.56 (7)	.54 (9)	.58 (6)	.36 (6)	0.6
Canada	.09 (17)	.00 (17)	.18 (14)	.09 (15)	0.4
Denmark	.65 (5)	.63 (5.5)	.67 (5)	.43 (4)	0.8
Finland	.67 (4)	.60 (8)	.73 (3)	.37 (5)	0.8
France	.27 (11)	.21 (12)	.32 (8)	.05 (16)	0.2
W. Germany	.43 (9)	.62 (7)	.23 (13)	.18 (11)	0.8
Ireland	.14 (15.5)	.28 (11)	.00 (17)	.18 (11)	0.4
Italy	.14 (15.5)	.17 (13)	.10 (16)	.14 (14)	0.2
Japan	.31 (10)	.47 (10)	.15 (15)	.04 (18)	0.2
Netherlands	.61 (6)	.80 (4)	.41 (7)	.21 (8)	0.6
N. Zealand	.22 (13)	.08 (16)	.36 (8)	.23 (7)	—
Norway	.97 (1)	.98 (2)	.95 (2)	.50 (2)	0.8
Sweden	.97 (1)	.93 (3)	1.00 (1)	.61 (1)	0.0
Switzerland	.43 (9)	.63 (5.5)	.23 (13)	.16 (13)	0.6
United Kingdom	.24 (12)	.16 (15)	.31 (10)	.19 (9)	0.4
United States	.02 (18)	.00 (18)	.04 (18)	.06 (17)	0.4

Panel B: Explanatory Variables

Nation	Organized Business I	Early Pacts II	Fascist Legacy III	Frag'd Right IV	Early Soc'm V	1950s Social Dems VI	1950s Christ. Dems VII
Australia	.00	.00	.00	.00	1.00	.00	.00
Austria	2.50	.00	1.00	.00	1.00	.45	.55
Belgium	1.00	.50	.00	1.00	1.00	.22	.50
Canada	.00	.00	.00	.00	.00	.00	.00
Denmark	3.00	1.00	.00	1.00	1.00	.76	.00
Finland	2.00	.00	.00	1.00	1.00	.26	.00
France	.00	.00	.00	1.00	.00	.28	.30
W. Germany	2.00	.00	1.00	.00	.00	.00	.75
Ireland	.00	.00	.00	.00	.00	.02	.00
Italy	1.00	.00	1.00	.00	.00	.16	.76
Japan	1.00	.00	1.00	.00	.00	.00	.00
Netherlands	2.00	.50	.00	1.00	1.00	.32	.61
N. Zealand	.00	.00	.00	.00	1.00	.00	.00
Norway	1.00	1.00	.00	.00	1.00	1.00	.00
Sweden	3.00	1.00	.00	1.00	1.00	.84	.00
Switzerland	3.00	1.00	.00	1.00	.00	.07	.28
United Kingdom	2.50	.00	.00	.00	1.00	.17	.00
United States	.00	.00	.00	.00	.00	.00	.00

Note: Rankings in parentheses in Panel A are for non-ordinal scales.
* Not ranked because of awkward number of ties and lack of New Zealand score.

Netherlands, Norway, Sweden, and Switzerland, and 0 for the remaining nations (Table 5.2, Panel B).

Fascist legacies also are dummy coded as ones or zeroes, 1 for Austria, Germany, Italy, and Japan, and 0 for the rest of the nations. *Right fragmentation* uses Kangas's (1992) scale for "fragmented Bourgeois blocs," which codes Denmark, Finland, Norway, Sweden, Switzerland, France, and Belgium as 1, and the remaining nations 0 (Table 5.2, Panel B).

Early social democratic government is a dummy variable coded 1 for nations with more than two years of social democratic participation in government (for Australia, Austria, Belgium, Denmark, Finland, New Zealand, the Netherlands, Norway, Sweden, and the United Kingdom) and otherwise 0 (Table 5.2, Panel B). Here participation in government requires at least 30 percent cabinet participation (thereby excluding Italy and Switzerland with their persistent marginal Left party participation). It should be noted that the nations in question encompass all of the clearly Christian Democratic party governments of the immediate postwar period that may be regarded as Center or Center-Left parties, as in the low countries and Austria, as opposed to Right and Right-Center parties, as in Germany and Italy (see Castles and McKinlay 1978). This virtually precludes a need for any separate measurement of Christian democratic governments, for during the immediate postwar years all nations except Germany with such governments are encompassed by those with social democratic governments (but see n. 10). *1950s social democratic government participation* is a measure of Social Democratic cabinet portfolios as proportional shares of all cabinet portfolios in the years 1950 to 1960. *1950s Christian Democratic Government Participation* measures Christian democratic cabinet portfolios as shares of all cabinet portfolios during these same years.

Economic openness is measured as the sum of a nation's imports and exports as proportions of GDP. Measures are for 1950 for the long-term analyses. (Data were not available for all cases before then for long-term analyses.) They are averaged for 1959 to 1961 for proximate analyses. Nation size is measured with the simple national population (in 1950 for long-term analyses and in 1960 for shorter run analyses).[6]

Again, simple ordinary least squares (OLS) multiple regression models are used to investigate hypotheses. Analyses are done in two

---

[6] Data for the measurement of economic openness and population are from OECD (1960–1995b, 1960–1995c); United Nations (1960–1995).

major groups, pre-1950 and post-1950, as well as subsets of these (e.g., pre-1945). To conserve scarce degrees of freedom imposed by a small sample, highly insignificant variables are excluded from final equations.[7]

Because a measure of social democratic political strength is included in the Left corporatist component of the tripartite scale and may introduce some element of operational tautology into relations between this scale and measures of social democratic strength, analyses are replicated by using an alternative to the tripartism scale. This measure of "the organizational power of labor," a key item in the Hicks-Swank scale (1992) was inspired by Cameron (1984, 164–166) and uses a product of a measure of union cohesion and a measure of union density to substitute for the Left corporatist component of the tripartite scale.[8] I refer to this measure as the "unionist" scale and to the new variant of tripartism as "union-centered" or "union corporatism." As an additional check on possibly unstable results, all models are estimated with and without the geographically, historically, and socioculturally distinctive Japanese case.

Findings

Pre-1945 models are presented in Table 5.3. They yield (following deletions), a strong positive effect of early pacts (statistically significant at the 0.05 test level). Nation size also achieves a notable effect, negative as predicted (but only significant at the marginal 0.10 test level). Organized business and fascist legacies have properly

[7] Stepwise deletion and entries of variables with t-statistics so small that their inclusions degrade the fit of models (i.e., increase mean square errors) are employed in a manner tailored to particular stages of analyses. For example, we begin with regression models including only pre–World War II independent variables and then delete variables one by one (beginning with the smallest t-statistic) that have absolute values of t less than 1.0 until all remaining regressors exceed this modest threshold. This averts inflation of standard errors and attenuation of statistical significance due to the inclusion of "irrelevant" variables in regressions (Wonnacott and Wonnacott 1985, 180–189) and Rao and Miller (1971, 60–68). See Appendix 5 for pre- as well as postdeletion reportage of findings.

[8] The measure of union cohesion is an average of three (proportional) measures—one of organizational unity, one of confederational autonomy and one of collective bargaining coverage—all drawn from Cameron (1984, Table 8.4) and extended with the help of Kenworthy (1995, Table 5.3). The measure of union density is a weighted average of the 1960s measure of union density used in Hicks and Kenworthy (1998) and of Kenworthy's 1970 to 1990 (1995, Table 5.3) measure of average union density across those 20 years. The measure is rescaled to vary between 0 and 1 before being combined with the similarly rescaled Lijphart and Crepaz (1991) index to create the alternative tripartism index.

Table 5.3. Long-run and More Proximate Models of Neocorporatism

Panel A: Models of Neocorporatism (Tripartite Measure)

	Long-term Models		Proximate Models
	Pre-1945 **I** Postdeletion	Post-1945 **II** Postdeletion	Post-1950 **III** Postaddition/deletion
Organized business	0.26 (1.28)	— —	— —
Early pact	0.36 (2.30[†])	0.62 (4.29*)	— —
Fascist legacy	0.18 (1.34)	0.41 (2.79*)	0.36 (2.92*)
Right fragmented	— —	— —	0.24 (1.94[†])
Size	−.31 (1.63[‡])	— —	— —
Openness	— —	— —	0.17 (2.29[†])
Early Social Democrat Government	— —	0.55 (3.84*)	0.28 (2.02[†])
1950s Social Democrat Government	— —	— —	0.58 (4.28*)
R^2 (adjusted)	0.512	0.705	0.811

Panel B: Models of Union Corporatist Variant of Tripartite Neocorporatism

	Postdeletion **I**	Postdeletion **II**	Postaddition/deletion **III**
Organized business	0.35 (1.86[†])	0.21 (1.27)	0.28 (2.36[†])
Early pact	0.43 (2.07[†])	0.46 (2.66[†])	— —
Fascist Legacy	0.18 (1.52[††])	0.38 (2.51[†])	0.28 (2.28*)
Right Fragmented	— —	— —	— —
Size	−.39 (2.19[†])	−.20 (1.25)	— —
Openness	— —	— —	0.31 (2.49*)
Early Social Democrat Government	— —	0.43 (2.62[†])	— —
1950s Social Democrat Government	— —	— —	0.66 (5.54*)
R^2 (adjusted)	0.572	0.704	0.797

Note: Standardized regression coefficients with absolute ts in parentheses.
*, [†] and [††] denote statistical significance at 0.01, 0.05 and 0.10 test levels, respectively.

signed effect estimates that are, at least, larger than their standard errors and are retained in models even though the estimates fall short of any conventionally used level of statistical significance.[9] Importantly, these effects should be regarded as meaningful, even if they turn out to be not explicitly reinforced by subsequent models. This is because subsequent models are distinct only because of the addition of *temporally subsequent* variables to them, variables that are quite unlikely to render earlier measured variables spurious in the typical perjorative sense of the term (Wonnacott and Wonnacott 1985). (Spurious in the perjorative sense of the term arises when an association between two variables proves to be dependent on effects of one or more common causes of the two variables, such as an association between voting and airplane ownership that occurs because affluence increases both the likelihood of voting and of airplane ownership. Instances of *non*-perjorative spuriousness, seldom referred to as spuriousness at all, arise when an association between two variables is revealed as dependent on an intervening mechanism between the two, as an association between affluence and voting would be by such variables as voting intention or showing up at the polls.) More to the point, the hypothesis that early pacts contributed to neocorporatist institution building—indeed, did so in some rather general and durable manner—seems vindicated.

In the next stage of analyses early social democratic participation in government, which captures 1945 to 1949 post–World War II variability in social democratic government, is added to pre-1945 models. Despite rather insignificant organized business and size effects on 1950s government, we have an historical model of mostly significant institutional effects.[10] Fascist legacies, early pacts, and early social democratic participation in government all vary strongly and directly with subsequent levels of neocorporatism.

Next, measures of 1950s social and Christian democratic participation in government are introduced into estimations, alongside the updated measures of economic openness and nation size. Indeed, as a further check against spuriousness due to the omission of relevant

[9] Results are robust in the face of the deletion, or inclusion, of Japan.
[10] These are highly significant effects, all meeting the 0.01 test level (in a nutshell, each unlikely to have arisen by as much as one chance in a hundred). Note that various alternatives to early social democratic government were examined: (a) a measure of average share of social democratic legislative seats instead of a dummy variable; and (b) a measure of combined 1945 to 1949 social democratic and Christian Democratic seats (for Austrian, Belgian, and Dutch Center-Left parties). These yielded weaker effects than the early social democratic variable that, after all, included Red-Black coalition partners.

variables, all institutional variables are reintroduced. After deletions of variables so weakly related to neocorporatism that their standard errors exceed their coefficients, both early and 1950s aspects of social democratic government emerge as sources of neocorporatism. This is especially true of 1950s social democracy, which has a standardized regression coefficient (interpretable much like a partial correlation) of 0.58 that is significant at the 0.01 test level. Fascist legacies, right fragmentation, and economic openness also emerge as a preconditions of neocorporatism.[11]

Here, contrary to Crouch (1993), the social democratic explanation of neocorporatism seems preeminent, although other institutional preconditions, namely fascist interludes, fragmented political rights, and early (consensual and directly quasi-corporatist) pacts seem important as well. Indeed, business organization, although it does have modest (indirect) effects in the pre-1945 model, falls out of the "proximate" model.

When the alternative union-centered measure of tripartism is used, however, results, somewhat less weighted toward a predominant social democratic role, simplify and reincorporate business organization into the proximate model (Table 5.3, Panel B). This replaces right fragmentation, attaining the 0.05 level of significance and a beta coefficient of 0.28, identical to that for fascist legacies. The effect of early socialist government, like that of right fragmentation, drops out, but that of 1950s social democracy increases in magnitude, attaining a standardized slope estimate of 0.66.[12]

Overall, social democratic government emerges as the foremost source of neocorporatism, particularly 1950s social democratic government. In addition, effects of 1950s social democracy are complemented by—or at least conduits for—more distal effects of social democratic rule in the 1930s and 1940s and political and economic pacts in which social democratic parties and allied unions figured

---

[11] Openness and nation size are not prohibitively collinear here, yet may stand in, to an extent, for each other. The model is unshaken by the removal or entry of Japan and "explains" over 80 percent of the variance in neocorporatism in recent decades. A strong case emerges for attributing neocorporatism largely to social democratic rule, both recent and during the seminal Great Depression, World-War and postwar years. And evidence also indicates important effects of a Right weakened by partisan fragmentation and of the fascist interlude (whether due to its broadly corporatist precedent or to reactions to statist/labor-repressive corporatist traits, we cannot say). Evidence for less direct contributions to neocorporatism by national smallness, economic organization (or organized-ness), and early consensual pacts—especially the last—also emerges.

[12] Models are identical with Japan deleted.

notably. Other sources of income security policy—fascist legacies, organized business, economic openness, and national smallness—emerge as well.

An alternative Boolean analysis of neocorporatist emergence is sidelined because it requires somewhat forced dichotomizations without adding elegantly to results[13]; however, the analysis does reinforce the adequacy of present variables and suggest the centrality of two: early social democracy (1950s rule is excluded because it is markedly nondichotomous) and organized business.

Social Democratic and Pre-Liberal Foundation of Neocorporatism

We live in a liberal democratic capitalist world with institutionalized safeguards against governmental infringements upon private property as well as individual persons (Dahl 1982), but this is a world whose tilt toward individual freedom over collective responsibility and associated market failures has been moderated by solidaristic legacies and cooperative institutions. These have roots in precapitalist as well as socialist legacies, in the City of God as well as the communism of Karl Marx.

Two grand legacies—one out of industrial society or industrial workers' responses to it, one out of traditional illiberal society—

---

[13] Tripartite neocorporatism is dichotomized, with 1s for all nations at least as neocorporate as Germany and Switzerland, and 0s for the eight other cases (see Table V.2). (Indeed, this dichotomization is used in some analyses of the next two chapters.) Moreover, the pre-1950s political-economic variables lend themselves rather easily to dichotomization. Fascist legacies (F), right fragmentation (R), and early social democracy (S) are already dichotomized. Organized business (O) is easily dichotomized, dubbing all values less than 2 "unorganized." (Excluding only 0 values would exclude very few nations.) Early pacts (P) are easily assigned to nations with scores great than 0. This done, a reasonable model for tripartite neocorporatism (C) emerges:

$$C = PfS + pFrB + fRS + PfRsB = Sf(P + R) + B(pFr + PfRs)$$

That is, early social democracy sufficed in never-fascist nations that were either characterized by early pacts (Belgium, Denmark, Netherlands, Norway, and Sweden) or fragmented rights (Finland and Belgium again). Organized business sufficed in either once-fascist nations that lacked right fragmentation and early pacts (Austria and Germany) or in never-fascist nations that lacked powerful early social democracy but had experienced early pacts and fragmented rights (Switzerland). Although these results may aggravate measurement error without gaining elegance, they are interesting. They suggest that early social democracy is necessary for most eventually neocorporatist nations (five of eight) and that Crouch's organized business is necessary for all three of the rest.

appear to underlie the emergence and development of neocorporatist institutions.

Social democratic political and labor movements—the nominally social democratic ones, whose name I have used loosely, and kindred labor and socialist movements—appear to have been notable forces contributing to the rise of neocorporatism. They appear to have done this by helping enact the seminal economic pacts of the 1930s, by initiating later pacts, and by governmentally nurturing fledgling neocorporatist institutions throughout the 1950s.

In addition, preliberal legacies of hierarchical, collectivist, and regulatory—as opposed to market—control of economic activity appear to have played a role in neocorporatist emergence and development. Organized business as conceptualized by Crouch (1993) as a collectivist, cooperative, and hierarchical organization of business (as opposed to a liberal, individualistic, competitive one) certainly contained residues of precapitalist, as well as preliberal, social philosophy and organization.[14] Fascist legacies certainly draw on traditional, illiberal forces, however much they are revised to accommodate democracy and labor in affecting tripartite neocorporatism. Although fascism arose with industrial as well as agrarian—and free-market as well as labor-repressive—capitalist support, agrarian upper classes with foundations in feudal status as well as capitalist asset certainly figured prominently in the rise and consolidation of fascism (Rueschemeyer, Stephens, and Stephens 1992). And although fascist ideologies certainly made modern appeals (bureaucratic, technological, mass-communicative), they certainly made reactionary appeals as well (illiberal, authoritarian, mystical) (Herf, 1984; Russchemeyer, Stephens, and Stephens 1992).

Conservative as well as socialist principles of community and solidarity appear to have figured in the origins of neocorporatism, just as autocracy and Catholicism seem to have figured alongside socialist worker mobilization in early consolidations of social insurance programs.

Whatever the conservative foundations of neocorporatism, the social democratic ones, also rooted outside of liberalism, are clear. Insofar as neocorporatism stresses the incorporation of organized labor into national political economic policy-making institutions, it may be regarded as an extension of social democracy. As such, neocorporatism may be regarded as empowering reformists, however

---

[14] Note that Crouch's (1993, 313–324) postindustrial guild power predicts organized business quite well. (For this and my coding of Crouch, $r = 0.64$).

emasculating this may appear to emphatically revolutionary commentators (e.g., Panitch 1981). Early worker mobilization provoked and cajoled major social reforms from traditional and liberal policy makers while working toward larger social transformations. Early social democratic governments legislated reforms at the cost of revolutionary idealism. Similarly, neocorporatism stably incorporated organized labor into economic and social policy making, albeit by making it hostage to sustained cooperation with business and the nation-state. In so doing, it placed the social democrat's income maintenance project, already extensively grounded in midcentury consolidations of major social insurance programs, on a doubly firm basis. Policy legacies and institutions of political economic power both came to support the project in many nations.

A P P E N D I X 5

Detailed Regressions

(See page 152 for Table A5.1)

Table A5.1. Long-run and More Proximate Models of Neocorporatism

	Panel A: Models of Neocorporatism (Tripartite measure)					
	Long-term Models				Proximate Models	
	Pre–World War II		Post–World War II		Post-1950	
	(I)	(II)	(III)	(IV)	(V)	(VI)
	Pre-deletion	Post-deletion	Post-addition	Post-deletion	Pre-deletion	Post-deletion
Organized	0.23	0.264	0.10		0.10	
business	(0.98)	(1.28)	(0.59)		(0.63)	
Early Pact	0.35	0.365	0.54	0.62	0.11	
	(2.04†)	(2.30†)	(3.00*)	(4.29*)	(0.45)	
Fascist Legacy	0.19	0.18	0.28	0.41	0.15	0.36
	(1.13)	(1.34)	(2.37†)	(2.79*)	(1.52‡)	(2.92*)
Right Fragmentation	0.04				0.13	0.24
	(0.16)				(0.76)	(1.94†)
Size	−.32	−.31	−.13		−.09	
	(1.17)	(1.63‡)	(0.79)		(0.53)	
Openness	0.01				0.13	0.17
	(0.01)				(0.39)	(2.29†)
Early socialist democratic			0.48	0.55	0.33	0.28
government			(2.76*)	(3.84*)	(1.58‡)	(2.02†)
1950s socialist democratic					0.58	0.58
government					(2.80†)	(4.28*)
1950s Christian democratic					0.22	
government					(1.06)	
R^2 (adjusted)	0.425	0.512	0.677	0.705	0.780	0.811

	Panel B: Models of Neocorporatism (Union Corporatism Measure)				
	(I)	(II)	(III)	(IV)	(V)
	Pre-deletion	Post-deletion	Post-addition	Post-deletion	Post-deletion
Organized	0.35	0.347	0.21	0.264	0.28
business	(1.57‡)	(1.86†)	(1.27)	(1.51‡)	(2.36†)
Early pact	0.43	0.432	0.46	−0.03	—
	(1.88†)	(2.07†)	(2.66†)	(0.12)	—
Fascist Legacy	0.49	2.69	0.38	0.40	0.28
	(1.22)	(1.53‡)	(2.51†)	(1.61‡)	(2.28*)
Right fragmentation	−0.04			0.12	—
	(0.15)			(0.59)	—
Size	−.36	−.38	−.20	−0.14	—
	(1.39)	(2.19††)	(1.25)	(0.79)	—
Openness	0.04			0.24	0.31
	(0.15)			(1.06)	(2.49*)
Early socialist democratic			0.43	0.17	—
Government			(2.62†)	(0.89)	—
1950s Socialist democratic				0.49	0.66
government				(2.16†)	(5.54*)
1950s Christian democratic				−.13	—
government					
				(.60)	—
R^2 (adjusted)	0.495	0.572	0.704	0.757	0.797

Note: Standardized regression coefficients with absolute Ts in parentheses.
*, † and †† denote statistical significance at 0.01, 0.05, and 0.10 levels.

CHAPTER SIX

The Growth and Crisis of the Welfare State

The corporatist strain in the evolution of modern capitalism no longer yields readily to interpretations based on such established dichotomies as . . . Left and Right.

(Katzenstein 1985, 191)

The midcentury consolidation of social insurance programs described in Chapter 4 left no nation spending as much as 10 percent of its gross domestic product for social insurance benefits. Yet by 1990, average spending among the affluent democracies had reached 20 percent of domestic income. Indeed, among the midcentury consolidators of Chapter 4—Australia, Austria, Denmark, Ireland, the Netherlands, New Zealand, Norway, Sweden, and the United Kingdom—spending for social benefits as a share of GDP had reached an average of 23 percent by 1980. Even among the midcentury nonconsolidators or laggards, it had already climbed to 17 percent of GDP. As a little manipulation of Table 6.1 reveals, expenditures for social benefits as a share of GDP increased by about 90 percent between 1960 and 1990, 96 percent for midcentury consolidators, and 84 percent for laggards. Indeed, social spending already had increased that 90 percent *by 1980*, 109 percent for consolidators and 71 percent for laggards. Thereafter, *welfare effort* (defined as public expenditure for social insurance and relief benefits and services as a share of GDP) actually fell by a fraction of a percent. Indeed, welfare effort then fell among midcentury consolidators by about 8.6 percent from its 1980 level, while it continued to rise at a 1980s rate of nearly 6.9 percent for what had been the midcentury

Figure 6.1. Welfare effort ("Welffort") over Time (1959–1989) for Midcentury Consolidators and Nonconsolidators ("Consol/Nonconsol").

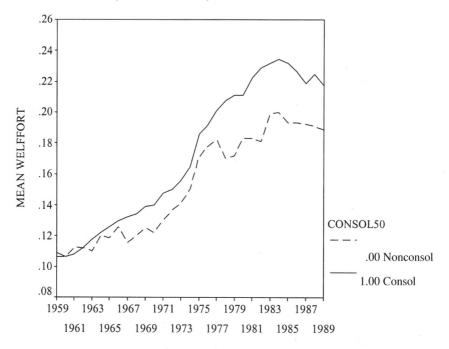

laggards. Figure 6.1 provides a bird's eye view of the initially accelerating, then U-turning and decreasing, trajectory of welfare effort broken down into two components, one for our earlier identified consolidators and one for laggards.

What are we to make of these social facts, these general increases, at first divergent but then convergent, in social spending effort? What brought them about? Why, to focus on Table 6.1, did some early consolidators—e.g., Australia, New Zealand, the United Kingdom— not keep pace with the others throughout most of the postwar period? Why, to focus on Table 6.1, was there a discernible post-1980 leveling off and even reversal?

Several theoretical perspectives vie for influence within the political science and sociology of the welfare state. Theoretical cleavages are especially sharply drawn within the literature on social spending in the post–World War II (and henceforth simply postwar) capitalist democracies. Nevertheless, I will argue here for an integrated explanation of postwar social spending stressing a range of political actors, institutions, and resources. These will vary beyond the bounds of particular current theoretical perspectives, yet be structured enough to offer

Table 6.1. Social Welfare Effort, 1969 to 1989 (Percentages)

	1960 ILO	1970 ILO	1980 ILO	1989 ILO	Percent Change 1960–89	Percent Change 1960–80	Midcentury[†] Consolidators
Australia	8.70	7.70	11.70	7.70	−11	34	1
Austria	13.80	19.50	22.40	23.80	72	62	1
Belgium	15.60	18.40	26.50	27.00	73	70	0
Canada	8.20	10.80	11.60	17.40	112	41	0
Denmark	10.40	14.80	26.90	27.60	165	159	1
Finland	9.30	12.70	18.60	21.00	126	100	0
France	12.70	15.30	26.80	25.90	104	111	0
W. Germany	16.30	16.40	23.00	22.20	36	41	0
Ireland	9.20	10.30	21.70	14.60	59	136	1
Italy	13.10	12.60	19.70	22.50	72	50	0
Japan	4.40	4.50	10.10	11.10	152	130	0
Netherlands	10.80	19.00	28.60	27.10	151	165	1
New Zealand	11.90	11.50	17.10	15.90	34	44	1
Norway	9.30	13.10	20.30	20.90	125	118	1
Sweden	11.10	18.80	32.20	33.40	201	190	1
Switzerland	9.90	10.10	13.80	13.20	33	39	0
United Kingdom	10.90	12.50	15.10	16.10	48	39	1
United States	6.70	9.50	12.70	11.70	75	90	1
MEANS (of means)	9.50	13.19	19.93	19.95	90	90	—

Social welfare effort is defined as social transfers and services for households as a share of GDP (here percentage share) based on data from the International Labour Organizations (ILO) 1960–1995; see Appendix 8 for details.
[†] See Chapters 4 and 5.

promise of an integrated account of recent social spending. Although I begin with an overall examination of variations in social spending as a share of domestic income, I eventually direct attention to the more specific question of post-1980 decelerations and even reversals in social spending, particularly to the possible roles of two favorite suspects for this "crisis" of the welfare state, demographic change and globalization.

To return to the disparate spending literature, however, the social democratic conception of the politics of social spending emphasizes the advancement of working-class interests by strong working-class movements, particularly social democratic (or Left) party governments (Stephens 1979; Korpi 1983, 1989). Statists argue that welfare effort is shaped by relatively autonomous state institutions and elites (DeViney 1984; Orloff and Skocpol 1984). According to pluralists, welfare effort is buoyed by groups mustering resources as varied as political participation, independent interest organization, and statutory entitlements (Pampel and Williamson 1988; Mahler 1990). Finally, according to societal (and global) determinists, societal and international—environmental dynamics (e.g., economic development, globalization) are key (Wilensky 1975; Piore and Sabel 1984).

Whereas all four perspectives make serious contributions, key claims from each remain controversial. For example, although Right party inhibition of welfare effort is broadly acknowledged, relative impacts of Left and Center parties remain unclear, indeed precarious in some recent studies (see Hicks and Swank 1992; and Beck and Katz 1995; and Hicks and Misra 1993). Although findings favoring the importance of pro-welfare effects of neocorporatism over those effects of Left partisan rule are lately prominent (e.g., in Hicks and Swank 1992; Hicks and Misra 1993; Crepaz 1996), Left partisan control of government appears never to have lost its core status within the social democratic research program. Results on the extent to which such particularistic (and pluralistic) groups as the elderly and unemployed matter for social spending vary widely (e.g., Pampel and Williamson 1989), as do findings regarding such core societal variables as affluence (Pampel and Williamson 1989; Hicks and Swank 1992). Also, pluralist and statist authors exaggerate their distinctiveness when they neglect such major pluralist works on political institutions as Dahl (1982) and Lijphart (1984). Thus, although the perspectives often substantially overlap, most studies portray a highly competitive and fragmented theoretical terrain.

Still, the postwar world is one of well-established programs, or at least program types, that many forces may be expected to contest. If a few large, bold actors were needed to introduce state-expanding, redistributive social programs before midcentury, a wide range of actors—all of the state's beneficiary groups (e.g., the elderly, the ill, the unemployed), including subsets of these (e.g., state pensioneers, the ill, retirees, the unemployed of stable and prosperous industries)—appear to have grown relevant to the politics of social programs. All groups of program beneficiaries—large and small, general, and highly program-specific—must now be considered potential participants in the politics of social policy. Moreover, both beneficiaries of programs that compete with social welfare programs for revenues and bearers of revenue burdens not manifestly offset by social program benefits can be expected to contest these programs' expenditures. In addition, such demographic dynamics as the trends and fluctuations in societal unemployment and age structure trigger entitlement spending. A complex of political forces is unleashed into the budgetary arena between beneficiaries and advocates for welfare and competing programs, not to speak of broader class forces in the party and interest association systems. Programs proliferate interests and processes that reproduce them. *A theoretical framework is required that is able to address a wide array of potential causal forces and organize them.*

In response to this challenge for theoretical integration, I elaborate an overarching political resource framework. To a large extent, this framework extends Korpi's (1983, 1989) "power resource" theory of the welfare state beyond its narrow repertoire of class actors, interests, and resources. Within a matrix of varied resources and orientations toward social spending, I consider an ample ensemble of actors and other social forces—voters, bureaucrats, economic growth, and dislocation. Yet, when all is said and done, I retain a role for class and class-linked forces that is at odds with earlier, wide-ranging, indeed pluralistic, frameworks. Moreover, the diversity of forces seemingly active in the determination of post–World War II social policy must be examined in light of two further issues. One is the extent to which variables from one or another perspective affects welfare effort. The other is historical context, particularly, the whole century-plus history of social insurance policy elaborated throughout this volume.[1]

In the next section I elaborate a political resource framework from the eclectic literature on the postwar welfare state. In doing this, I bring together strands of four major perspectives on welfare spending—social democratic, statist, pluralist, and environmental—and I identify pertinent contributions from each perspective to the overarching model. Regression analyses of social spending then follow.

Theory

Political Resource Theory

Resource theories of politics range from the world-historic and metatheoretical formulations of Lenski (1971) and Rogers (1974), respectively, to the interest-group formulation of Truman (1971), the social movement formulation of Gamson (1975), and the class/welfare state power resource theory of Korpi (1983). To quote Hicks and Misra (1993),

> They share a common focus on the empowering role of resources for the realization of outcomes that advance actors' perceived interests. . . . Korpi's (1983) power resource theory is especially germane to an interest in social spending, although its scope merits expansions. Korpi's theory focuses upon the "tripartite corporatist" actors, namely, labor, capital and the state, and

[1] To an extent, this framework sharpens that of Hicks and Misra (1993).

upon a set of matching resources comprised of "means of production" (for capital), "human capital" (for labor), and "collective action capacities" (for state and labor especially) (Korpi 1983). In particular, state organization is a collective action resource for the state, and, indeed, all actors.[2] In fact, as the institutional basis for authoritative decisions in final phases of the policy process, Korpi's state organization is presented as a proximate source and *sine qua non* for all public policy. However, for capital and labor, "collective action capacities" principally involve interest organizations such as voluntary associations, interest-group confederations, and political parties. Regarding the present concern with state policy outputs, Korpi's (1983, 25) "general hypothesis is that the presence of reformist parties in government can bring public policies closer to wage earner interests." By implication, the presence of nonreformist parties in government distances policy outputs from wage earner interests. (671–672)

Rogers (1974) makes a useful distinction between the instrumental resources (e.g., votes) wielded by particular actors and the infra-resources that serve as preconditions for diverse actors' uses of instrumental resources (e.g., political democracy). Here I define *instrumental resources* as *specific resources used by specific actors to realize their perceived interests*. I define *infraresources* as *resources that broadly facilitate diverse actors' pursuits of their interests by empowering their actions, conditioning their uses of specific instrumental resources or systematically operating to their advantage*.[3]

I include both instrumental resources, such as collective action capacities of the type stressed by Korpi (1983), and infraresources, such as the revenue-generating capability of society in my "political resource" framework. Resources are highlighted in Table 6.2.

Like Korpi, with his stress on reformist and nonreformist parties, I also distinguish between pro- and anti-welfare orientations of actors

[2] In effect, however, these collective action capabilities are regarded as disproportionately important for labor. State organization aside, collective action capacities are conceived as disproportionately empowering labor: capital, with its means of production, can fare quite well in a laissez faire environment and/or as a congery of uncoordinated interests. Still, labor's collective action capability is implicitly regarded relative to that of (an always efficacious) capitalist capability (see Korpi 1983). Progress defining independent dimensions of capitalist collective action capabilities is acknowledged as a major imperative for future theoretical development.

[3] A resource that can be said to capacitate a particular type (or a few particular types) of actor(s) and only (or preponderantly) that actor (or those actors) is an instrumental resource. An infraresource may not only capacitate diverse actors, it may precondition the use of particular instrumental resources. Innumerable actors may employ infraresources, many of them useful for a particular type of actor, that is, "token" to the resource's "type" (see Levine, Sober, and Wright 1986).

Table 6.2. A Political Resource Framework for Explaining Welfare Effort

Principal Resource (Instrumental or infraresource)	Welfare Orientation of Actor/Institution		Main Theoretical Advocate
	Pro-welfare	Anti-welfare	
Instrumental Resources			
Governmental authority over state	Reformist party (e.g., **Left and Christian Dem. governments**)	Antireformist party (e.g., **other party governments**)	Social democratic
Subgovernmental and legal (administrative) authority	Welfare-entitled citizens (e.g., **unemployment and elderly rates**)	Other (and otherwise) entitled citizens	Statist (pluralist)
Interest organization	Organized beneficiaries (e.g., **elderly rate share of population**)	Other organized groups	
Electoral influence	Lower status voters (e.g., marginal voters high **turnout**)	Higher status voters (e.g., regular voters; low turnout)	Pluralist
Infraresources			
State structure	Nationally organized (e.g., **cooperative veto points**)	Generally organized (e.g., **exclusionary veto points**)	Statist
Organization of interest organization	Organized employees (e.g., **neo-corporatism**)	Disorganized employers (**neo-corporatism**)	Social Democratic (pluralist)
Domestic systemic bias	General public (e.g., **high per capita GDP**)	Disproportionately tax burdened	Industrial (structural Marxist)
International systemic bias	Moderate stable international environment (e.g., high **openness**)	Extreme/runaway international environment (e.g., very high **openness**)	International

(including institutions) and systemic processes (Table 6.2). My logic is fundamentally political. Not only are both varieties of resources ascribed political functions, both are assumed to generate welfare spending via the omnibus conduit of final, authoritative state action (Hicks and Misra 1993, 614). Action may be relatively automatic, as in governmental or administrative implementation of extant statutes and policy-routines, or it may be relatively discretionary, as in a more novel, contingent, or loosely programmed translation of demands into policy. The plausibility of any economic explicans not subordinated to the mediation of politics, and thus the plausibility of any distinctly economic theory of welfare policy, is denied (see Skocpol and Amenta 1986, 134–137; but see Wilensky 1975). Although opposed to any simple economistic determinism, this resource-centered logic is hardly a logic antithetical to class. Indeed, the focus of my framework is a policy domain, the welfare state, that is, among other things, progressively redistributive (Hicks and Swank 1984a; Kenworthy 1999). Moreover, class actors such as Left parties and class-linked institutions such as neocorporatism figure prominently within the framework. Still, the current resource framework is one calculated to consider a wide range of factors and give credit where it is (as empirically adjudicated) due.

I specify causes of welfare expansion as combinations of particular political resources and specific welfare orientations of particular actors or institutions (Table 6.2). For example, combining the resource governmental authority with pro-welfare orientation yields socially reformist parties as pro-welfare actors. At a more operational level, it yields social and Christian democratic party governments as specific variables. To provide a second example, the combination of interest organization with a pro-welfare orientation generates organized labor (and the variable neocorporatism). As these examples illustrate, the actual variables deployed for analysis may stress actors (reformist parties) or resources (neocorporatism). They may stress instrumental resources the actors wield (e.g., state authority for governing parties) or infraresources such as neocorporatism that more complexly advantage some actors, organized labor and the large public of all employees more generally, for the case of neocorporatism. In Table 6.2, I conserve space by folding the identification of actors into the names of causes.[4] For example, I fold reformist parties into reformist party government. As further ad hoc reference to still unelaborated causes jeopardizes clarity, we leave further discussion of specific causes to the systematic elaboration of my framework.

In terms of the framework, then, I declare welfare policy determination to be a process in which actors, including some state ones, pursue their interests in welfare policy on the basis of their political resources. These actors are broadly defined to include institutions. They have, as a result of structured games among variously bureaucratically and strategically arranged actors or institutionally inscribed norms, missions, values, and orientations toward such objects as income security and equality. Resources are varied and include infraresources such

---

[4] I ground relations between social spending and its causes in politics, that is, in causal mechanisms involving the stages of the policy process: agenda setting and formulation, legislation, appropriations, and implementation (Anderson 1984), especially where actions of specific actors are concerned. For a more formal elaboration of resource theory that, unlike mine, pits them against "social action" theories, see Korpi (1985).

as revenue capacities and state structures, as well as instruments matched to the hands of particular actors.

The Social Democratic Perspective

For social democratic students of social spending, the central political actors are "reformist" parties. For most "social democratic" authors, these "reformist" parties are solely Left (i.e., social democratic, socialist, labor, and communist) parties (e.g., Hewitt, 1977; Cameron 1978; Esping-Andersen 1985; Hicks and Swank 1992; Hicks and Misra 1993); however, for other social democrats, reformist parties may also include Christian democratic parties (Stephens 1979; Wilensky 1981; Huber, Stephens, and Ragin 1993), as well as, more rarely, progressive liberal parties (as in Hibbs 1987). The key social democratic proposition has been that increases in Left party government augment welfare effort. This suggests the corollary proposition that increases in Christian Democratic party government augment welfare effort. The uses of governmental authority for the formulation, legislation, and implementation of policy, which should be familiar, helps ground our proposition.[5]

A second social democratic determinant is neocorporatism, a system of interest articulation between society and state and most especially one of the incorporation of cohesive labor movement organizations (union and party) into the policy-making process of state and labor market. (Lange and Garrett 1985). This tends to empower employees relative to employers, especially insofar as the former are well organized (Lange and Garrett 1985; Hicks and Swank 1992). It contrasts with the highly fragmented mode of pluralism singled out by Dahl (1982) for such decentralized polities as the United States. I hypothesize that neocorporatism buoys social spending. Several authors already have, in effect, viewed the presence of neocorporatism as an infraresource conditioning the politics of social welfare, in particularly reinforcing the effects of Left party. (Cameron 1984; Hicks and Misra 1993; Garrett 1998a).

It merits noting that views of some Marxian social democratic authors resemble those of some industrialism (and neopluralism) theorists of domestic societal determinants discussed later.

Statist Perspective

For statists, authoritative control over state organizations and their operations constitutes the principal political resource, whereas state

[5] See n. 4.

authorities constitute the principal political actors (Skocpol 1985; Padgett 1981; Orloff and Skocpol 1984; Evans, Rueschemeyer, and Skocpal 1985; Ashford 1986; Weir et al. 1988; Kamlet and Mowery 1987). Although we have already acknowledged the state's pervasive role in grounding governmental power over policy making, we have not discussed the structure of the state itself.

Statists discuss internal organizational (and interorganizational) structures of states as sources of social policy. Huber, Stephens, and Ragin (1993) have most succinctly focused discussions of the state structures as potential cause of social spending by focusing attention on features of states' de facto constitutions as sets of veto points obstructing reformist policy making. They draw attention to the federal (versus unitary) aspect of states as sources of disadvantage to working-class actors who are (relative to business actors) unlikely to uniformly organize across a set of subnational jurisdictions, even when their overall national electoral and productive clout is large (see also Dahl 1982; Lijphart 1984; Immergutt 1989; Skocpol 1992). Federal, as opposed to unitary, governments offer *relatively more potentially labor-exclusive veto points for obstructing welfare reforms* (Korpi 1983; Dahl 1982; Hicks and Swank 1992). Again echoing Lijphart (1984) and Immergutt (1989), statists draw attention to the greater opportunities for similarly exclusionary (or competitive) vetoes in systems of bicameral legislatures (with twice the legislative hurdles) and presidential systems (an extra legislative hurdle).

Importantly, Huber et al. (1993) also underscore Lijphart (1984) on the importance of consensual government when they consider single-member-district/plurality modes of electoral accounting as sources of veto points and regard systems of proportional representation as their antithesis.

Huber, Stephens, and Ragin (1993) do neglect the important theoretical point that proportional representational (PR) systems— electoral systems that select party shares of representatives in proportion to votes cast for given parties—create consensual orientations and practices from the increasing number of legislatively consequential, partisan, veto actors (to use Tsebelis's (1995, 293) term) that they spawn; however, the solution to this theoretical anomaly is simple in light of Tsebelis's (1995) original treatment of veto points and actors. Some veto points provide incentives to cooperation. In particular, some veto points, although they raise obstacles to cooperation (e.g., proliferating parties), operate within common institutional arenas. In such shared contexts, potential obstacles to action become actual incentives to it by defining common problems (e.g., ineffective and illegitimate performance). Moreover, common settings, missions, and so on become means to overcoming the common problems. Such at least appears to be the case for legislatures elected by means of PR: The costs of gridlock motivate cooperation, and the effort generates more than isolated cooperative actions, cooperative norms. To solve the anomaly of cooperative veto points, one must theoretically treat these inclusionary veto points as exceptional variants of what are for the most part exclusionary veto points that counsel a stress on exclusionary dimensions of state structure. Semantically, one may avoid confusion by treating the two types of veto points as separate components (each potentially complex) of a more encompassing variable. If this variable is stipulated as *exclusionary*, as it is here, then measures of particular exclusionary (or competitive) aspects of state social structure are directly related to it (e.g., might be *summed* to contribute to its measurement); measures of particular inclusive aspects of state structure are inversely related to it (e.g., might be subtracted from exclusionary measures to contribute to its scoring). The opposite, of course, holds for the social structure or veto points *inclusively* conceived. Exclusionary and inclusionary state structures might, of course, be separately stipulated without any consideration of a single, comprehensive, state-structural variable; however, I have, in the interest of simplicity, foregone that possibility here. I stress exclusionary state structure as a single variable; and I hypothesize that exclusionary social structures impede welfare effort.[6]

Another set of potential statist influences stresses policy-maker frames (theories, routines, and so on) for responding to economic conditions. Prominent among these are policy-maker norms and statutes prescribing upward adjustments of benefit levels to rising price levels (Hicks and Swank 1992). Cost-of-living allowances (statutory COLAs and more discretionary ad hoc equivalents) are political resources for program beneficiaries. Studies indicate that inflation,

---

[6] One potentially prominent state sector likely to be in competition with the welfare state for limited revenues and thus spending is the "warfare state," the state's military component. Consideration of this has occasionally yielded the hypothesis that the military spending effort crowds out and reduces the welfare spending effort (Griffin, Devine, and Wallace 1983; Kamlet and Mowery 1987; Hicks and Misra 1993; Huber et al. 1993). Further potentially important factors (of no perspective reviewed here so much as a distinctive conflict theory) includes protests and strikes (Griffin et al. 1983; Hicks and Misra 1993); however, the foregoing variables have yielded inconsistent, spotty, or highly contingent findings. Moreover, in this book more than in a journal article aimed preponderantly at specialists, I wish to avoid unnecessary complexities. Accordingly, I exclude the military and conflict variables from analyses.

by cuing revisions of payment rates as well as by subsidizing these upgradings via bracket creep, increases welfare spending; indeed, it does so somewhat in excess of increases in real income (Kamlet and Mowery 1987; Pampel and Williamson 1988; Hicks and Swank 1992). Our resource view of COLAs warrants the hypothesis that inflation buoys welfare effort.

Pluralist Perspective

Pampel and Williamson (1988, 1989) have revived the core pluralist emphasis among comparative students of the welfare state. This is the stress on group empowerment by means of citizenship, interest associations, and electoral leverage. They have, in other words, highlighted the political importance of groups of needy citizens with vested interests in benefits from the major extant welfare programs (old age and retirement pensions, unemployment compensation, and so on). Of course, "needy" groups not only activate extant statutes, thus increasing social spending when their numbers swell, they also influence the contents of underlying statutes as organized voting blocks and lobbyists (Pampel and Williamson 1988, 1989). Nonetheless, entitlement statutes serve as a most reliable resource for the needy: If interest groups have some power to initiate, sustain, and upgrade entitlement statutes, statutes themselves empower citizens to draw individually on program benefits. Furthermore, program utilization, although everywhere substantial, is a variable and an object of struggle (Isaac and Kelly 1981; Palme 1990). Programs do not, overall, depoliticize their automatic beneficiaries. Rather, they tend instead to galvanize political association and consolidate iron triangles of interdependent group, administrative, and governmental interests (Truman 1971; Gamson 1975; Skocpol 1985). In short, group members attain entitlement benefits, both as the collectively organized and as the individually (but categorically) entitled. With both mechanisms in mind, I hypothesize that the weight of needy groups such as the aged and unemployed within the population positively affects welfare effort.[7]

Pluralists have also argued that newly mobilized voters (disproportionately low status and pro-welfarist) tend to augment

[7] The paternalism and centralization factors from Hicks and Swank (1992) are not used here, the former because of spotty findings (e.g., Huber et al. 1993), the latter because of overlaps with the more readily interpretable measure of veto points drawn from Huber et al. (1993).

welfare outlays (Dye 1979; Pampel and Williamson 1988).[8] I adopt this hypothesis.

Environmental Approach: Industrialism Perspective

Authors such as Wilensky (1975) and Kerr (1983), often typed as industrialism theorists, have stressed the importance of societal economic capabilities and resources as preconditions for social spending (see Kerr 1983; Myles 1989). In addition, neopluralists like Lindblom (1977) have, restating neoMarxist propositions, emphasized the "structural power of capital" (Block 1977) over government policy by a sequence of effects, extending from the appropriation of profits to fiscal abundance, operating without any necessarily political intentions on the part of capitalists (Block 1977; Lindblom 1977; Przeworski and Wallerstein 1988). In brief, profits, as the principal fount for investment, can fuel economic growth and affluence. These, in turn, buoy revenues and electoral popularity, two key supports of governments (Hibbs 1987). Thus, government spending is contingent upon factors that sustain these supports. More to the point, it is dependent on the infraresources of growth and affluence (and ultimately profits).[9] I hypothesize that economic affluence facilitates welfare effort if only though the medium of political action.

Environmental Approach: International Perspective

Increasingly, scholars have turned to situating domestic welfare states in international context. Cameron (1978) and Katzenstein (1985) have directly linked the welfare state to a nation's openness to the international economy, trade in particular, arguing that greater openness (as we saw in the last chapter) pressures nations to cushion their citizens against economic adversity (see also Garrett 1998b). Yet, somewhat more recently, scholars have also turned to seeing the international economy as a source of pressures for moderation, modification, and retrenchment of social policy (Piore and Sabel

---

[8] Similarly, party competition, because of the pro-welfare appeals offered median voters by competing parties, might augment welfare effort (see Mueller 1979, chaps. 6–8). The typically assumed pro-welfare tilt of median voters, however, is uncertain. For example, independent voters are unpredictable. Moreover, evidence for the hypothesis had been spotty (Pampel and Williamson 1989; Hicks and Swank 1992; Hicks and Misra 1993).
[9] See Przeworski 1985 on profits and investment; Hicks and Misra 1993 on revenues; and Hibbs 1987, pt. III, on popularity.

1984; Piore 1995; Turner 1993). Some scholars have been ambivalent (Rodrik 1997).

Economic Openness

Much attention has been given to possible effects of economic openness upon neocorporatism. For Katzenstein (1985) open economies are particularly vulnerable economies. Economies are open to the extent that domestic consumers are dependent on imports and domestic producers and that wage-earning consumers, in turn, are highly dependent on exports (Cameron 1978, 1249; Katzenstein 1985, 81–87). When economies are open, cooperation is encouraged by the large and unpredictable impact of the international market on the domestic economy: key state and economic actors cooperate to ensure and buffer populations against "developments they can never fully control" (Katzenstein 1985, 236; Wallerstein 1987). This argument is offered by Katzenstein (1985) to establish economic openness as the crucial causal mechanism linking small states to cooperative institutions, neocorporatism in particular. It is economic vulnerability and openness, manifest correlates of small states, not size per se, that directly grounds causal relations between state smallness and neocorporatism for Katzenstein (1985). Recently some scholars have stressed inhibiting effects of openness on social spending. Net inhibiting effects are argued to obtain for a combination of reasons. One is because increased openness increases the substitutability of domestic labor and goods to foreign labor and goods, creating pressures for states to cut public deficits and debts that depress investment and aggravate trade deficits, as well as cut public income subsidies that (via their revenue costs) augment corporate wage bills. The second is that these pressures come to swamp any contrary effects for public compensation of the victims of international economic competition (Ruggie 1996; Rodrik 1997).

Macroeconomic Eras

The 1973 OPEC (the Organization of Petroleum Exporting Countries) oil shock is widely regarded as a watershed between two macroeconomic eras with contrasting implications for social policy formation (Schmidt 1983; Hicks and Swank 1992; Pampel and Williamson 1989). Macroeconomic stagflation, the unraveling of the Keynesian reconciliation of interventionist government and economic growth, and the emergence of antistatist movements and governments, all appearing in tandem in the years following the 1973 to 1974 OPEC oil shock, transformed the global economic context politically and ideologically, as well as economically. Although the new era has been associated with an upward hike in welfare effort due to a massive triggering of entitlements by the swelling ranks of the unemployed and poor, it is generally thought to have eroded the material and philosophical (*sic* orthodox macroeconomic) bases for discretionary forms of welfare expansion (Roubini and Sachs 1989). For example, decreased economic growth is argued to have exacerbated zero-sum trade-offs in policy, thereby intensifying citizen competitiveness and eroding public altruism. An earlier Keynesian consensus in macroeconomic theory that legitimized ample state spending broke up under such pressures as stagflation with its Hobson's choices between inflationary high unemployment and job-cutting price stability. Net of our controls for measures of need, we expect the additive impact of the post-OPEC period to be a simple drop in welfare effort and its rate of expansion.

Again, our principal propositions are summarized in Table 6.2. Here, explanatory variables are emphasized by bold-face type. Hypothesized effects are apparent from their placement under either pro-welfare orientation or antiwelfare orientation. The last column identifies the theoretical perspective given political resources and associated causes of welfare effort. Examples of particular determinants are emphasized by bold type to pinpoint a variable's special relevance to explaining social spending effort and anticipate actual operational variables used in data analyses.

To highlight some theoretical issues, the social democratic perspective emphasizes the resources of governmental authority, interest organization, and domestic systemic bias—social and Christian democratic rule, neocorporatism, and prosperity, more specifically. Statists, at least in contrast to social democrats, stress administrative authority and state structure. In particular, they anticipate the extent to which state structures open up or close off opportunities for groups to exercise power and influence over actual policy. Pluralists view electoral leverage and interest organization as key resources, although they stress the operation and, through demand overload, the cumulative effect of "atomized" interests in relatively *un*structured interest-group systems. Theorists of domestic social systems stress their overall resource capabilities (e.g., affluence or per capita GDP), whereas theorists of international systems stress international incentives and threats to the stability and prosperity of domestic material resources.

Overall, I do not claim to have tightly synthesized social demo-cratic, political-institutional, and other theories, along with all of their distinctive premises and logics. I claim merely to have organized the principal explanatory factors from these theories of social spending within a single framework. This has a less sharply focused logic than the originating perspectives. Nevertheless, it has a logic of its own. This is a logic of specific actors, the interests they pursue, and the resources they wield, all situated within the major political-institutional contexts of governments and state administration of electoral, societal, and international arenas. In short, it is a logic of action by resource-empowered, socially embedded, and goal-oriented actors.

Models, Measures, and Methods

Models

My focus is on welfare effort or spending for welfare benefits as a share of the GDP (Cameron 1986; Pampel and Williamson 1989; Esping-Andersen 1990). *Welfare spending* is defined here and by the International Labor Organization (ILO) as government spending relating to schemes, transfers, or services. These must (a) grant cura-tive or preventive medical care, maintain income in case of involun-tary diminution of earnings, or grant supplementary income to persons with family responsibilities; (b) be legislatively sanctioned; and (c) be administered publicly or quasi-publicly.

Measures

This work analyzes welfare effort in the 18 large and continu-ous post–World War II democracies during the years (1960–1989) for which complete and comparable data are available. Operationalized variables are outlined in Table 6.2 and detailed in the Appendix 6; However, a few immediate comments here may help to clarify our measures.

Welfare effort is measured by the ratio of welfare spending to GDP and is measured with the ILO expenditure data and GDP resource data (cf Y in Appendix 6). It is used in lieu of more nuanced measures of welfare benefits (e.g., proportional income maintenance or replace-ment rates) as the conventional measure of welfare spending effort rel-ative to economic capacity pioneered by Wilensky (1975), as well as a serviceable indicator of welfare "rights").[10] GDP's lesser vulnerability to distorting trade and exchange rate fluctuations makes it preferable to gross national product (GNP) data. Total expenditure data on social welfare spending from the ILO (1960–1995) improve on the comprehensiveness and comparability of analogous Organization of Economic Cooperation and Development (OECD) data by including health spending and some "in-kind" benefits (e.g., Pampel and Williamson 1988).[11] Hopefully, a sense of welfare efforts variation across our eighteen nations during the 1960 to 1982 period has already been provided by Table 6.1 and Figure 6.1.

Partisan government variables are measured as follows (and as detailed in Appendix 6). Social democratic participation in government and Christian democratic cabinet participation principally are measured in terms of proportional shares of cabinet positions for social democratic and Christian democratic types of parties, respectively. They are also measured as indices of cumulative (1946 to present) party government, following Huber et al. (1993).

Neocorporatism is measured as a composite of two measures that themselves distill an extensive literature on the measurement of this institution. To do this, I draw upon two past efforts to measure neocorporatism. These are the factor analytically constructed scales of Lijphart and Crepaz (1991) and Hicks and Swank (1992). To reinvoke

[10] Our 1980 values of welfare effort correlate 0.69 with Esping-Andersen's (1990, 52) measure of decommodification for the same year. Welfare effort is W/Y, where W is welfare spending and Y is aggregate income. It can be restated as $(B*P)/Y$, where B is a count of the beneficiaries and P is a per-beneficiary payment rate. Thus, welfare effort resembles a coverage-weighted income-replacement ratio; and controlling for (or residualized on) measures of P, such as measures of need, resembles P/Y, a simple income replacement ratio. The Esping-Andersen (1990, 52–54) measure is an index of income replacement weighted by coverage and adjusted for waiting and coverage duration for health, unemployment, and pension program benefits.

[11] Aggregate or summary social spending is targeted, first, to maintain continuity with the bulk of the literature on welfare effort (e.g., Wilensky 1975; Hicks and Swank 1984b; Pampel and Williamson 1988; Pampel and Stryker 1990; Mahler 1990; Esping-Andersen 1990). Second, it is used because top-down theorists of budgetary processes stress the causal priorities of such large aggregates over their components (pensions, family allowances, and so on), which are decided on as shares of the more encompassing aggregates (Kamlet and Mowery 1987). Moreover, although expenditures on subcategories of social spending may work as an alternative, functionally equivalent tools of social policy and analysis of aggregate spending is parsimonious as well as important. Finally, analysis of specific programs, although imperative, must lie beyond the present, already complex effort. Better post-1980 data on social spending have arguably become available recently from OECD (1994, 1996). (See Swank, 1997.) However, measures of welfare effort for these data (both for 1980–1989 and for 1961–1989 with OECD measures spliced to ILO ones) correlate around 0.95 with the ILO data employed.

terms from the previous chapter, scores for both the former authors' generalized neocorporatist scale and the latter's Left neocorporatist scales were standardized so that they would vary neatly between 0 and 1. They were then averaged together into one final composite scale. I refer to this third composite scale as a tripartite neocorporatism scale because it offsets the generalized scale's marginal disregard of labor's tripartite role by including the labor-centered Left corporatism scale. Further elaboration of this scale, along with scores, may be found in Chapter Five (see especially Table 5.2, Panel A).

The principal statist variable is a measure of constitutionally defined structural veto points taken from Huber et al. (1993). This is a measure that codes three types of exclusionary veto points (federal, bicameral, and presidential) high for exclusiveness, and one type of cooperative point (PR) low for nonexclusiveness, which is to say high for its opposite (plurality-election/single-member districts).[12] I measure inflation as the annual percentage change in a nation's cost of living index. I leave definitions of measures of the pluralist variables of voter turnout (the proportion of citizens eligible to vote who are actually voting), the unemployment rate (the proportion of the economically active seeking working), the elderly's share of population, all quite self-explanatory, to Appendix 6 for further description. Industrialist and global measures of affluence and openness, respectively, are, in turn, (a) per capita GDP (logged for less skewness and stronger fit), and (b) the sum of exports and imports as a proportion of GDP.[13]

To avoid simultaneity bias and to curtail specification searching (or fishing) for optimal lags, explanatory variables are lagged as follows. Zero and one-year lags (averaged) will be used for variables that seem likely to have some immediate automatic effects as entitlement or revenue triggers (rates of unemployment and old age, the natural logarithm of GDP per capita). In order to capture a full range of policy

[12] For consistency with Huber et al. (1993), Swiss referenda gain one point for Switzerland's competitive score. Note that, in a strictly statistical sense (as in a more technical paper), utilization of separate competitive and consensual veto point measures would be ideal (see Hicks and Misra 1993, n. 30). For the sake of clarity on potentially arcanely technical matters, a single composite measure is used here.

[13] With consideration of these variables—plus military spending and protests and strikes in n. 6 and party competition in n. 8—the full range of principal variables in recent studies is largely covered. A potential exception is state size measured in terms of state employees as a share of population, the bureau voting variable of Hicks and Swank (1992) and Hicks and Misra (1993). This has been dropped because of the absence of data for many nations much beyond 1980, the cutoff in the key source used for previous studies (OECD 1986).

action lags (covering everything from prompt enactment of a program to slow legislative movements through monitoring, legislative, budgetary, and implementation stages), moving averages of variables, lagged one through four years, are used for each of two (social democratic and Christian democratic) cabinet share (or participation in government) variables. One-year lags are used for remaining variables (economic openness, pre-OPEC era, voter turnout).[14] The two temporally invariant structural variables, neocorporatism and veto points are, as operationally unchanging contexts, unlagged.

My basic model, expressed with concise symbols (and longer, clearer variable names), is

(Eq. 1)   Welfare effort $= f (X_1$ [Left cabinet], X_2 [Christian democratic cabinet],
X_3 [Neocorporatism], X_4 [constitutional structure],
X_5 [unemployment rate], X_6 [aged as a percent of population],
X_7 [economic openness], X_8 [GDP per capita(ln)],
X_9 [pre-OPEC era], X_{10} [voter turnout], X_{11} [inflation])

Estimation

The pooling of time series ($t = 29$ years) and cross-sectional units ($n = 18$ nations) permits large-sample analyses ($N = 522$) drawing on temporal and cross-national variation; however, it also presents estimation difficulties unless data are remarkably well behaved (Kmenta 1988, chap. 12; Johnston 1984, chap. 10; Stimson 1985). Errors are typically autocorrelated within units and heteroscedastic, as well as autocorrelated across units, thereby degrading estimator precision. To correct for these maladies, I estimate multiple regressions using SHAZAM's "pool" procedure, with simultaneous applications of a simple AR(1) correction for autoregressive errors and of the "hetcov" implementation of Beck and Katz's (1995) panel corrected standard errors (PCSE) procedure.

---

[14] In order to take account of a plausible range of action lags, party-strength measures were cumulated over that range of years that proved consequential. Distributed lag effects of partisan measures upon welfare effort were examined for years *t*-6 through *t* by using Almon distributed lags (see Johnston 1984, 352). The consequential range proved to be *t*-1 through *t*-4 for both party rule measures.

Specification and Analysis

First, we estimate a model with $X_1, X_2, \ldots, X_{10}$ all included. Next, we estimate a model that deletes variables that have not met a lenient standard of retention.[15] This criterion is a t-statistic greater than or equal to 1.0 in absolute value, the minimum level required of a variable if its inclusion in a regression is not to degrade its goodness of fit (e.g., reduce its R^2 corrected for degrees of freedom).

Results are displayed in Table 6.3. The initial, or predeletion, equation fits the data well with its corrected R^2 of 0.858 (and its indication of negligibly autocorrelated errors). In this equation, all variables are statistically significant and correctly signed, except the two partisan cabinet variables and the marginally significant inflation variable. After deletion of the Left Cabinet variable, which had an estimate that was both anomalously signed and smaller than its standard error, model fit slightly improves. All retained variables are now statistically significant except Christian democratic cabinet, although inflation remains only marginally significant. Most variables seem quite substantively as well as statistically significant. In particular, standardized beta coefficients (which vary largely between 1.0 and −1.0 and may be interpreted much like correlation coefficients) are moderate or, at least, noteworthy in size (i.e., >.15) for all variables retained in the equation, except the slightly less potent OPEC and turnout.

In standardized terms, aged population share, unemployment rates, and neocorporatism have the largest effects (Table 6.3, revised equation). The first two of these are variables that straddle statist and pluralist perspectives, fitting the former insofar as they automatically translate demographic and economic aggregates into social spending by automatically triggering entitlements and expanding the number of recipients of benefits. They are pluralistic to the extent that they capture any influence of the elderly and unemployed as interest groups and voting blocks.

The next most statistically notable effects on welfare effort are those of neocorporatism and exclusionary state-structure. Consistent with our theory and consistent with its origins in cooperative institutions, politics of social reform, and social democratic rule, neocorporatism has a substantial positive effect of 0.237. Consistent with our theory about both exclusionary and cooperative veto points, ex-

---

[15] I simplify by means of a term-at-a-time backward deletion of terms with absolute values of t-statistics below 1.0. (The term with the smallest such t is removed from each estimation until no such insignificant terms remain; and terms with disqualifying t and theoretically anomalous signs are removed first of all.)

Multiple Regressions of Welfare Effort on Explanatory Variables

ariable	Initial Equation			Revised Equation		
	Estimated Coefficient	T-Ratio 492 df	Partial Beta Coefficient	Estimated Coefficient	T-Ratio 493 df	Partial Beta Coefficient
flation	0.0354	1.37[‡]	0.021	0.0339	1.31[‡]	0.020
eft cabinet	−0.0041	−0.95	−0.021	—	—	—
hristian Democratic cabinet	0.0094	0.83	0.034	0.0130	1.14	0.047
eocorporatism	0.0523	3.77*	0.229	0.0541	3.56*	0.237
onst'l Structure	−0.0056	−2.80*	−0.176	−0.0053	−2.65*	−0.167
nemployment rate	0.4051	6.15*	0.218	0.4044	6.13*	0.217
ged percent of population	0.7889	4.32*	0.290	0.7093	3.68*	0.261
onomic openness	0.0338	3.82*	0.139	0.0355	3.90*	0.147
DP per capita (ln)	0.0104	3.08*	0.135	0.0110	3.22*	0.143
ost-OPEC era	0.0158	4.10*	0.119	0.0155	4.92*	0.117
oter turnout	0.4228	2.08[†]	0.070	0.0412	2.03[†]	0.069
onstant	−0.3479	−1.60[†]	0.000	−0.0295	−1.31[†]	0.000

Durbin-Watson = 1.850
rho = 0.0452
R²: observed and predicted = 0.858
(corrected for df)

Durbin-Watson = 1.859
rho = 0.045
R² = 0.861
(corrected for df)

ote: Initial equation with "base" variables; revised equation after deletion and entry of variables.
[†], [‡] denote significance at the 0.01, 0.05, 0.10 test levels, respectively.

clusionary state structure has a negative effect of −.167 on welfare effort. As a negative effect of exclusionary structure may be reconstrued as a positive one of cooperative state-structure, the following broad stroke may be painted: cooperative institutions, both within the state and at its boundary with organized interests—cooperatively structured states and neocorporatism—promote welfare effort.

Additional effects take us beyond the polity to its domestic and international economic environments. One is the positive one of GDP per capita, which probably operates by creating "resource slack" (whether by means of automatically expanding revenues or augmenting the tax base) for social policy makers contemplating legislative expansions of programs. A second is the positive, pro-welfarist effect of economic openness (beta = .147), which has been argued to pressure states into buffering their citizens against international economic volatility, indeed, into compensating them for its shocks so they will support efforts to sustain exposure to these shocks' economically disciplining and productive spin-offs. A third, is the positive effect of OPEC (beta = 0.117), which may be regarded as tapping a particular historical set of compensatory responses to international shocks.[16]

Overall, the effects of the unemployed and elderly, with their direct access to statutory entitlement mechanisms and possibly complementary influences as lobbyists and voting blocks, are straightforward. So are the effects of openness and the post-OPEC period, as these can be assumed to exacerbate actual and perceived needs for welfare effort.[17] Economic product, on the other hand, clearly helps empower societies to address the kinds of needs, uncertainties, and entitlement dynamics addressed by unemployment and old age, economic openness, and oil shocks. Again, partisan rule effects are quite lacking (but see Appendix 6 on cumulative rule).[18]

The findings in Table 6.3 on political institutions, for example, neocorporatism and state structure, may seem a bit obscure in their operations. Had empirical results yielded strong effects of reformist partisan governments, findings would have been more straightforward. We might simply have said that Left or Left-Center partisan actors tend to enact increases in welfare effort when they govern, but how do institutions such as neocorporatism and competitive state structures—hardly straightforward actors, if actors at all—"enact" policy? By what mechanisms do they do so? Of course, part of the likely story has already been spelled out or suggested. Neocorporatist systems, by incorporating labor, give it voice and commit it to participation

[16] Analyses were replicated by using the OECD data on transfers to households, which exclude evaluations of nonmonetary benefits such as goods in-kind (e.g., food stamps) and such services as unbilled health care, and by using the alternative union-centered measure of tripartite corporatism, which substitutes a measure of union strength for the Left corporatism index of Hicks and Swank (1992) (see Chapter 5, c. Table 5.3). Replications, reported in Appendix 6B, yield almost the same pattern of results as Table 6.3. The *transfer equation* differs from the analogous equation of Table 6.3 only in yielding a significant positive effect of Christian democratic government, a finding consistent with the greater effects of Christian democratic rule found for transfer effort relative to more encompassing welfare effort in Huber et al. (1993). (In the initial transfer equation, neocorporatism falls below the *t*-criterion, but it rebounds to significance in the "revised" equation after the deletion of the anomalously Left Cabinet variable.) The union corporatism equation of Appendix 6B (Panel B) almost exactly replicates the revised equation of Table 6.3. (See Chapter 5 on "union corporatism.")

[17] In fact, OPEC correlates 0.534 with unemployment in the data for the Table 6.4 analyses, whereas openness captures that increasing dependence on trade near the heart of globalization scenarios of increased economic vulnerability.

[18] I question results that, like those of Huber et al. (1993), use cumulative measures of social democratic and Christian democratic government, and I detail them in Appendix 6C. In brief, cumulative models use measures of cumulative partisan government, typically cumulated from 1946 through to the year of any particular case. These are likely to tap and exploit any time trend in welfare effort and to be counters for time when social Christian democratic rule is the norm. They are ineffectual in Appendix 6C's analyses, except for indirect, long-run effects of pre-1960s cumulative rule.

in policy negotiations. By so doing, they involve labor in exchange networks in which welfare benefits arise as complements to, and as substitutes and general lubricants for, the main union business of collective bargaining. After all, policies that augment the social wage (the public wage for those outside the market) will tend to advance worker interest; and to be pursued regardless of governmental partisanship. Still, how can static measures of the mere extent of corporatist and other cooperative institutions, not measures of their operational processes, get at temporally varying aspects of policy?

Neocorporatism can most simply affect policy over time by helping to shape the impacts that temporally variable forces have on it. For example, neocorporatism might augment policy responsiveness to Left government or unemployment, whereas structures of the formal state that have been conceptualized in terms of exclusionary veto points do the opposite. To examine such possibly demonstrable mechanisms for institutional impact, I computed statistical interactions between dichotomized variants of each of the two institutional variables and each of the temporally lively (process-oriented) regressors.

Such interactions simply estimate parameters for products of such structure/process pairs of variables that tell us whether effects of the lively process-oriented variable are functions of the more temporally inert structural ones. I dichotomize the structural variables for easier interpretation. This done, we may decipher the interaction estimates for each structure-process pairing algebraically, as follows: an estimate of a structural effect on the relation of process-oriented variable to the outcome variable. In other words, they are estimates for differences in the welfare consequences of lively variables across the categories of the dichotomous (here structural and temporally static) variable. We will see that such interactions also are useful for estimating the effects of each continuous variable within either category of each (dichotomous) structural variable. Neocorporatism is dichotomized to equal 1 for Austria, Belgium. Denmark, Finland, Germany, the Netherlands, Norway, Sweden, and Switzerland, the eight nations highest on the tripartite corporatism index used here, and the remaining nations studies are coded 0. This is a simple choice, as it is both conventional and divides cases at the substantial gap between Switzerland and (the less tripartite corporatist) Japan (see Chapter 4, Table 4.2). Veto points are dichotomized to equal 1 for the five cases with values over 2 on its 0 to 7 level scale: Australia, Canada, Germany, Switzerland and the United States; the rest of the 18 nation cases are coded zero.

Results for the analysis are quite striking for the case of neocorporatism, as well as interesting for that of structural veto points. For the former institution, neocorporatism interacts significantly (at the 0.05 level of statistical significance) with three of the more temporally lively or processual regressors and has an interaction-term estimate that is significant at the marginal 0.10 test level (and arguably notable) for turnout as well (Table 6.4, Panel A.) More specifically, neocorporatism interacts strongly and positively with unemployment rates, the elderly's population share, and per capita GDP. This is to say, welfare effort is more responsive in corporatist than in noncorporatist nations—both to the share of unemployed persons in the labor force and the share of elderly persons in the population. Welfare effort in corporatist nations is also relatively more responsive to variations in per capita GDP, and to levels of need and demand. In addition, there is also some indication that higher levels of voter turnout yield higher returns in welfare effort in corporatist than in noncorporatist societies. These shifts in policy responsiveness as we move from noncorporatist to corporatist contexts are instructively presented, not merely in terms of the significance of differences between noncorporatist and corporatist states, which is what all the interaction findings of Table 6.4, Panel A, provide.

Interactions become more informative when we examine levels of estimates in each of the two contexts defined by a structural dichotomy. Panels B and D of Table 6.4 help us see this additional information. In Panel B, we can see that the responsiveness of welfare effort to economic affluence is statistically significant in corporatist cases only (t equaling 5.30 here but less than 1.0 elsewhere). Similarly, we see that the responsiveness of welfare effort to unemployment rates and shares of elderly in populations is much greater (roughly twice as great) in corporatist contexts than it is in noncorporatist contexts. Raw metric coefficients for rates of the unemployed and of the elderly jump from 0.268 and 0.591, respectively, in noncorporatist cases, to 0.620 and 0.967 in other cases; and standardized coefficients for analogous variables jump from 0.144 and 0.218 to 0.333 and 0.356. The t-statistic for voter turnout shifts from a marginally significant 1.416 in noncorporatist cases to a fully significant 2.43 in corporatist ones.[19]

[19] Category-specific coefficients in Table 6.4, panels B and D, are coefficients for continuous variables in contexts defined by one or the other category of a nominal variable involved in interactions (e.g., for corporatist or noncorporatist contexts). Technically, the corporatism-specific slope for a continuous variable (e.g., unemployment) is the slope estimated for it in an equation for which the corporatism variable is coded 1 for *non*corporatism and 0 for corporatism. (It is the opposite for the slope of unemployment in noncorporatist contexts: This is the slope for unemployment in an equation for which noncorporatism is coded 0 and corporatism is coded 1.) Category-specific, standardized estimates must be compared across context with some caution because their magnitudes vary in part with context-specific variances.

Table 6.4. Statistical Interactions between Dichotomized Structural Variables and Welfare Effort: Figures on Interactions and Category-Specific Coefficients for Processual Variables

Panel A: Neocorporatist Interactions: Corporatist Coefficients Minus Noncorporatist Ones

	b	t	B
Left cabinet	−0.0015	(−0.19)	−0.008
Christian Democratic cabinet	0.0183	(1.08)	0.052
Unemployment rate	0.3514	(2.99)*	0.143
Aged percent of population	0.3754	(3.01)*	0.379
Economic openness	0.0113	(0.78)	0.067
GDP per capita (ln)	0.0173	(4.19)*	0.266
Post-OPEC era	0.0049	(0.87)	0.032
Voter turnout	0.0244	(1.52)‡	0.159
Inflation	−0.0269	(−0.54)	−0.014

Panel B: Neocorporatist Interactions: Category-Specific Coefficients

	Noncorporatist			Corporatist		
	b	t	B	b	t	B
Christian Democratic cabinet	0.0370	(0.231)	0.013	0.0221	(2.037)‡	0.042
Unemployment rate	0.2682	(3.063)*	0.144	0.6203	(7.227)*	0.333
Aged percent of population	0.5910	(2.978)*	0.218	0.9674	(4.577)*	0.356
GDP per capita (ln)	0.0029	(0.681)	0.038	0.0202	(5.300)*	0.263
Voter turnout	0.0303	(1.416)‡	0.050	0.0547	(2.434)*	0.091

Panel C: State-Structural Interaction: Exclusionary ESTIMATES Minus Inclusionary Ones

	b	t	B
Left cabinet	−0.0120	(−1.30)‡	−0.030
Christian Democratic cabinet		(too multicollinear to estimate)	
Unemployment rate	0.0490	(0.44)	0.019
Aged percent of population	−0.9974	(0.15)	−0.076
Economic openness	−0.2200	(−1.41)‡	−0.069
GDP per capita (ln)	−0.0118	(−2.99)*	−0.166
Post-OPEC era	−0.0094	(−2.05)†	−0.051
Voter turnout	0.0095	(0.58)	0.049
Inflation	−0.0135	(−0.27)	−0.006

Panel D: State-Structural Interactions: Category-Specific Coefficients

	Exclusionary state structures			Inclusionary state structures		
	b	t	B	b	t	B
Left cabinet	−0.0145	(−1.841)†	−0.075	−0.0026	(−0.529)	−0.013
Economic openness	0.0134	(0.820)	0.055	0.0354	(3.696)*	0.146
GDP per capita (ln)	0.0040	(0.953)	0.052	0.0158	(4.101)*	0.205
Post-OPEC era	0.0084	(1.871)†	0.063	0.0178	(5.180)*	0.134

Note: Raw (b) and standardized (B) coefficient estimates; t-statistics are in between in parentheses
*, †, and ‡ denote significance at the 0.01, 0.05, 0.10 test levels, respectively.

For the case of exclusionary veto points, results of only two interactions are significant at the 0.01 level: negative results for GDP and OPEC (Table 6.4, Panel C). In particular, welfare sensitivity to economic product and the OPEC oil shocks are both positive and significant in nations with relatively inclusionary, cooperative states but are nullified in nations with relatively exclusionary, competitive states. Estimates for state structure's interactions with Left rule and trade openness are also significant at the marginal 0.10 level. Left rule apparently has counterproductive, antiwelfarist effects in exclusionary states that shift into mere ineffectiveness in more inclusionary states. Trade openness evokes pro-welfarist, compensatory responses in nations with relatively inclusionary, cooperative states that vanish (yet are not reversed) in nations with relatively exclusionary, competitive states.

So, not only have rates of unemployment and old age, economic openness and oil shocks, domestic product and voter turnout substantially determined levels of welfare effort in affluent democracies during recent decades. In addition, two political structures—neocorporatist structures of interest intermediation and exclusionary (e.g., federal, nonparliamentary) structures of formal states—complement these more temporally lively processual effects and shape them, shifting their magnitudes and even their directions. More details would be helpful regarding underlying mechanisms for the highly significant interactions involving neocorporatism and characteristically pluralist policy determinants, needy aged and unemployed, economic resources, and mobilized electorates. Very likely, labor's strong, robust position within neocorporatist arrangements has meant neocorporatist pressures for benefit and eligibility statutes that structure a high (and largely automatic) degree of responsiveness to rates of unemployment and old age. (For example, union wage moderation probably earned them social side payments to grease labor market bargains, as in Lange and Garrett [1985]). Very likely, relatively high tax rates implied by neocorporatist labor incorporation have structured a high (automatic) responsiveness to the relatively high tax base denoted by high GDP (see Hicks and Misra 1993). Very likely, turnout is not only relatively higher in neocorporatist contexts; it is also, due to labor mobilization, relatively conducive to social spending appeals for votes.[20]

---

[20] Very likely, the residual of economic risk and hardship captured by the post-OPEC period is relatively conducive to compensatory social insurance where state structural veto points are fewer. Very likely, the social-spending orientations of Left governments are facilitated by, for example, unitary states that grant such governments a single, nation-level set of policy levers.

Conclusions and Implications

Empirically and substantively, these findings speak to many indeterminancies in past research. Effects of affluence and unemployment upon welfare effort, spottily supported in past studies, are affirmed here. As regards any recent primacy of Left (or Catholic) party government variables for social democratic theorists, results counsel skepticism. Present analyses unearth scant evidence for direct welfarist effects of measures of partisan government; however, *long-run*, indirect effects of social democratic (and, more equivocally, Christian democratic) participation in government clearly do emerge (see Table A6C.2). Loosely interpretable as legacies of postwar reformism, these seem best interpreted as indirect effects of postwar partisan reformism channeled through largely social democratic–constructed neocorporatist institutions, although signs of some complementary effects net of neocorporatist conduits emerge.

If the at least partial eclipse of direct social democratic effects by neocorporatism appears puzzling, it need not remain baffling. First, past findings concerning the partisan welfare linkage have been disparate. True, a tradition of pro-welfarist effects of social democratic parties has been recently prominent in the literature (see Hicks and Swank 1984b; Esping-Andersen 1990, Chap. 4; Hicks and Swank 1992; Huber et al. 1993; and Hicks and Misra 1993). Nevertheless, some authors within this tradition have often found small or contingent effects of Left rule (e.g., Hicks and Swank 1992; Hicks and Misra 1993) or have found relatively larger, more robust effects of Christian democratic parties (e.g., Huber et al. 1993). Moreover, evidence of very general, non-Rightist, pro-welfarist rule has been consistent in one prominent line of work (Castles and McKinlay 1978; Castles 1998). Furthermore, evidence of antiwelfarist Left party effects and pro-welfarist Right party effects has stood out in some studies of pension effort (e.g., Pampel and Williamson 1989, Chap. 3; and Williamson and Pampel 1993, 192–198, respectively); and evidence of a strong, postwar Center-Right advancement of social insurance policy stands out in, at least, the recent landmark qualitative study of Baldwin (1990). The absence of distinct, direct Left-party findings should not be extremely unsettling. They are much anticipated.

Second, Christian and social democratic contributions to the social insurance state are not entirely lacking for postwar welfare effort. Not only is an ample effect of Christian democratic rule recorded for transfer effort (see n. 16), indirect legacies of 1946 to 1960 Left party rule are documented (again, see Appendix 6C, Table A6C.2). In addition, as social democratic rule dominated welfare reform in the 1930s and 1940, and as social democrats largely erected the neocorporatist institutions so prominent in welfare expansion during recent decades, social democratic boosts to welfare effort are implicit in neocorporatist ones. Moreover, labor unions are broadly constitutive of neocorporatist arrangements, whereas social democratic governments are supportive of routine neocorporatist operations (e.g., Garrett 1998a). Indeed, social democratic rule may be (as Chapter 7 shall detail) as crucial to neocorporatist survival as it was to its emergence.

Third, both the extent of nonconservative social insurance reform during the 1930s and 1940s and the degree of basic social insurance program consolidation by the early 1950s were *very* extensive. Together with the neocorporatist incorporation of union political prominence, they may be supposed, true to Baldwin (1990), to have established an extensive "risk class" of social insurance supporters of every partisan stripe by the 1960s. This convergence of electoral majorities and partisan actors on some degree of support for the social insurance state, at least through the often proclaimed retrenchments in Britain of the Tories of Thatcher and after, is likely to have muted partisan difference in social insurance politics for most of the 1960 to 1989 period studied and analyzed here. In short, the post-1960 partial eclipse of social democratic welfarism by neocorporatism welfarism hardly deprives the social insurance state of social democratic energies.[21]

What of the relative explanatory powers of alternative theoretical perspectives and not just alternative forms of working-class power? For more general theoretical adjudications, we must address a wider range of findings.

In one sense of theoretical dominance, that based on a preponderance of relevant variables from one particular theoretical perspective, no single perspective emerges as preeminent. Instead, factors associated with every perspective play consequential roles in the determination of social spending. This conclusion is consistent with our introductory reading of the previous literature, even as it is at odds with the narrowly parochial claims of past studies. *If theoretical dominance requires explanatory monopoly by the variables of a particular elementary perspective, none emerges.*

In a second sense of theoretical dominance, one that weighs the extent of each perspective's effects and allows for synthetic, integrative perspectives, results seem more theoretically focused. Findings seem to converge on (a) a trio of processual variables that bridge plu-

---

[21] Search for partisan effects early in the 1960–1989 period might reveal some.

ralist and statist theories; (b) a pair of structural variables that bridge statist and social democratic theories; and (c) a common convergence on the interface between state and society. Turning to the first of these foci, the processual trio consists of unemployment, aging, and affluence variables that, whatever their policy relevance as indicators of political demand and influence, are inexorably linked to state budgets by relatively automatic, technical mechanisms. Two of these, rates of unemployment and old age (or retirement), are strongly linked to policy via conduits of statutory entitlement: They gauge eligibilities for policy benefits that seldom go unutilized by potential beneficiaries. The third member of the trio, affluence, automatically sets revenue levels for a given set of well-implemented tax rates; and revenues have been shown to almost automatically generate commensurate expenditures (e.g., Kamlet and Mowery 1987).

This pluralist-statist trio is complemented by (a) neocorporatism, which entails an interpenetration of organized societal interests and the formal state; and (b) aspects of the formal state that inhibit or promote the inclusive aggregation of societal interests into policies, indeed, the aggregation here of class interests in progressively redistributive welfare policies (see Hicks and Swank 1984a, 1985; Kenworthy 1998; and Chapter 7, n. 12). The two structural variables help shape the impacts of society on state.

What the two *sets* of variables, processual and structural, share are a common location at the interface between state and society *plus* involvement in the mediation (from one end or the other) of societal forces by state structures. These processual and statist commonalities suggest the power of a statist framework that is also attentive to group and class influence. Closer to home, they suggest a state-centered variant of resource theory much like that proposed as a frame for this chapter's analysis or, similarly, a polity-centered approach like that of Skocpol (1992) that stresses the organizing role of the state for all that impinges on it. *Insofar as theoretical dominance weighs the extent of a perspective's impacts and allows for synthesis, support emerges from present analyses for something like Hicks and Misra's political resource theory* or, similarly, for Skocpol's polity-centered framework (1992).

In a third sense, one that places welfare effort *in historical perspective, present findings suggest a social democratic approach attentive to the power of the state to frame the ways in which societal forces determine policies* (not a statism cum class but class-analysis cum state). The strong mediating force of neocorporatism in the generation of welfare effort is, as we saw in Chapter 5, deeply rooted in processes of class compromise and social democratic governance. The lesser mediating force of state structure captured by effects of exclusionary state structure (or veto points) likewise shares roots in moments and legacies of class compromise and suppression, as in the concessions to labor constituencies and parties inscribed into turn-of-the-century adoptions of proportional systems of representation and implicit in the *divide et impera* of federalism (e.g., Katzenstein 1985; Skocpol 1992). If history calls for a greater recognition of the centrality of class politics, however, it also historicizes class. It should now make apparent, even more than when historical discontinuities in policy determination were first noted in Chapter 4, that the modes of class politics are historically specific.

Insofar as theoretical dominance not only allows for synthetic approaches but takes account of the historical long run (here, social insurance from its 1880s inception to date), a class perspective that foregrounds state contingencies for class politics takes on special prominence. However, this class-centered perspective merits extended historical delineation and may, paradoxically, be undercut by a declining importance of class. (See Chapter 8.)

Before returning to any discussion of this history over the five- or six-score years encompassed by this work, it is wise to turn first to the current history of welfare effort and of social policy more generally. For this, a return to the trajectory of welfare effort in recent decades is useful.

As we saw with Figure 6.1, welfare effort reflects the history of midcentury program consolidation, running a higher course for consolidators, and reveals a common pattern not merely of S-shaped growth to limits but of retrenchment. This last pattern of deceleration and retraction speaks to the crisis of the welfare state, of a possible recent turning point in its history.

This chapter's findings suggest refinements of the picture in Figure 6.1. What does welfare effort's trajectory look like examined for corporatist and noncorporatist nations, as opposed to midcentury consolidators and nonconsolidators? How does it look for combinations for these two types, which can perhaps tie together processes extending from midcentury back toward Bismarck and from midcentury forward toward century's end? How do trajectories appear if they are adjusted for (graphed "net of") the strong, substantially automatic pressures of population aging and secularly increasing unemployment?

A look at Figure 6.2, which plots values over time of welfare effort separately for corporatist and noncorporatist nations, shows a pattern of development much like that in Figure 6.1, only this new figure singles out neocorporatist nations rather than midcentury consolidators as welfare leaders. Now the two time paths are more distinct, more con-

Figure 6.2. Welfare effort over time (1962–1989). Neocorporatist and non-neocorporatist ("neocorp") without (A) and with (B) adjustments for population and unemployment effects on welfare effort.

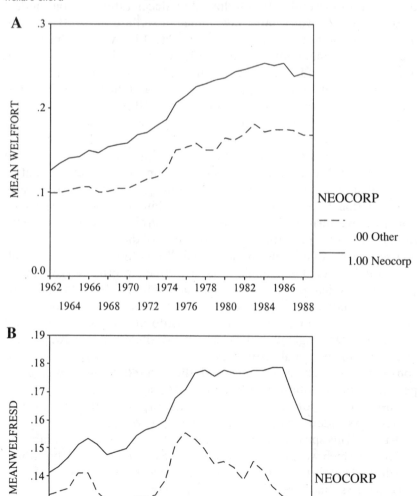

sistently and widely apart, suggesting a greater relevance for neocorporatism than consolidation to the development of welfare effort. Also the S-pattern of acceleration followed by deceleration is a bit moderated in Panel A, which plots raw values of welfare effort. If we turn, however, to the need-adjusted values of Panel B—values adjusted for the effects of unemployment and elderly population—the similarity with the pattern of Figure 6.1 is sustained. The divide between the corporatist and noncorporatist paths is widened and the S-shape is accentuated by the sharp 1980s declines in welfare effort.

If we turn to Figure 6.3's plots of raw welfare effort, we see in Panel A a clear ranking of the two corporatist curves above the two noncorporatist curves and a similarly clear ranking (blurred only in the mid-1960s) of the pathway of corporatist consolidators above that of corporatist non-consolidators.[22] Apparently, corporatism and early consolidation both matter, and their combination proves especially potent. If we turn to the need-adjusted figures of Panel B, we see a rather different pattern. Corporatist consolidators sustain a high course relative to all other nations. The three other sets of nations all appear to be caught in a tangle, although some pattern emerges among this large residual of nations by the mid-1980s. By 1984, the path for corporatist nonconsolidators assumes the second highest course. At about the same time, the path for noncorporatist consolidators, until then lost in the tangle with the other two of the three intertwined trajectories, falls below all others, even that of the noncorporatist, non-consolidators such as Canada and the United States. Thus, early program consolidation, which seemed for a while to have buoyed welfare effort in noncorporatist as well as corporatist nations, appears to have expended all of its independent pro-welfarist effects by the mid-1980s. This speaks directly to the devolution of the Anglo-laborite societies, (which were close to the corporatist nations in 1959 but which had dipped below the virtually Left-less Anglo-settler nations of North America less than three decades later), a point worth revisiting.

Looking to the future, what I see in Figure 6.3 is, first, the vigorous welfarist development of the strongly social democratic consolidators of midcentury, when neocorporatist consolidation followed on the heels of social-insurance consolidation; second, an ample welfarist development of neocorporatist nations, where the advantages of a full midcentury consolidation were lacking and the roughly "random walks" of noncorporatist nations across the decades. Adjusting for the

[22] To adjust values of welfare effort for unemployment and old age, unstandardized residuals were rescaled to regain realistic (positive) minimum values (i.e., original minimum values).

Figure 6.3. Welfare effort by combinations of mid-century consolidations and neocorporatism. (A) Effort for four sets of nations. (B) Effort adjusted for age and unemployment for four sets of nations.

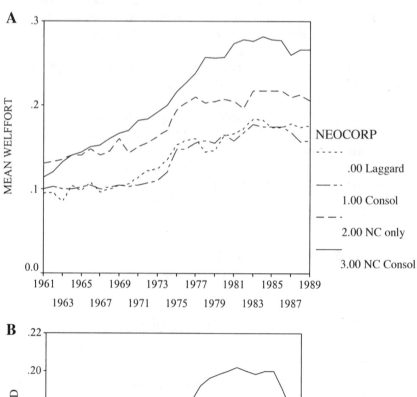

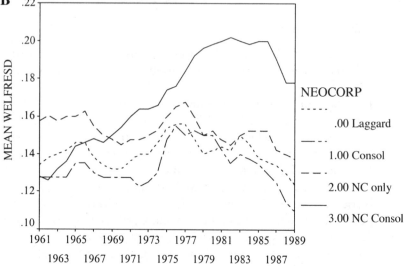

upward pressure of aging and unemployment on welfare effort, an actual downturn of welfare is evident from the mid-1970s onward for all but the neocorporatist consolidators. For these nations—Australia, Austria, Belgium, Denmark, the Netherlands, New Zealand, Norway, Sweden and the United Kingdom—leveling and decline came perhaps more precipitously when they did arrive around 1985.

There must be underlying causes for Figure 6.3's image of welfare effort leveling off and then falling back into the incontrovertible retrenchment of actual decline (especially once automatic forces of population growth and unemployment upwardly pressuring welfare effort are factored out). Welfare effort, demographically adjusting, is getting smaller. One candidate for an explanation comes especially to mind: globalization (e.g., Rodrik, 1997; Western 1997). To this and retrenchment I turn in the next chapter.

A P P E N D I X   S I X

A. Measures and Data Sources

Overview of Variables

Y: Welfare effort. Total social welfare expenditures as proportions of GDP, from International Labour Organization (selected years, a).

X_1: Left cabinet. Four-year average (t-4 through t-1) of Left-Party cabinet participation (portfolios as proportions of total cabinet portfolios). Party classifications data are from Castles and Mair (1984), and Swank (1991); cabinet participation data from Browne and Dreijmanis (1982) and Keesings.

X_2: Christian democratic cabinet. Strictly analogous to Left Cabinet.

X_3: Neocorporatism. Average of Lijphart and Crepaz's (1991) corporatism scale and Hicks and Swank's (1992) Left corporatism scale after the two were rescaled to vary between 0.0 and 1.0.

X_4: Exclusionary veto points. Constitutional structure scale from Huber et al. (1993).

X_5: Unemployment rate. Unemployed as proportion of economically active population averaged across t and t-1; data from OECD (1960–1995b).

X_6: Aged population. The number of persons at least 65 years old age and over; data from United Nations (1960–1995), average of 0 and 1-year lags.

X_7: Economic openness (see Chapter 5).

X_8: Economic product. The natural logarithm of GDP/population with data from OECD (1960–1995b); measured at t and t-1.

X_9: Post-OPEC. Equal to 1 for 1975 and later; otherwise equal to 0.

X_{10}: Turnout. Valid voters as proportions of eligible voters at most recent election; from Mackie and Rose (1974; selected years).

X_{11}: Inflation rate. Annual percentage change in consumer price index; data from International Monetary Fund, selected years. Measured at t-1 in analyses. Investment openness. See Appendix 7.

Data Sources

Principal data sources include Browne and Dreijmanis's *Government Coalition in Western Democracies* (New York: Longman 1986); the International Labor Organization's *Yearbook of Labor Statistics* (Geneva: author, selected years, b); the International Monetary Fund's *International Financial Statistics* (New York: author, selected years); Keesings Publications' *Keesings Contemporary Archives* (London: Longman, selected years); Thomas Mackie and Richard Rose's *The International Almanac of Electoral History* (London: Macmillan 1974), and "General Elections in Western Nations" in *European Journal of Political Research* (selected years); New York Times Index (selected years); the Organization in Economic Cooperation and Development's *Employment in the Public Sector* (Paris: author 1982), and *Economic Outlook: Historical Statistics 1960–1983* (Paris: author 1985), and *National Accounts of OECD Nations* (Paris: author, 1960–1995c), and *Main Economic Indicators* (Paris: author, selected years, b), and *Labour Force Statistics* (Paris: author, selected years, c); Fred C. Pampel and Robin Stryker's State Context and Welfare Development in Advanced Industrial Democracies, 1950–1980 (presented at Workshop on Inequality and Distributional Conflict, Stockholm 1988); Stein Rokkan's *Citizens, Elections, Parties* (New York: McKay 1970); Robert Summers and Alan Heston's "Improved International Comparisons of Real Product and its Components, 1950–1980," in *Review of Income and Wealth* (41: 207–262, 1982); and Michael Wallerstein's "Union Organization in Advanced Industrial Societies" in *American Political Science Review* (83: 481–501, 1989). Any sources referenced in the previous section that are not listed here are available in the Reference section.

B. Additional Regressions: Variations on Table 6.3

Table A 6B.1. Additional Regressions

Panel A: Multiple Regressions of Transfer Payments As Proportion of GDP on Explanatory Variables of Table 6.3

Variable Name	Initial Equation			Revised Equation		
	Estimated Coefficient	T-Ratio 492 df	Partial Beta	Estimated Coefficient	T-Ratio 494 df	Partial Beta
Inflation	0.0017	0.10	0.001	—	—	—
Left cabinet	−0.0022	−0.93	−0.014	—	—	—
Christian Democratic cabinet	0.0152	1.76†	0.070	0.0200	2.38*	0.09
Neocorporatism	0.0082	0.83	0.046	0.0021	1.98†	0.11
Constitutional structure	−0.0046	−4.62*	−0.183	−0.0037	−3.90*	−0.14
Unemployment rate	0.2932	5.69*	0.200	0.3175	6.38*	0.21
Aged percent of population	0.6432	5.36*	0.300	0.5079	4.11*	0.23
Economic openness	0.0276	3.26*	0.145	0.0290	3.34*	0.15
GDP per capita (ln)	0.0107	3.91*	0.177	0.0115	4.10*	0.19
Post-OPEC era	0.0119	4.95*	0.115	0.0114	4.65*	0.11
Voter turnout	0.0188	1.43‡	0.040	0.0192	1.44‡	0.04
Constant	−0.0098	−0.79	0.000	−0.0041	−0.28	0.00

Durbin-Watson = 1.57   rho = 0.001
Corrected R²: observed and
predicted = 0.872

Durbin-Watson = 1.644
rho = 0.122
R² = 0.883

Panel B: Multiple Regressions of Welfare Effort on Alternate Union-Centered ("Union Corporatism" Measure of Tripartite Corporatism) and Explanatory Variables of Table 6.3

Variable Name	Initial Equation			Revised Equation		
	Estimated Coefficient	T-Ratio 492 df	Partial Beta	Estimated Coefficient	T-Ratio 494 df	Partial Beta
Inflation	0.0373	1.43‡	0.022	0.0336	1.30‡	0.02
Left cabinet	−0.0047	−1.08	−0.024	—	—	—
CD cabinet	0.0068	0.57	0.025	—	—	—
Union corporatism	0.0584	2.88*	0.235	0.0521	2.49*	0.21
Constitutional structure	−0.0059	−2.99*	−0.185	−0.0055	−2.89*	−0.17
Unemployment rate	0.3938	6.00*	0.211	0.3894	6.25*	0.20
Aged percent of population	0.7284	3.27*	0.268	0.7987	4.06*	0.29
Economic openness	0.0328	3.56*	0.135	0.0383	4.53*	0.15
GDP per capita (ln)	0.0111	3.04*	0.144	0.0093	2.71*	0.12
Post-OPEC era	0.0157	4.92*	0.119	0.1504	4.83*	0.1
Voter turnout	0.0373	1.82†	0.062	0.0428	2.07†	0.07
Constant	−0.0236	−1.03	0.000	−0.0333	−1.55‡	0.00

Durbin-Watson = 1.833   rho = 0.055
R²: observed and predicted = 0.868

Durbin-Watson = 1.814
rho = 0.063   R² = 0.872

*, †, and ‡ denote significance at the 0.01, 0.05, 0.10 test levels, respectively.

C. Analyses of Welfare Effort with Cumulative Measure of Partisan Government

Huber et al. (1993) use cumulative measures of social democratic and (broadly) Christian democratic government. These cumulative measures sum prior annual scores of partisan rule (varying annually from 0 for *no* rule by a party type to 1 for *sole* rule by the type) from the year of origin (1946) through to whatever present time t an observation denotes. Updates of these cumulative measures of social and Christian democratic rule were available from Huber et al.'s "The Comparative Welfare State Data Set," available at http://www.lissy.ceps.lu/compwsp.html. Accessed: August, 1998.

With their alternative measures, Huber et al. (1993) estimate significant, positively signed effects of Left and Christian democratic cabinet participation on welfare effort with high t-statistics for both social and Christian democratic (in fact, Protestant as well as Catholic, Right as well as Left) measures, especially the latter. These effects extend a considerable series of studies that have found welfarist effects for Left and Catholic parties on welfare effort (e.g., Cameron 1978; Stephens 1979; Wilensky 1981; Schmidt 1983; Hicks and Swank 1992; Hicks and Misra 1993; Garrett, 1998a). They also yield rather stronger—less conditional and more highly significant—findings than most studies using noncumulative measures.

Presumably, cumulative measures are used to operationalize the idea that because policy outputs accumulate over time from past policies they are functions of *cumulative histories* of political variables. (Huber et al. are not explicit on the point.) This reasonable notion carries some liabilities, however. Cumulative measures essentially combine (a) cross-sectional (one-per-nation) or static measures of legacies of partisan rule from origin (1946) until the first time periods in a data set (here 1960); and (b) more dynamic, post–1960 temporally variable measures of partisan rule (here for each "present" observation through 1989). Such static measures are likely to tap no more than effects of vague legacies, and such dynamic measures are likely to act partly as proxies for time, capitalizing on correlations with any trend in welfare effort. (For example, in heavily social democratic nations such as Norway and Sweden, Left ones essentially count years.)

In Huber et al. (1993), measures of social democratic government (LEFTCAB) and neocorporatism (CORP, as measured with the Lehmbruch coding listed in Table 5.2) are reported as highly collinear ($r = 0.607$) and as, more generally, plagued by multicollinearity. As a result of its high reported collinearity with LEFTCAB, as well as relatively high measurement error, CORP is excluded from analyses, whereas LEFTCAB is retained (Huber et al. 1993, 730). Here I examine what happens when, contrary to Huber et al. (1993), measures of neocorporatism are used alongside cumulative Left (and Catholic) government; when the former is concluded to be neither prohibitively multicollinear nor especially troubled by measurement error (certainly no more than LEFTCAB); and when neocorporatism substitutes for partisan rule rather than vice versa. As high multicollinearity of a focal measure with other variables should result, first, in some attenuation of its effects and, second, in attenuation of *other* variables' effects, a standard is available for assessing whether cumulative Left government or neocorporatism should be deleted from regressions: So far as multicollinearity and measurement error are concerned, the variable with lower significance is best deleted. (I also examine effects of static and dynamic components of cumulative variables.)

Table A6C.1 displays regressions of welfare effort on measures of cumulative social democratic government and cumulative Christian democratic government (drawn as LEFTCUM and CNCRCUM, respectively, from "The Comparative Welfare State Data Set") and on regressors of the revised model of Table 6.3. Cumulative measures never attain the absolute-t criterion for retention in equations, much less significance at any utilized level (Table A6C.1, Panel A).

Still, social democratic government might have some pro-welfarist effects, effects that are soaked up in Panel A by the measure of neocorporatism. Such masked effects of cumulative measures might be visible if estimated with a control for the "union corporatism" measure of neocorporatism (introduced in Table 5.3, Panel B) that eschews any items measuring social democracy as such. Resulting estimates, however, still yield no significant, or even retainable, partisan effects (Table A6C.1, Panel B).

Any effects of cumulative (or noncumulative) partisan measures that neocorporatism might mask should certainly be unmasked by estimations without controlling for neocorporatism. Table A6C.2 reports estimates of the basic models of Table 6.3 without neocorporatist controls. Panel A looks at both regressions with the partisan (Current) regressors of Table 6.3 and at ones with cumulative measures of Table A6C.1, yielding some news: The measure of cumulative social democratic rule (Cum Left Cabinets) has a significant, positive effect on welfare effort when neocorporatism is excluded. The measure of cumulative social democratic rules has no remotely significant effects. Still a notable partisan rule effect has been estimated.

Table A 6C.1. Regressions of Welfare Effort on Cumulative Cabinet Participation

Panel A: Multiple Regressions of Welfare Effort on Cumulative Cabinet Participation and Tripartite Neocorporatism

Variable Name	Estimated Coefficient	T-Ratio 492 df	Partial Beta	Estimated Coefficient	T-Ratio 494 df	Partial Beta
Inflation	0.0390	1.52‡	0.023	0.0349	1.34‡	0.021
Cum Left cabinet	0.0088	1.12	0.113	—	—	—
Cum CD cabinet	0.0004	0.92	0.045	—	—	—
Neocorporatism	0.0468	2.83*	0.205	0.0492	3.22*	0.216
Constitutional structure	−0.0034	−1.51‡	−0.105	−0.0053	−2.65*	−0.163
Unemployment rate	0.4204	6.60*	0.226	0.4038	6.39*	0.217
Aged percent of population	0.7529	4.19*	0.277	0.8600	5.17*	0.316
Economic openness	0.0324	3.30*	0.133	0.0379	4.48*	0.156
GDP per capita (ln)	0.0073	2.00†	0.095	0.0084	2.64*	0.110
Post-OPEC era	0.0152	4.96*	0.115	0.0150	4.85*	0.114
Voter turnout	0.0485	2.36†	0.080	0.0505	2.46*	0.084
Constant	−0.0406	−1.81†	0.000	−0.0459	−2.20†	0.000

Durbin-Watson = 1.877 rho = 0.038
R^2: observed and predicted = 0.853

Durbin-Watson = 1.829
rho = 0.057 R^2 = 0.905

Panel B: Multiple Regressions of Welfare Effort on Cumulative Cabinet Participation and Alternate Union-Centered ("Union Corporatism") Measure of Neocorporatism

Variable Name	Estimated Coefficient	T-Ratio 492 df	Partial Beta	Estimated Coefficient	T-Ratio 494 df	Partial Beta
Inflation	0.0039	1.53‡	0.023	0.0440	1.32‡	0.020
Cum Left cabinet	0.0011	1.42	0.138	—	—	—
Cum CD cabinet	0.0004	0.78	0.040	—	—	—
Union corporatism	0.0445	2.04*	0.179	0.0540	2.46*	0.217
Constitutional structure	−0.0035	−1.45‡	−0.107	−0.0054	−2.78*	−0.168
Unemployment rate	0.3991	6.30*	0.214	0.3880	6.18*	0.208
Aged percent of population	0.7094	3.44*	0.261	0.7925	3.96*	0.292
Economic openness	0.0325	3.10*	0.134	0.0376	4.34*	0.155
GDP per capita (ln)	0.0075	1.92†	0.098	0.0094	2.72*	0.122
Post-OPEC era	0.0151	4.83*	0.114	0.0150	4.81*	0.114
Voter turnout	0.0419	2.02†	0.070	0.0436	2.10†	0.072
Constant	−0.0285	−1.27	0.000	−0.0338	−1.54†	0.000

Durbin-Watson = 1.862
rho = 0.0393
R^2: observed and predicted = 0.850

Durbin-Watson = 1.817
rho = 0.062
R^2 = 0.872

*, †, and ‡ denote significance at the 0.01, 0.05, 0.10 test levels, respectively.

This preliminary emergence of support for post-1960 partisan rule effects, however, is open to the charge that it simply capitalized on trending in data during the period analyzed. To check on this possibility, I reestimated the cumulative model of Panel A after

Table A 6C.2. Additional Regressions of Partisan Cabinet Variables

Panel A: Multiple Regressions of Welfare Effort on Current and Cumulative Measures of Partisan Rule Absent a Control for Neocorporatism

Variable Name	Current			Cumulative		
	Estimated Coefficient	T-Ratio 492 df	Partial Beta	Estimated Coefficient	T-Ratio 494 df	Partial Beta
Inflation	0.0031	1.19	0.018	0.0387	1.50	0.023
Normal/cum left cabinet	−0.0036	−0.84	−0.018	0.0015	2.12*	0.197
Normal/cum CD cabinet	−0.0041	−0.32	−0.015	0.0001	0.24	0.012
Constitutional structure	−0.0064	−3.33*	−0.202	−0.0034	−1.41‡	−0.105
Unemployment rate	0.3347	4.71*	0.180	0.3775	5.87*	0.203
Aged percent of population	1.2015	7.49*	0.441	0.9655	5.33*	0.355
Economic openness	0.0388	3.79*	0.160	0.0362	3.61*	0.150
GDP per capita (ln)	0.0052	1.57†	0.067	0.2958	0.88	0.038
Post-OPEC era	0.0154	4.73*	0.116	0.0147	4.61*	0.111
Voter turnout	0.0352	1.69†	0.058	0.0354	1.69†	0.059
Constant	−0.0440	−2.03*	0.000	−0.0339	−1.57†	0.000

Durbin-Watson = 1.802   rho = 0.073
Corrected R²: observed and predicted = 0.817

Durbin-Watson = 1.8305
rho = 0.056
R² = 0.819

Panel B: Multiple Regressions of Welfare Effort on Measures of Cumulative Partisan Rule, Pre- (and Post-) 1960 without Neocorporatism

Variable Name	Initial			Revised		
	Estimated Coefficient	T-Ratio 492 df	Partial Beta	Estimated Coefficient	T-Ratio 494 df	Partial Beta
Inflation	0.0035	1.38	0.021	0.0419	1.62†	0.025
Cum left cabinet, 1946–60	0.0047	2.83*	0.314	0.0048	2.78*	0.318
Cum CD cabinet, 1946–60	0.0031	3.02*	0.204	0.0023	2.24*	0.145
Cum left cabinet, 1962–89	0.0007	0.72	0.054	—	—	—
Cum CD cabinet, 1962–89	−0.0007	−1.08	−0.060	—	—	—
Constitutional structure	−0.0016	−0.60	−0.050	−0.0012	−0.43	−0.037
Unemployment rate	0.4200	6.57*	0.225	0.4249	6.12*	0.228
Aged percent of population	0.6532	3.09*	0.240	0.7958	3.88*	0.293
Economic openness	0.0438	4.78*	0.180	0.0350	3.66*	0.144
GDP per capita (ln)	0.0104	2.72*	0.134	0.0090	2.77*	0.116
Post-OPEC era	0.1456	4.67*	0.110	0.0150	4.84*	0.113
Voter turnout	0.0266	1.27	0.044	0.0272	1.30	0.045
Constant	−0.0323	−1.20	0.000	−0.0390	−1.57†	0.000

Durbin-Watson = 1.830   rho = 0.088
Corrected R²: observed and predicted = 0.916

Durbin-Watson = 1.852
rho = 0.056
R² = 0.843

*, †, and ‡ denote significance at the 0.01, 0.05, 0.10 test levels, respectively.

decomposing each initial cumulative measure into two components. I operationalize the two-component structure by creating static measures of cumulative rule for 1946 to 1960 and for dynamic ones for 1962 to 1989. (For heuristic clarity, I innocuously chose 1961 to end the static span.) In particular, for Left parties I create Cum Left Cab, 1946–1960, equal to the 1960 value of cumulative Left cabinet for all observations; and I create Cum Left Cab, 1962–1989, equal to the Cumulative Left Cabinet minus Cum Left Cab, 1946–1960 (per observation). For Christian democratic parties, I create Cum CD Cab, 1946–1960, equal to the 1960 value of Cumulative CD Cabinet (per observation); and I create Cum CD Cab, 1962–1989, equal to the (annually varying) Cumulative CD Cabinet minus Cum CD, 1946–1960.

Regressions of welfare effort on the two static and the two dynamic components reveal that *partisan estimates are both statistically significant and sensibly signed for the two static components only* (Table A6C.2, Panel B). These are the estimates for Cum Left Cab, 1946–1960 (beta and t equal to 0.314 and 2.83, respectively, before deletion of dynamic terms and equal to 0.318 and 2.78, respectively, after deletions) and Cum CD Cab, 1946–1960 (beta and t equal to 0.204 and 3.03, respectively, before deletion and 0.145 and 2.24, respectively, afterwards). These findings indicate that earlier estimates of undecomposed cumulative rule conflated robust (long-term) cross-sectional effects of partisan rule with fragile and indecipherable "effects" of time-varying, post-1960 rule. This is perhaps most clearly evident for the revised Cum CD Cab, 1946–1960, raw effect estimate of 0.0023 in Table A6C.2, Panel B, which roughly averages the raw Cum CD Cab, 1946–1960, and Cum CD Cab, 1962–1989 (0.0031–0.0007) (see Table A6C.2).

In any case, evidence emerges for post-1960 effects of pre-1961 social and Christian democratic participation in government. This I take to capture long-run indirect effects of these variables that are preponderantly channeled by the intervening emergence of neocorporatism (see Chapter 3). After all, Chapter 5 revealed that early and 1950s social democratic rule predicts neocorporatism. These corporatism-mediated effects may be complemented by legacies other than neo-corporatist ones, legacies such as extensive, nonpartisan legitimation of welfare effort and its constituent programs, especially where early Red-Green and Red-Black reforms emerged, and unions were strong, before midcentury (see Chapters 3 and 5).

CHAPTER SEVEN

Course and Causes of the Crisis

Until now, the crisis was invariable *endogenous* to the welfare state. . . . The current crisis is, in contrast, essentially a manifestation of *exogenous* shocks . . . global economy . . . aging population.

(Esping-Andersen 1999, 3)

Much attention has lately been given to the issue of welfare state "crisis," "retrenchment," and "dismantling" (Jones 1993; Pierson 1994, 1996; Blank 1994; Esping-Andersen 1996; George and Taylor-Gooby, 1996; Rhodes 1997; Rodrik 1997; Swank 1997, 1998b; Garrett 1998a, 1998b; Huber and Stephens forthcoming).

For example, in the United States, the scope and universality of income maintenance programs has been limited by missing programs (e.g., family allowances); exclusive sectoral and work-history requirements (e.g., as in unemployment and retirement insurance); and various particularistic criteria (e.g., old age for Medicare). As a result, means-tested programs have been the mainstays of antipoverty policy (Gordon 1988). Yet, in 1996, the three-core means-tested programs were attacked: cuts in Medicaid were debated, cuts in Food Stamps were legislated, and Aid for Families with Dependent Children was eliminated.

In Sweden, perhaps the nation most characterized by a full repertoire of generously funded, universalistic social insurance programs, benefits and coverage rates have been shaved recurrently since the mid-1980s (Swank, 1997, 1998b). For example, in 1983, the pension benefit for part-time workers was reduced from 65 percent to 50 percent of income. During the 1989 to 1992 period, the base income used to calculate social benefits was twice reduced by 3 percent, and co-payments and other user charges were introduced for certain public medical services. In 1994 the basis for major pension reform was initiated in Sweden where, for instance, the earnings-related portion of the public pension was slated for shifting from one's "best 15 years" of earnings to one's lifetime trust-fund contributions (Plough and Kvist 1996; Swank 1998b).

Pierson (1994) offers a two-sided conception of the "crisis of the welfare state." This "crisis," if it exists, might be a crisis of programmatic retrenchment, of actual atrophy in welfare state programs. Or it might be a crisis of systemic retrenchment, of signs in the welfare state's environment that portend an onset, or intensification, of programmatic retrenchment. In the last chapter, Figures 6.2 and 6.3 revealed a degree of crisis. Yet the time paths of welfare programs and some of their major hypothesized causes merit a closer look. What might more refined indicators tell us about the possible crisis of the welfare state? In programmatic terms, attention should be turned to extant policy. In systemic terms, attention should be directed toward explanatory dynamics that might portend future crisis. In this regard, Pierson counsels a stress on political dynamics; however, the most discussed crisis scenario to date, the globalization scenario, merits a close look as well. If globalization—increasing international interdependence—is indeed a principal driver of whatever programmatic welfare retrenchment has so far occurred, and if globalization is, as often assumed, a process in inexorable advance, then globalization trends might bear truly "systemic" portents.

Present analyses have identified neocorporatism as a crucial political foundation of the welfare state. Moreover, commentators point to neocorporatism as a system in possible "crisis" (e.g., Katz 1993; Lange, Golden, and Wallerstein 1995). Some point to what might well be the systemic crisis par excellence, a collapse of tripartite neocorporatism (Western 1997).

I turn now to time plots of welfare output over time that might reveal programmatic retrenchment and some possible causes of systemic retrenchment—societal aging, globalization, and the like. This leads not only to revised analyses of welfare effort, but also to fresh analyses of actual turning points in—literal retrenchments of—welfare effort.

Programmatic Retrenchment?

This is not the place to provide a definitive, finely grained answer to the question, How much programmatic retrenchment has there been to date? As increases in the number of entitled individuals may occasion veritable explosions in social spending under extant legislation, and do so even in the face of some cuts in coverage and benefits per beneficiary, specialized data are optimal for answering that question. The sort of data in question, however, such as the extent to which the incomes of the unfortunate are sustained during spells of misfortune by program coverage and income replacement rates, remains just short of the public domain as I write.[1]

Useful complements to the data already analyzed here are available, however. OECD (1994, forthcoming) has generously made available estimates of the social wage for workers in 18 focal nations of the post–World War II portion of this inquiry. The *social wage* is the amount of money that a worker, severed from the labor market, will earn merely by virtue of his or her citizenship (plus, where relevant, proof of serious resolve about reentering the labor force). The data in question are compiled from data on unemployment compensation, general public assistance, and the like, and are compiled for the social wage of a worker at (a) the median income and at (b) 67 percent of that income. Despite arguable limitations, these data on the social wage for economically average and poor workers are independent of shifting populations of persons eligible for program benefits. These data allow a closer look at social benefits.[2]

In addition, it is possible to construct a useful measure of public pension benefits with International Labour Organization (ILO) data on pension spending and figures on domestic income and persons over 65 years of age. The particular measure I construct is the welfare benefit per person of 65 years of age or older as a proportion of per capita income. Although this measure is biased to the extent to which *private* pensions are extensive and merit attention as sources of social security, it is otherwise a serviceable proxy for public income replacement for the elderly. As public pension programs constitute the most expensive type of social insurance program, some indication of their generosity, adjusting for a nation's age structure and affluence,

---

[1] The principal project producing such data is that of Walter Korpi and his colleagues at the Stockholm Institute for Social Research, bits of whose data have been used, with acknowledgments, in Chapters 1 and 3 of this work (e.g., Korpi 1989; Palme 1991).

[2] These data are not used here in analyses because they are only estimated biennially and because they seem to indicate questionably austere "social wages" for Italy and Switzerland and questionably generous ones for France. The former rank eighteenth and seventeenth, respectively, among our nations on social wages despite ranking seventh and twelveth, respectively, on Esping-Andersen's (1990, 48–54) index of overall decommodification and 15th and 3rd, respectively, on his closely relevant index of the decommodifying aspect of unemployment insurance.

is important. This proxy for the social retirement wage should be helpful.

Data on public health care benefits are more elusive. Health-care benefits are divided among income transfers and services, precise market prices and vaguer public "costs," clear public expenses and subsidized private ones, and costs of direct medical expenses and compensation for pay lost due to sick days off. Because preparation of data necessary to overcome these challenges is still in progress (e.g., Kangas 1991; Korpi forthcoming), I construct a new single measure from readily available data sources. In particular, I construct a measure of public expenses for sickness and maternity benefits as a proportion of gross domestic product (GDP), a kind of index of "public health care effort."

An examination of Figure 7.1, which displays time plots of the data in question from roughly 1962 to 1992, reinforces yet refines the image of some degree of welfare state "crisis" projected by the figures given at the end of Chapter 6. Time lines are displayed for four subsets of nations introduced in the previous chapter. These are (a) corporatist midcentury consolidators, which consists of neocorporatist nations that consolidated all major forms of income-security programs by the aftermath of World War II; (b) corporatist nonconsolidators; (c) noncorporatist consolidators; and (d) a residual of what I will call "laggard" regimes. (See Chapter 4 and 5 on the consolidator and corporatist characterizations, respectively, and Chapter 6 on both.)

Figures 7.1A and B suggest a pattern of general "leveling off" (decelerating increase) more than of retrenchment (decrease), although some slight retrenchment is evident. For the case of benefits to the average worker, the pattern is clear. Leveling off roughly describes all groups of nations; however, some decrease in the social wage is evident for all except the neocorporatist nonconsolidators (NC only in Fig. 7.1A). For the case of benefits to poorer workers, leveling off again seems clear for all categories of nations except for the neocorporatist nonconsolidators (Fig. 7.1B). (These actually appear to have decreasing benefits after 1989, but the reversal is surely too slight and short-lived to be reliable.) Both sets of neocorporatist consolidators and laggards seem engaged in a degree of retrenchment by 1990, whereas the noncorporatist consolidators (Consol)—Australia, New Zealand and the U.K.—are on a course of very gradual retrenchment dating back to the economic troubles of the mid-1970s.[3]

---

[3] Discussion of consolidating and nonconsolidating nations, neocorporatist and non-(neo)corporatist nations can be found in Chapters 4 and 6.

Figure 7.1. Time lines for four income security outputs. (A) Average worker social wage (AVESOCWAG), 1959–1994. (B) Poorer worker social wage (POVSWAGE), 1959–1994. (C) Social retirement wage (PENOLDG): Per capita public pension as a proportion of per capita GDP, 1961–1989. (D) Public health care effort (HEALTHG): Public spending as share of GDP, 1961–1989.

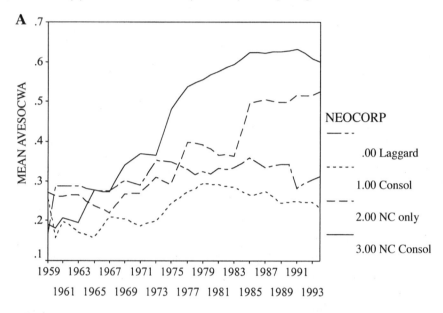

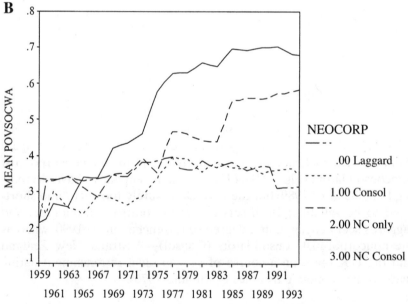

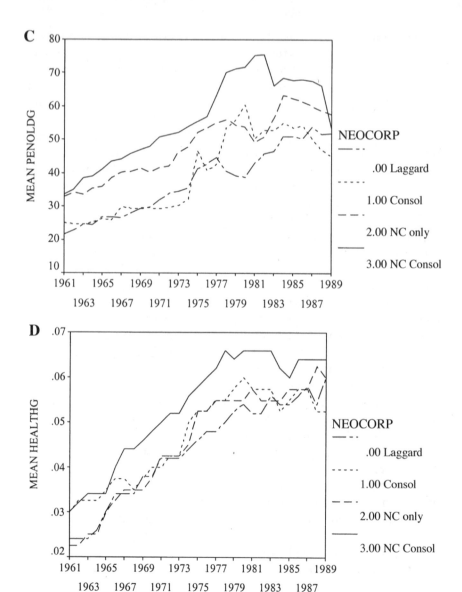

C

MEAN PENOLDG

NEOCORP

.00 Laggard

1.00 Consol

2.00 NC only

3.00 NC Consol

D

MEAN HEALTHG

NEOCORP

.00 Laggard

1.00 Consol

2.00 NC only

3.00 NC Consol

Turning to my measures of the social retirement wage, a nearly general pattern of retrenchment is evident. Interestingly, the only exception to this pattern occurs for the laggards, which appear to be engaged in steady catch-up.

Turning to *public health care effort*, a simple measure of public health care expenditures as a share of GDP, I see a doubly striking pattern emerge. A very steady increase in heath-care effort up until a modest, late 1980s deceleration stands out. So does a nearly parallel upward advance of the time lines, all increasing in tandem, laggards never far behind and always closely following the movements of national types just ahead of them. Clearly, growth in public health care expenditures is a widespread process with common features—lack of notable retrenchment in expenditures. This is so despite clear exceptions, such as the Swedish shift toward surcharges noted earlier. It is so even though there is reason to expect more cost inflation and less advance in effective health service among the lower spenders (Hollingsworth et al. 1992).

Overall, leveling off emerges as a more long-standing, general pattern than retrenchment; however, one is tempted to extrapolate retrenchment as an extension of the pattern of deceleration onto a flat plateau. Retrenchment is sometimes manifest. It is clear, if not quite universal, for the case of pension programs. It seems evident for the case of the social wage everywhere except in the set of corporatist non-consolidators, signaling something of the retreat of the residual welfare state suggested by Pierson (1994). For laggards, retrenchment for average and poorer workers signals something more: an incipient unraveling of even that "residual" welfare state that leaves the amelioration of income insecurity and poverty to minimum benefits of last resort for the most disadvantaged (Titmuss 1983). Yet this unraveling is advancing slowly and is hardly completed.

In short, a little actual programmatic retrenchment is evident, if we use the term to mean retreat to a policy position previously behind the lines. Retrenchment is rampant if, stressing motion over location, we use the term to describe a shift from taking new ground to holding old ground after surrendering some. Clearly, some retrenchment has occurred. But what more can we generalize about programmatic retrenchment? What of systemic retrenchment, the accumulation of political economic trends threatening more serious programmatic retrenchments to come?

Systemic Retrenchment

Describing Domestic Determinants

The model of the previous chapter helps direct attention to the domestic determinants of welfare policy (see Table 6.3). That model's findings lead one to ask whether increasing unemployment and societal aging have recently shown signs of generating such extreme enlargements of welfare programs that benefits or eligibility, or both, must eventually be cut back? Does domestic product threaten to contract, undercutting the resource base for programs even when their ameliorative effect is most needed? Does the globalization of trade, summarily captured by increases in the openness of nations to international trade, mandate a new frugality in macroeconomic management, management of social spending in particular?

Demographic Threats. Such correlates of population as increasing ratios of beneficiaries to contributors for public pensions pose urgent challenges to fiscal order and economic health and already have occasioned much study. Indeed, Figure 7.2A indicates that the increase in the elderly's share of population is dramatic enough to provide a compelling prima facie explanation for the rather sharp and extensive cutbacks in spending effort for public pension effort (demographically adjusted) that are evident in Figure 7.1C. Figure 7.2A charts a seemingly inexorable rise in the elderly's share of the population. It shows that this ascent took a particularly high and precipitous course in just those neocorporatist societies where welfare effort tended to be greatest (see Figures 6.1–6.3). An imperative for major pension reform to curtail an unproductive drain on societal resources is not inconsistent with these data. Nevertheless, Leone (1997) has noted a tendency for commentators to exaggerate the threat of societal aging. For example, pundits have often highlighted rising ratios of pension recipients to contributors without noting declining ratios of dependent populations—children plus retirees—to working populations. Despite such exaggerations, however, reductions in child dependents hardly offset pressures on public budgets caused by increases in retirees. The case for a degree of budgetary crisis rooted in societal aging is strong (Feldstein 1997); however, it is a highly technical and complex issue that is amply addressed elsewhere (e.g., Myles 1989; Ruggie 1996). Accordingly, it requires no detailed treatment here.

Domestic Economic Threats. High sustained or growing unemployment rates may pose similar challenges to social policy by generating exorbitant demands for it. True, they may augment pension spending by promoting pressures for early retirement in slack labor markets, by placing upward pressure on the social wage (e.g., by depressing wages and triggering reactions against shifts toward more temporary and part-time work), and by simply lengthening the queue of those eligible for entitlements. Where more direct impacts of unemployment are concerned, one emphasis in the literature has been on increased

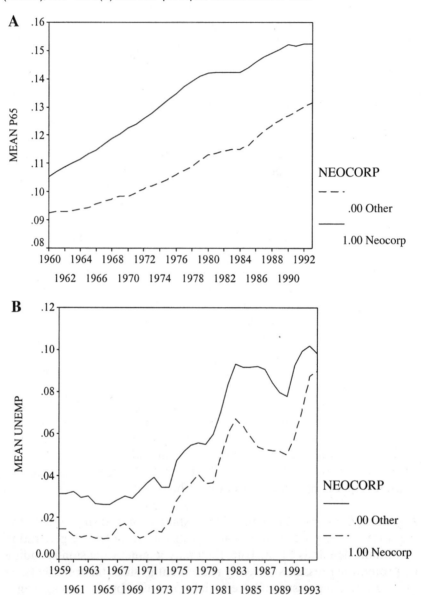

Figure 7.2. Time lines for three social indicators: Old age, unemployment and real per capita GDP. (A) Proportion of the population at least 65 years old (1960–1993). (B) Unemployment rate (UNEMP), 1959–1994. (C) Real GDP per capita, U.S. dollars, 1962–1993.

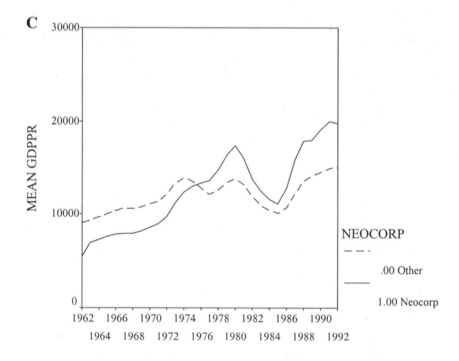

C

MEAN GDPPR

NEOCORP

– – ·

.00 Other

1.00 Neocorp

(entitled!) demand for social spending, unemployment compensation in particular; bloated welfare rolls; and burgeoning social outlays (Roubini and Sachs 1989).

Unemployment may reflect and exacerbate deteriorating economic production and state revenues, however. As we see in Figure 7.2B, increases in unemployment rates, although not so steady as those in the elderly, are quite ominous. Although our examination of differential social wages (see Figs. 7.1A, B) suggested that unemployment is better ameliorated in neocorporatist nations, it has been argued that the social wage delays the unemployed's return to work (Bruno and Sachs 1985; Blank 1994; OECD forthcoming). Indeed, the argument continues, obstacles to layoffs and wage cuts in neocorporatist labor markets aggravate underlying problems, slowing adjustments to mounting international economic competition (Bruno and Sachs 1985). Moreover, the copious revenues needed to finance the social wage in neocorporatist nations exacerbate the challenge of international competition. Do data on domestic product support this line of reasoning?

Direct examination of real, per capita GDP indicates some

slowdown and much increased volatility since the 1970s, but it shows rather different patterns for corporatist and noncorporatist nations (Fig. 7.2C). For the former, recession is not clearly evident until about the time of the second, 1979 oil shock associated with the price hikes of the Organization of Petroleum Exporting Nations (OPEC) (Fig. 7.1C). Thereafter, however, production is extremely volatile, with a 1980 to 1985 recession and another post-1989 one. Despite the sharp rise from the early 1980s recession and some subsequent growth, 1993 income barely exceeded the 1980 level.

In the noncorporatist nations, recession, marked by 1974 to 1977 dips, recurred more modestly in the early 1980s and post-1989. After 1979, income growth is higher than in the neocorporatist nations (about 10 percent versus 1 percent), although it is lower (about 10 percent versus 40 percent) if we go back to a 1973 benchmark.

Overall, the neocorporatist nations must be said to have weathered the 1970s better that the noncorporatist ones, however, their marginally worse performance since 1979, in particular since 1989, indicates that challenges to the welfare state posed by sluggish macro-economic production may be, if anything, greater in neocorporatist than non-(neo)corporatist nations (see Mishra 1993; Scharpf 1999). Demographic and economic pressures for a growing social security state look greater in the more rapidly aging neocorporatist states with their worsening, if slightly lower, unemployment figures. Economic resources for sustaining the welfare state look more threatened in neo-corporatist nations. Can these impressions survive a deeper, more analytical look? And what of economic forces impinging from beyond national borders, such as the much-touted trend toward increased economic globalization?

International Economic Threats: Globalization

The Openness Literature

What of globalization? Two perspectives dominate thinking about the policy effects of globalization viewed as a process of world-wide international market integration. One may be called the competitiveness perspective, and the other the compensation perspective.

The more conventional competitiveness view argues that globalization brings international competitive pressures for more efficient (competitive, laissez-faire free market) structure and performance. Such performance, in turn, demands less social spending (economic regulation, and so forth). Globalization here is three-pronged, involving international markets for goods and services, international markets for nonportfolio direct foreign investment (DFI) in productive facilities, and international financial markets.

Most analysts regard income transfers as almost categorically "uncompetitive" (Pfaller and Gough 1991; Pierson 1994). Generous welfare benefits reduce market competitive discipline on labor, creating upward pressures on wages while dulling incentives for labor force participation and mobility. In addition, government spending must be funded by tax increases or borrowing. Taxes erode income from asset holding, whereas borrowing increases debt and interest rates. Both thereby depress investment. Internationally, funding welfare spending not only may increase prices for goods abroad, thereby undercutting the competitiveness of domestic goods on foreign markets, it also may provoke appreciation in domestic currency or exchange rates (as foreign financial investment rushes in to profit from increased domestic interest rates) and thereby dampen export competitiveness.

Increased trade makes domestic producers more vulnerable to any expansion in the competitiveness of foreign goods relative to domestic ones and to volatile terms of trade. By so doing, it places downward pressure on social expenditures, for these soften market discipline and depend for funding on tax increases that raise domestic production costs. Increased flows of domestic-to-foreign and foreign-to-domestic direct investment may likewise discipline government budgets. Increased domestic-to-foreign investment may index relocation of productive capacity to sites overseas where labor is less costly and production can be more internationally competitive. This entails at least some transitional loss of jobs. It exerts pressure on government to cut taxes that might aggravate such loses. Increased foreign-to-domestic direct investment may indicate that foreign producers are relocating from abroad in ways that offset exports of production and employment, but foreign investment will be attracted (and retained) by roughly the same tax incentives that retain domestic investment. Emigrating capital may seem more relevant, but if emigrating capital often leaves behind highly visible victims who dramatize the costs of competitiveness, immigrating capital allays such costs. Moreover, capital must be kept from emigrating. Internationally mobile capital, ingoing or outgoing, largely consists of big, articulate firms that may advantageously parlay the costs of business "exit" into a probusiness politics of "voice."

Degradation of domestic competitiveness by domestic social

benefits and their tax costs is often theorized especially for low-skill/low-cost industries, where competition from foreign producers is expected to be more likely (Greider 1997; Rodrik 1997); however, international competitiveness and its accentuation by domestic social spending is not confined to low-skill/low-wage markets. For example, high-tech services may be wanted in newly industrializing economies. Moreover, financial markets—for stocks and other equities, for bonds and for currencies themselves—may also discourage social spending, for social spending tends to displease financial actors whose retaliatory movements of capital may be swift.

The compensation view focuses not on the direct economic costs of social spending but on the indirect economic benefits of this spending's political economic consequences (Polyani 1944; Ruggie 1983; Katzenstein 1985; and even Rodrik 1997). According to this view, social spending ultimately benefits economic efficiency by sustaining political support for the free trade essential to globalization. More specifically, globalization generates short-run dislocations and resulting risks and injuries (some quite long-term enough, though, for their victims). They tend to generate social insurance against (and actual public amelioration of) the costs of dislocation (Rodrik 1997; Garrett and Mitchell 1997; Swank 1997, 1998b). Such social policy is sustainable because, besides yielding some direct economic benefits, it makes the tonic of globalization socially palatable (Ruggie 1983; Rodrik 1997; Garrett and Mitchell 1997; Garrett 1998b). Ruggie (1995, 508) has argued that social spending has been constitutive of "the compromise of embedded liberalism. . . . Societies were asked to embrace the change and dislocation attending international liberalization. In turn, liberalization and its effects were embraced by the newly acquired domestic economic and social policy goals of governments." In fairness, this same author (1996) has also argued that increased globalization caused a swamping of social spending benefits by their costs—and a case for government retrenchment.

Rodrik (1997) appears torn between the competitiveness and compensation views. Indeed, he attempts to theoretically reconcile these within a single economic model. In his summary of the implications of this model for social policy, he writes, "An increase in openness makes domestic capital more responsive to changes in international prices and correspondingly magnifies the amplitude of fluctuations in real wages. Hence, labor becomes worse off due to increased exposure to risk, even if the mean (expected) real wage remains the same. To restore the expected utility of workers to its reservation level, the government has to increase income transfers and raise the tax on capital" (1997, 88–89). (To clarify, this "reservation" level is some "decent," state-assured minimum.)

> This strategy works as long as the openness of the economy and the international mobility of capital are not too high. However, when openness crosses a certain threshold an attempt to compensate labor by increasing the tax on capital becomes self-defeating. Past that threshold, the flight of capital and erosion of real wages at home would more than offset the value of income transfers. In an extremely open economy, therefore, the government loses its ability to compensate workers through the tax system. (pp. 88–89)

Not surprisingly, empirical evidence on the competitiveness and compensation theses is rather contradictory.

This is much the case for variables taken to affect social spending. In particular, it is the case for tax rates (e.g., Cameron 1978; Garrett 1998a; Rodrik 1997; Swank 1998a) and for government consumption and for total spending (e.g., Rodrik 1997; Garrett 1998b; and Swank 1997, 1998b). If we confine attention to social spending (typically operationalized here with ILO benefit measures), however, empirical findings tilt toward the compensation thesis. Not only has simple trade openness quite consistently been found to augment social spending (e.g., Hicks and Swank 1992; Huber et al. 1993; Rodrik 1997; Garrett 1998b; Swank 1997), variants of it that have been weighted by "risk" (or volatility in terms of trade) or confined to trade with low-wage foreign competitors have all yielded the same "compensatory" result (Rodrik 1997; Garrett and Mitchell 1997). In addition, measures of direct foreign investment flows (as in Swank 1997, 1998b), trade liberalization (Quine 1997; Swank 1997, 1998b), and financial integration, as indexed by the covered interest-rate differential or CID (Shepherd 1994; Swank 1997; Garrett and Mitchell 1997; Garrett, 1998b), have found the same compensatory pattern of openness generating social spending.

Research has not yet addressed Rodrik's (1997, 89–90) idea of a threshold beyond which "the flight of capital and the erosion of real wages" robs government of its ability to "compensate."[4] I next attempt to redress this neglect of possible—initially compensatory but eventually competitive—nonlinear effects of openness. I do so for measures

---

[4] Rodrik's (1997, 1998) examinations of product terms for risk and openness variables might be construed to imply a test for the threshold idea, yet no such intention is explicit. Indeed, the positive signs of slopes for such product terms are, if relevant to his "threshold" notion, inconsistent with it. Rodrik, however, claims no such relevance and I don't presume to disagree with him.

of trade and, following Swank (1997), direct investment openness. (I also do so very tentatively for scarce, temporally truncated CID measures of financial integration.)

Describing Openness. Assuming that globalization does impose cost on economies, what do the time paths of globalization measures portend? Two such paths are examined in Figure 7.3, one for trade openness and one for direct investment openness. *Trade openness* is measured as the sum of a nation's imports and exports expressed as a proportion of its GDP (see Appendix 6A.1). Investment openness, defined as foreign direct investment, following an index from Swank (1997), is measured as the sum of FDI flows into and out of a nation (expressed as a proportion of its GDP).

Figure 7.3A indicates that trade openness did in fact increase rather dramatically from the early 1970s into the mid-1980s, especially in neocorporatist nations; however, the time lines in question also indicate distinctly, if modestly, declining levels of trade openness since the mid-1980s. These declines are small among noncorporatist nations (from about 49 to 46 percent of GDP), especially when compared with the rather substantial declines in openness experienced since the early 1980s in neocorporatist nations (from about 95 percent of GDP to 85 percent of it). Overall, the present trends—roughly stable for two decades in the noncorporatist nations, high but declining in the neocorporatist nations—hardly seem threatening. Yet threats from them should not be flatly discounted. Rates of trade openness may be so high in neocorporatist nations as to be quite unsustainable without severe consequences for economic and policy performance. After all, the severe recession that struck corporatist nations in the early 1980s coincided with these nations' 80+ percent levels of trade openness.

Investment openness (IO) tells a more dramatic tale. This skyrocketed between 1984 and 1990, especially in neocorporatist nations. It rose from about 1 percent of GDP in both sets of nations to about 3 percent in noncorporatist nations and to something over 4 percent in corporatist ones. Despite subsequent drops, it concludes the present examination (in 1992) at over 2.5 percent in neocorporatist nations and at about 2 percent in noncorporatist ones. Here are trajectories that might indeed portend havoc *if* investment openness has destructive potential with respect to social spending.

It does appear to be potentially harmful for social spending. True, on the one hand, competition from foreign investors *within* one's borders might seem to offer large compensation in the way of jobs and

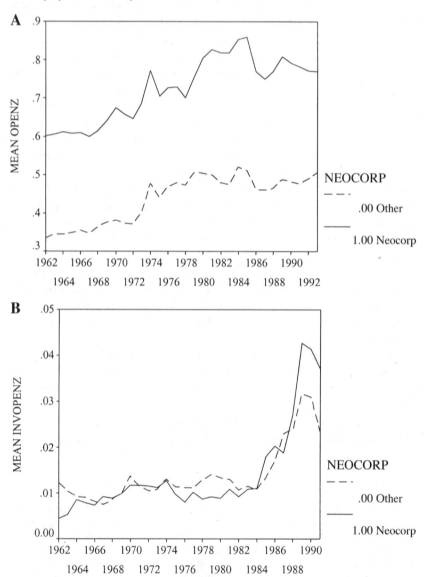

Figure 7.3. Time lines for measures of "globalization." (A) Trade openness (imports and exports as proportion of GDP), 1962–1993. (B) Investment openness (inflows and outflows of direct investment as proportions of GDP), 1962–1991.

incomes; however, on the other hand, investment openness helps provide employers, domestic as well as foreign, with a credible threat of economic relocation as a political tool. Domestic producers may point to the reality of domestic capital flight to justify demands for

lower tax burdens and the like. Similarly, FDI raises the risk relocation (relocation or repatriation, call it what you will) from moment of
investment (Przeworski and Wallerstein 1988; Gill and Law 1988;
McKenzie and Lee 1991).[5]

Can these impressions survive a deeper, more analytical look?
Univariate economic trends in variables, even when differentiated by
separate corporatist and noncorporatist figures, provide only a shallow
basis for assessing consequences of these trends for future social
policy. This is especially so for variables such as unemployment and
economic product. In actuality, these forces have so far tended to
sustain welfare spending. In speculation, they have so far merely
appeared to augur retrenchment. Nonetheless, light can be thrown on
this assessment in a number of uncomplicated ways.

One concern about the implications of economic performance
for the welfare state involves claims that processes of globalization
depress welfare spending—albeit at a deep and not readily observable
level. Although the last chapter offered no evidence of negative
trade-openness effects upon welfare effort—indeed, it provided
estimates of *positive* compensatory trade-openness effects—IO was
not examined. Now I turn to analyses of IO as well as trade openness.
In addition, I probe for possible antiwelfarist threshold effects of
openness measures, that is, test for possible nonlinear effects of
openness.

Second, more direct attention to the question of retrenchment is
possible than regression analyses of levels of welfare effort alone
permit. To focus analytical attention on retrenchment per se, I analyze
turning points in nations' trajectories of welfare effort by using event-
history (or survival) analyses in a manner reminiscent of Western's
(1997) analysis of bargaining decentralization. (As bargaining decen-

---

[5] Neither high levels nor changes in openness are confined to the European Union
or, more pertinently for present analyses, the European Economic Community.
Mean levels of trade and investment openness are 0.667 and 0.0157, respectively,
for the pre-Maastrich member of the EEC and are 0.473 and 0.0112, respectively,
for nonmembers (during the 1962–1990 period). Although these levels are significantly
different from each other at the 0.01 test level, these levels are even more significantly
different from zero for all nations, and rates of annual *change* in trade and investment
openness are *not* significantly different. Moreover, time lines for these levels and
changes are remarkably similar. Openness appears not to be an artifact of European
economic integration. Moreover, if an eventual supranational European state might
seem to portend an eventual transformation of the meaning of openness by escaping
its constraints on public-goods provision, the more likely suprastate*less* confederational structure of the future (like the current) European Union means no such
thing.

tralization entails a deterioration of the neocorporatist foundation of postwar welfare states, I also allude to complementary analyses of turning points toward bargaining decentralization.)

In short, I next return to the analysis of globalization and levels of welfare effort. After that, I turn to analyses of globalization and policy retrenchment as such.

International and Political Threats: Welfare Policy Reanalyzed

Welfare Effort Revisited

In the last chapter, economic openness was considered as a possible cause of welfare effort under the view, conventional in the welfare-state literature, that trade openness is especially important and leads to welfare outlays aimed at compensating citizens for the pain of adapting to a volatile and competitive economy. Trade openness was measured as a ratio of imports plus exports to GDP and presumed to have stimulative effects on welfare effects. IO was not considered; only simple linear effects of trade openness were. Furthermore, the analytical focus was on *levels* of welfare effort, not welfare retrenchment as such.

Here I test for effects of what Swank (1997) has dubbed "investment openness," as well as for threshold effects of effects of trade openness. Investment openness consists of the flow of FDI capital in productive assets like firms and capital goods (not more elusive financial investments in bonds, currency, and the like) in and out of a national economy relative to its scale of economic activity. (See Appendix 7 for measures and data sources.)

Finally, following suggestions in Rodrik's (1997) theorizing about the impacts of openness upon social spending, I test for possible turning points in these impacts. In particular, I test for inverted-U-shaped relations of openness to welfare effort. More specifically, I test for relations in which openness may, beyond some point, switch over from augmenting welfare effort to reducing it. One may easily do this by specifying squared, as well as raw, terms for each initial measure of openness. Specifically, one checks for the presence of quadratic functions by testing whether both raw and squared terms are statistically different from zero. If they are, one may confidently conclude that quadratic functions obtain. If these have positively signed raw terms and negatively signed squared terms, the quadratics are inverted-U shaped, or hump-shaped, and welfare effort declines beyond some point.

The new hypotheses are three. One (N1) is that the square of trade openness is negatively related to welfare effort. A second hypothesis (N2) is that the raw term for IO is positively related to GDP. The idea here is that, up to some point, IO tends (like trade openness) to pressure governments to cushion and recompense citizens for its costs by means of increased welfare spending. These costs may be job losses and wage cuts due to new competition from foreign-owned plants and reallocations of domestic investment—and whole plants—to overseas. The third (N3) is that the square of IO is negatively related to welfare effort. This is, in effect, a test for a range of IO for which increases in IO reduce welfare effort. This may obtain because the costs of recompensing victims of foreign investment are seen as less than the benefits of foreign investment in new plants and jobs and from income repatriated by a nation's domestically centered, but foreign-investing, capitalists. In particular, it may occur because, in a context of ample international movements of FDI, business benefits *politically* from the threat of investment and plant relocation to overseas sites. That is, business uses this threat as a political resource in seeking favorable legislation, e.g., cuts in taxes and in forms of spending that inflate business' tax burden without providing offsetting benefits (but see Swank, 1998a).

Tests for this wider range of openness hypotheses are performed within the context of the "revised" equation of Table 6.3. Only the new explanatory variables required by the new hypotheses modify that equation. These new variables are a measure of direct investment openness, of FDI flows as a percentage of GDP, plus squared terms for both trade openness and investment openness (see Appendix 7).[6]

Results of reanalyses of levels of welfare effort presented in Table 7.1 provide no evidence of negative effects of trade openness beyond some threshold.[7] This variable continues to have only significant positive effects (for its raw or unsquared term); however, it provides statistically significant support for exactly the hypothesized quadratic relations of IO to welfare effort. These relations consist of positive or

[6] A measure of CID that studies by Garrett (1998b) and Garrett and Mitchell (1999) suggest to be the optimal measure of the international integration of particular financial markets was gathered from Shepherd (1994), but it was only available for 1978 to 1989, and use of it, both raw and squared, is confined to ancillary analyses (see n. 8).
[7] Note that in quadratics if the raw term for a variable X has a negatively signed coefficient, but the squared term has a positively signed one, then, for lower ranges of X, the function is negative, but as X increases the weight of the squared term begins to overwhelm the raw term, progressively reducing the magnitude of the negative slope until at some point it turns positive (see Wonnacott and Wonnacott 1985).

uations	Initial Equation			Revised[a]		
	Estimated Coefficient	T-Ratio 490 df	Partial Beta	Estimated Coefficient	T-Ratio 491 df	Partial Beta
flation	0.0401	1.58‡	0.024	0.0390	1.53‡	0.023
hristian democratic cabinet	0.0114	0.96	0.041	0.0119	1.02	0.043
eocorporatism	0.0574	3.72*	0.252	0.0558	3.59*	0.245
onstitutional structure	−0.0054	−3.18*	−0.169	−0.0055	−3.17*	−0.172
nemployment rate	0.4143	6.31*	0.222	0.4126	6.36*	0.222
ged % of population	0.6275	3.08*	0.231	0.6455	3.29*	0.237
DP per capita (ln)	0.0290	1.83‡	0.119	0.0324	3.24*	0.134
st-OPEC era	0.0116	3.43*	0.151	0.1142	3.38*	0.148
ter turnout	0.0155	5.05*	0.117	0.1541	5.03*	0.116
onomic openness	0.0450	2.27†	0.075	0.0444	2.25†	0.074
penness squared	0.0003	0.02	0.002	—	—	—
▪	0.3000	2.03†	0.058	0.3020	2.04†	0.058
▪²	−5.3215	−2.83*	−0.062	−5.3078	−2.83*	−0.062
onstant	−0.0244	−1.02	0.000	−0.0263	−1.19	0.000

Durbin-Watson = 1.852	Durbin-Watson = 1.86
RHO = 0.049	RHO = 0.047
R^2 (observed & predicted) = 0.799	R^2 = 0.815

▪te: Initial equation with "base" variables; revised following stepwise deletions/entries of variables.
Revised models follow any deletion of "base" variable with t statistics < |1.0|.
▪, and ‡ denote significance at the 0.01, 0.05, 0.10 test levels, respectively.

stimulative effects of investment openness on welfare effort for lower ranges of IO and negative or dampening effects for higher ranges of IO. Apparently some combination of increased international competitiveness and increased antiwelfarist corporate clout dampens welfare effort, or at least did so as national openness to flows of direct investment approached the high levels of the late 1980s.[8]

Specifically, we find (averaging across the very similar equations of Table 7.1) that welfare effort is a quadratic function of IO. Controlling for variables other than IO

$$\text{welfare effort} = 0.300 \times \text{IO} - 5.321 \times \text{OI}^2.$$

This function maximizes its contribution to the generation of welfare effort for a value of IO of about 0.03 that lies considerably beyond the 1962 to 1989 IO mean of 0.0135. This is a mean investment level

[8] Analysis of 1978 to 1989 data with raw and squared measures of CID yielded no remotely significant estimates.

approximated by the Netherlands in the early 1970s and Australia, Finland, the Scandinavian nations, and the United States in the early 1980s. Beyond the 0.03 threshold, investment openness begins to depress welfare effort, mostly doing so for the nations with the highest levels of investment openness (around 0.08, or 8 percent of GDP). As may be gleaned (or recollected) from Figure 7.3B, the highest levels of IO are a phenomenon of the late 1980s. The highly DFI-open nations include Belgium, the Netherlands, New Zealand, and the United States in the late 1980s—nations that contrast with those very low on DFI (in and out), such as 1960s Austria, Denmark, Finland and Switzerland, and Japan throughout the 1960s and 1970s.

In short, Table 7.1's reanalysis of the determinants of welfare effort provides no support for hypothesis N1: trade openness has strictly linear, if positive, effects on welfare effort; however, the new analysis supports hypotheses N2 and N3, namely that relations of IO to welfare effort describe an arch beyond whose peak increasing DFI means less welfare effort.

What of actual retrenchment, precisely defined in terms of turning points toward reduced welfare effort? What are the determinants of this?

Welfare Retrenchment in Focus

So far I have modeled levels of welfare effort; however, levels models may be too dominated both by short-run fluctuations in welfare effort and by secular increases in welfare effort to model retrenchment well. Retrenchments consist of turning points toward relatively long-term decline in welfare effort.

To identify any turning points, indeed to discover whether turning points exist, welfare effort, averaged over two years for a little smoothing, was examined. Specifically, it was plotted versus time twice for each of the 18 nations under investigation. Plots were done first for unadjusted welfare effort and then for welfare effort adjusted for effects of two of its principal sources of automatic variations.[9] These are unemployment and societal aging, which drive up welfare effort by pressing on the triggers of statutory entitlement as they rise. These two power-

[9] Welfare spending effort was adjusted by "residualizing" it on unemployment and old age, that is, by replacing raw welfare effort with residuals from a regression of welfare effort on measures of unemployment rates and population shares of persons at least 65 years old (see Appendix 6A). ($R^2 = 0.40$)

ful need or demand variables were the most consequential for variations in welfare effort in Table 6.3 and are the most precipitously upward trending variables to emerge from the figures of this chapter. Evidence for turning points was strong overall; indeed, it was surprisingly unambiguous concerning the dating of turning points. To only slightly stylize nations' welfare trajectories over time, each nation tended to hit a peak level of welfare effort sometime between the OPEC oil shock of 1973 to 1974 and the 1989 completion of the currently available ILO data series on welfare benefits. Each nation's series showed a rather dramatic downturn in need-adjusted welfare effort following this same point. I designate these points of inflection in the plots of welfare effort as retreat points.

Only two exceptions to the pattern just described arose. One emerged for Canada, where post-1976 drops in welfare effort, sharp for need-adjusted series and moderate for unadjusted ones, were followed by a strong 1980s recovery that eventually converged on a second, 1987 reversal. The other occurred in Sweden, where decline after identical 1983 peaks for both series was very modest and was followed by a partial recovery of welfare effort in both. In the Canadian case, I stayed with the principle of selecting the series maximum as its turning point, and the arguably second 1987 turning point was ignored. In the Swedish case, I stayed with the same principle despite the modest character of Swedish retrenchment.

Principal datings of "retreat points" are reported in footnote "a" to Table 7.2. As a check on the robustness of results, I construct and analyze two additional supplement measures of "retreat points," "early" and "late" ones, to supplement to "core" one analyzed in Table 7.2 (see Appendix A7B).

I analyze rates of movement toward retrenchment by using event history analysis (Allison 1982; Western 1997, chaps. 10–11). A simple time-dependent mode of event-history analysis that models the effects of time on retrenchment as a simple quadratic, operationalized by means of the inclusion of raw and squared terms for the year, is used. Retrenchment is coded 0 for each year before the retreat point and 1 for the retreat point itself. Observations for years succeeding retreat points are deleted, yielding a total of 371 nation-year observations, and rates at which nations approach retreat points—present for every one of the 18 nations studied—are analyzed by using logistic regression (after Allison 1982).

Explanatory variables in logistical regressions, which are a variant of multiple regression that specializes in the analysis of dichotomous outcomes, are those of the last chapter's analysis of welfare effort,

Table 7.2. A Model of Retrenchment: Causes of Welfare Effort Turning Points.[a] (Revised Model Following Deletion of "Base" Variable with t-Statistics < |1.0|)

Explanatory Variables	Equation for[1] "Core" Datings[a]		
	b	Wald χ^2	R
Year	−78.10	1.60	0.00
Year^2	0.020	1.62	0.00
Social Democratic cabinet	−3.58	5.42[†]	−0.15
Christian Democratic cabinet	—	—	—
Neocorporatism	—	—	—
Constitutional structure	1.007	9.60*	0.23
Unemployment rate	44.64	7.79*	0.20
Aged percent population	—	—	
GDP/population (ln)	—	—	—
Inflation	—	—	—
Economic openness	11.47	3.39[†]	0.10
Openness^2	−6.42	3.31[†]	−0.10
IO	—	—	—
IO^2	−5679	6.20[†]	−0.17
Constant	−71,753	5.61[†]	
−2 Log likelihood		65.36	
	Percent 0s predicted	99.72	
	Percent 1s predicted	50.00	
	Percent total predicted	97.30	

[a] Dates for "retreat points" or retrenchment turning points for "best" measure, in parentheses: Australia (1977), Austria (1986), Belgium (1984), Canada (1976), Denmark (1982), Finland (1986), France (1984), Ireland (1982), Germany (1984), Italy (1982), Japan (1984), the Netherlands (1984), New Zealand (1989), Norway (1986), Sweden (1983), Switzerland (1977), United Kingdom (1984), United States (1977).

* and [†] denote significance at the 0.01 and the 0.05 test levels, respectively.

complemented by a few more. In addition to the variables of Chapter 6's analysis—social democratic cabinet strength, Christian democratic cabinet strength, neocorporatism, exclusive state structure, the unemployment rate, the elderly population share, the natural logarithm of GDP real per capita, a dichotomous variable for the pre-/post-OPEC contrast, and measures of voter turnout and trade openness—a few more variables are added to analyses: the raw and squared year terms mentioned earlier plus a squared variant of the measure of trade openness and raw and squared versions of IO.[10]

For core model of retrenchment, 99.72 percent of non-retrenchment points are correctly predicted, but a far more modest 50 percent of "retreat points" are correctly predicted (more technically, the log-likelihood statistic gauging goodness of fit is a satisfactory

[10] See n. 7.

65.36). Nevertheless, a number of statistically significant "effects" of hypothesized explanatory variables emerge. (See Table 7.2.) In particular, exclusive state structure markedly promotes welfare retrenchment (R = 0.23), consistent with its reduction of welfare effort in the levels model(s) of Table 7.1. (See Table 7.2.) A second political force, social democratic cabinet participation, delays retrenchment (R = −.15). Interestingly, the *higher* the unemployment rate, the *higher* the likelihood of retrenchment, indicating that, despite the tendency for *increases in unemployment* to increase welfare rolls and bloat welfare effort, high levels of unemployment—perhaps portending demand overload—*increase the likelihood of retrenchment.* The relative strength of unemployment exerts pressures on welfare rolls and expense, that ultimately shift nations into retrenchment. The R for unemployment equals 0.19, second only to the R for state structure, and seems to warrant Huber and Stephen's (1996, 1998) stress on unemployment as a principal source of retrenchment.

Trade openness has a quadratic relation to welfare for the first time in this investigation. However, it contrasts with that for investment openness in analyses of welfare effort: trade openness appears to first dampen welfare policy (by promoting retrenchment) and to subsequently shift into supporting it (by resisting retrenchment). Investment openness now has a simple, inhibiting effect on retrenchment (R = −.11) that persists for all levels of investment openness. (The terms introduced for "Year" and "Year squared" in order to capture any time dependence are modestly—almost significantly—negative and positive, respectively.)

Overall, significant anti-welfarist effects (*pro*-retrenchment effects) emerge for exclusionary state structures as in models of welfare effort. Significant pro-welfarist effects (*anti*-retrenchment effects) emerge for social democracy, social democratic government apparently appropriating the role of welfare-state guardian from neocorporatism where social policy turning points, as opposed to mere increments in social-policy funding, are at stake. Consistent with Stephens and Huber (1998), unemployment emerges as the key force driving retrenchment. However much increasing unemployment may incrementally ratchet up welfare effort, as the rolls of those eligible for social insurance are enlarged, unemployment also pressures for shifts toward spending cuts and fiscal austerity. Findings from the supplementary models of Appendix A7B support those of Table 7.2. However, it merits noting that two domestic variables that were inconsequential in the "core" model of Table 7.2 are consistently consequential in the "early" and "late" models of Table A7B.1. One is per capita real GDP, which has persistently negative effects on retrenchment across the two analyses of the Appendix. These negative affluence findings suggest that affluence is less conducive in practice to the private-sector absorption of globalization's human costs than it is to sustained public-sector compensation. The second variable that emerges from the supplementary analyses as persistently relevant to retrenchment is the elderly share of the population, or old age. However, old age has contrasting effects across "early" and "late" analyses. In "early" analyses where the benefit of any doubt in dating retrenchment points goes to the earlier dating, elderly populations appear to resist retrenchment. This is consistent with Pierson's (1996) stress on a "new politics" in which program beneficiaries constitute effective constituencies for program continuity, indeed expansion. In "late" analyses larger elderly shares of populations appear to pressure for retenchment, suggesting that demographic pressures on spending turn eventually into demographic pressures for social spending cuts, trumping any partially offsetting grey-lobby defense of retirement spending—and apparently trumping Pierson's "new politics" with neoliberal politics.

As for the overall pattern of openness findings, evidence again emerges for contradictory openness effects that pressure welfare policy first one way and then the other. Now, however, it is trade rather than investment openness that has a quadratic relation to social policy; and the quadratic relation for trade now involves initially anti-welfarist pressures that eventually turn pro-welfarist and inhibit retrenchment. Despite this contrast with findings for the welfare effort models of Tables 6.2 and 7.1, present findings resemble those for welfare effort in two regards. First, they indicate more overall support for the "compensatory" thesis that globalization promotes welfare state growth; and, second, they do once again indicate a complex, contradictory pattern of globalization effects on welfare states in which globalization sometimes spurs retrenchment. (These patterns are supported by the supplementary analyses of appendix Table A7B.1.)

Importantly, globalization's impacts on welfare states may largely depend on policymaker responses to *perceived* effects of welfare states on economies. Perception here appears complex, although perhaps leaning toward pessimism (Rodrick 1997; Swank 1997; Garrett 1998b). Perceptions ideally should depend on reality. But what is this reality? How effective or ineffective are welfare states in the attainment of their goals? Just how benign or pernicious are they with regard to economic performance?

As for strong negative by-products of welfare spending, the case that welfare spending undercuts economic growth has spotty empirical support at best (Dowrick and Nguyen 1989; Castles and Dowrick 1990; Bean 1994; Slemrod 1995). Furthermore, the case for pernicious aggregate economic effects of welfare state's neocorporatist pillar has been soundly rebutted, if not reversed (Alvarez, Garrett, and Lange 1991; Alesina and Perotti 1997; Hicks and Kenworthy 1998). Moreover, the charge that welfare states betray their distributional ends seems squarely reversed by empirical findings: Welfare states appear to be progressively redistributive (e.g., van Arnheim, Corina and Schotsman 1982; Hicks and Swank 1984b; Kenworthy 1998). The reader can be well assured that the welfare state is neither so distributively ineffectual nor so economically costly as to make its radical dismantling merely a matter of time.[11]

[11] As we saw in Chapters 5 and 6, extant measures of neocorporatism are temporally invariant, or virtually so. We may, however, empirically examine the one aspect of neocorporatism on which sufficient information is available to permit some analyses of change (Golden, et al. 1993; Lange et al. 1995; Western 1997; Hicks and Kenworthy, 1998): decentralization of national wage bargains. In a working paper (Hicks, 1998), I have preliminarily analyzed the causes of bargaining decentralization, however, the number of decentralizing turning points is small—only a half dozen. (I am more stringent than Western (1997), about the degree of initial centralization required before subsequent decentralization can be assessed.) This limits the robustness of analyses.

What I find from my rather tentative analysis of bargaining decentralization is heavily contingent upon whether a nation is a relatively long-standing, strongly neocorporatist nation or not (Hicks 1998). In particular, net of other factors, more corporatist nations are less likely to dismantle centralized wage bargains. What this apparent oxymoron actually tells us is that centralized wage bargains have been disproportionately subject to dismantling in relatively noncorporatist nations in which bargains emerged later on, nations such as Australia, Italy, and New Zealand. In more long-standing neocorporatist nations, inflation and trade openness have tended to increase the likelihood of dismantling, although high unemployment rates have tended to inhibit these changes. In neocorporatist nations, work councils have inhibited bargaining decentralization (see Western 1997). However, central Left governments have been central to bargaining dismantling in Australia and New Zealand. Right and Left parties, respectively, have tended to be pitted for and against dismantling in the long-standing neocorporatist nations in which room for bargaining decentralization is greatest. Consistent with Western (1997), relatively rapidly increasing wages and salaries have tended to encourage dismantling in all contexts. In short, aspects of economic competitiveness—trade and investment openness—have contradictory impacts on the bargaining cornerstone of neocorporatism. This appears to be also buffeted by Right government but steadied by Left government, work councils, and neocorporatism itself.

Conclusions and Discussion

Causes of the Crisis

Economic openness appears to have contradictory consequences for social spending. Consistent with work by Garrett and collaborators (Garrett 1998a, 1998b; Garrett and Mitchell 1997) trade openness appears to have principally compensatory, pro-welfarist impacts on social spending. It seems principally to affect welfare spending by generating increases in spending that are readily interpretable as increases in efforts to ensure against—or compensate for—the costs of globalization.[12] Increasing national openness to flows of FDI appears, beyond a point, to provide some marginal pressure for incremental reductions of (income security–enhancing and redistributive) welfare effect.

In addition, trade competition, alongside such threats to successfully engaging in it as increasing wage and revenue shares of domestic income, appears to exert pressures for the decentralization of centralized wage bargains. With threats to these components of neocorporatism, an additional threat to welfare states emerges.

Some aspects of economic competitiveness do appear to strike at the foundations of welfare states. To what extent they do so because they bring inexorable economic threats or because they evoke ideologically construed (or inflated) responses from policy makers is hard to say.

The net welfarist impacts of openness are reinforced by the efforts of Left governments and by a range of institutional forces linked (to this day) to the workers' movement that helped construct the neocorporatist welfare state. Left-party governments are most prominent in this chapter's core analyses (see Tables 7.1 and 7.2), but worker councils (which represent workers independently of unions within firms) and neocorporatism itself also appear to help fend off bargaining decentralization (see Western 1997 and n. 11.)

In Chapter 6 I concluded that Left parties have largely been supplanted by neocorporatist institutions, as well as by the automatic responsiveness of extant welfare statutes to demographic and economic needs and demands, as sources of welfare effort. Here I further conclude that, as obstacles to the retrenchment, Left parties

---

[12] A simple eighteen-nation regression of decommodification on transfer effort with data from Hicks and Kenworthy (1998) yields a significant positive relation of transfers to decommodification.

persist as pillars of welfare states. Where the protection of extant income-security programs is concerned, social democracy remains pro-welfarist. It is not entirely eclipsed by the movement of neocorporatism to the center of the postwar political economic galaxy.

These findings round out this work's account of the course and the causes of income security policy since Bismarck. In the context of this large topic, the direct continuing relevance of social democratic government to the preservation of neocorporatist institutions and welfare state regime is notable. Union-tied parties, although partially eclipsed by the neocorporatist system of interest organization and policy concertation to which such parties helped give rise, have not become irrelevant to income-security policy or collective bargaining. Some apparent implications of global imperatives to the contrary, Left parties actively oppose the dismantling of both the welfare state and its neocorporatist institutional foundations.

For closer looks at the program-specific details of welfare state policy and politics, I refer readers to Castles (1998), Huber and Stephens (forthcoming), and Korpi (forthcoming). For more detailed examinations of the supply-side policies of social democratic neocorporatist states, I recommend that readers turn to Boix (1998) and Garrett (1998a). For an economically and institutionally nuanced examination of globalization's impacts on recent political economic policies of affluent democracies, readers may turn to Scharpf (1999), Swank (1987, 1998a, 1998b) and should await Swank (forthcoming).[13] Hopefully, the present analyses and the narrative they cap can help put these works in historical perspective.

In the next, final chapter I turn to the larger historical (meta-) narrative, but first a review of the last three chapters to help set the stage for that wrap-up.

---

[13] For other versions of the "big picture," see Huber and Stephens (forthcoming), and Wilensky (1998). Swank (1997) deserves special mention here as the most sophisticated analysis of globalization and welfare effort in OECD nations available as of the writing of this work. Its findings support the main lines of this work's conclusions on the topic, despite a far richer set of political control variables. These findings include strong state-structural effects in line with present ones, albeit with decentralization and PR measures separated (consistent with Hicks and Misra, 1993, footnote 30, if not with the present stress on minimizing control variables for heuristic purposes); neocorporatism effects but a lack of partisan rule effects; a similar array of economic and demographic effects; complex (contingent if not non-linear openness) effects tilted toward supporting the "compensation" hypothesis.

Welfare Politics since Midcentury

During the decade or two following the conclusion of World War II, labor unions within the relatively affluent capitalist democracies were incorporated into neocorporatist institutions of labor market governance. Union-based parties had found extensive admission into the halls of government by the late 1940s (Chapter 4), but it was in the 1950s that the social democratic workers movement helped consolidate the construction of those neocorporatist institutions that would shape mature postwar welfare states (Chapter 5). This amply social democratic construction of neocorporatism is depicted by the arrow running from social democracy to neocorporatism in Figure 7.4.

Once in place, neocorporatism became the principal worker instrument—perhaps the principal political instrument—for the advancement of social insurance policy. Social democratic governments, broadly defined to include all governments with social democratic—social democratic, socialist, or labor party—participation, had set the pace of social policy reform during the Great Depression and World War II. By the 1960s, neocorporatism had replaced social democratic government as the preeminent class-linked source of income security advances. (Better to receive social insurance benefits in the moderately neocorporatist Germany than in the moderately labourite United Kingdom.) Indeed, the signs that emerge in this study of disproportionally social democratic welfare advances after the 1950s are confined to effects of Left democratic rule out of the same pre-1960s period in which neocorporatist institutions were erected. By the 1960s social insurance policy had attained broadly nonpartisan legitimacy, which it would retain into the late 1970s and beyond. Fluctuations in government partisanship no longer were of much account for social policy performance. Neocorporatism raised levels of welfare spending effort primarily by augmenting policymaker responsiveness to conventional pluralist processes of societal affluence (and revenue availability), group need and demand, and electoral participation. Figure 7.4 depicts these processes of neocorporatist impacts on welfare effort, particularly their magnifications of the impacts of pluralist factors.

Although this largely social democratic story provides focus and continuity to my explanation of social insurance policy determination, and largely shapes Figure 7.4, it hardly exhausts explanation.

For example, political institutions and aspects of domestic and global economies matter. State institutions structurally conducive to exclu-

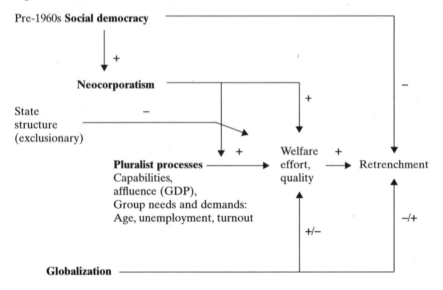

Figure 7.4 Post–World War I Welfare-State Politics: Institutionalization and Deinstitutionalization.

sionary politics, like federalism and winner-take-all electoral districts, dampened welfare spending at least as much as neocorporatism buoyed it. (See the arrow from state structure to welfare effort in Fig. 7.4 and the last chapter's Table 6.3.)[14] Demographic and political pressures from the unemployed, levels of prosperity (and revenue resources), and participatory electorates substantially drove welfare effort, albeit more vigorously in neocorporatist systems. Forces of globalization exercise additional, contradictory effects on both welfare effort and its retrenchment. Whereas the risks and vulnerabilities connoted by trade openness appear to have promoted compensatory social spending, FDI appears to have joined in the generation of such compensatory social spending only up to a point (reached somewhere in the 1980s in a number of nations). Beyond that threshold, investment openness appears to have motivated policy makers more to provide low-tax, laissez-faire incentives to business than to provide compensations for risks and hardships to citizens.

[14] In interactive relations not noted in Figure 7.4, antiwelfarist, or at least counterproductive, social democratic effects emerge where exclusionary state structures are more prominent, however, these are small in comparison with those involving neocorporatism. In addition, exclusionary state structures intensify the positive responsiveness of welfare effort to OPEC shocks.

Globalization provides an entree to discussion of the study of actual welfare retrenchment—actual direct reversals in trajectories of national social spending—introduced here. For retrenchment as such, globalization also emerges as a contradictory force. (Similar effects—first inhibiting, then accelerating—are found for trade dependence upon neocorporatist dismantling, an ominous portent for welfare state vitality.) In Figure 7.4, combined "+" and "−" characterizations of the arrow from globalization to retrenchment depict globalization's contradictory effects.

With welfare program retrenchment, social democracy reemerges from its partial eclipse by neo-corporatism in Chapter 6. Now, Left governments pit themselves against Right efforts to dismantle the welfare state.

The preceding few pages provide a simplified account of income-security policy since mid-century. This account is integrated into the longer story of social welfare politics since 1880 in the next and final chapter.

A P P E N D I X   S E V E N

A. Measures and Data Sources

Welfare effort. See Appendix 6A.1.

Welfare effort retrenchment. See Table 7.2, n. 1.

Social wage. Biennial data from OECD Database on Unemployment Benefit Entitlement and Replacement rates, OECD (forthcoming), described in OECD (1994).

Social retirement wage. Pension benefit expenditures from ILO (1960–1995). Data on population at least 65 years old and GDP from sources listed below and in Appendix 6A.

Public health care effort. Data on public health spending (sickness and maternity benefits) from ILO (1960–1995). Data on GDP from sources listed below and in Appendix 6A.

Poverty measures. See Kenworthy (1997) for details on data from LIS.

Left cabinet, Christian democratic cabinet and Right cabinet. See Appendix 6A.
Neocorporatism. See Appendix 6A.
Exclusionary veto points. See Appendix 6A.
Unemployment rate. See Appendix 6A.
Aged population. See Appendix 6A.
Trade openness. See Appendix 6A.
Investment openness. Direct investment inflows and outflows in millions of US dollars as a proportion of GDP from IMF, Balance of Payment Statistics, Washington, DC, 1960–1995. (See "economic product" for GDP.)
Economic product. See Appendix 6A.
Post-OPEC. Equal to 1 for 1975 and later; otherwise equal to 0.
Turnout. See Appendix 6A.
Price level. See Appendix 6A.
Inflation rate. Percentage change in price level from t-1 to t.

B. Supplementary Analyses of Retrenchment

Data for many nations suggested two downturns, one during the 1970s and a second during the 1980s. This occurred even while for most nations one point of sustained reversal in welfare effort from a peak level was manifest. As a check on both the robustness of results and on the possibility of different causes for relatively early and late retrenchments, I constructed two additional measures of "retreat points." One was a measure of "early" points, the other a measure of "late" reversals. I always dated any "early" retrenchments for a nation at the earlier of any two apparent reversals (or in the case of a single reversal at the single reversal point). I always dated "late" reversals at the times of second reversals (if any). Dates of "early" and "late" retreat points are listed in footnotes a and b, respectively, to Table A7B.1.

I analyze rates of movement toward retrenchment using "event history" models closely analogous to the model of Table 7.2. Totals of nation-year observations are 318 for "early" measures and 395 for "late" measures. Rates at which nations approach "retreat points" are once again analyzed using logistic regression as advised by Allison (1982).

Table A7B.I. A Model of Retrenchment: Causes of Welfare Effort "Turning Points."[a]

Explanatory Variables	Equation for 1 "Early" Datings			Equation for 2 "Late" Datings		
	b	Wald χ^2	R	b	Wald χ^2	R
Year	350.53	6.08†	0.18	−34.78	0.09	0.00
Year²	−0.088	5.32†	−0.18	0.089	0.09†	0.00
Social Democratic cabinet	−3.81	4.59	−0.14	−1.52	1.20‡	−0.00
Christian Democratic cabinet	7.48	7.47*	0.20	—	—	—
Neocorporatism	3.93	1.53	0.00	5.50	2.73†	0.07
Constitutional structure	0.62	5.32*	0.16	0.43	1.67	0.00
Unemployment rate	44.71	2.38‡	0.05	42.90	5.94*	0.16
Aged percent of population	−41.89	2.45‡	−0.06	41.29	1.77	0.04
GDP/population (ln)	−0.33	4.70†	−0.14	−0.30	2.38‡	−0.05
Inflation	—	—	—	21.89	2.31‡	0.05
Economic openness	18.34	3.40†	0.10	−10.28	2.46‡	0.06
Openness²	−13.82	3.49†	−0.11	3.99	1.34	−0.00
IO	—	—	—	74.37	1.12	0.00
IO²	−5363	3.53†	−0.11	−4608	2.70‡	−0.07
Constant	31,858	6.07		−32,258	0.93	
−2 Log likelihood		64.49			64.17	
Percent 0s predicted		99.67			99.20	
Percent 1s predicted		41.18			55.56	
Percent total predicted		96.52			97.22	

Note: (Revised model following deletion of "base" variable with t-statistics < |1.0|).

[a] Dates for "retreat points" or retrenchment turning points for "early" measure, in parentheses: Australia (1977), Austria (1986), Belgium (1976), Canada (1976), Denmark (1982), Finland (1976), France (1984), Ireland (1982), Germany (1976), Italy (1976), Japan (1984), the Netherlands (1979), New Zealand (1978), Norway (1986), Sweden (1983), Switzerland (1977), United Kingdom (1984), United States (1977).

[b] Dates for "retreat points" or retrenchment turning points for "late" measure, in parentheses: Australia (1987), Austria (1986), Belgium (1984), Ganada (1987), Denmark (1982), Finland (1986), France (1984), Ireland (1982), Germany (1984), Italy (1982), Japan (1984), the Netherlands (1984), New Zealand (1989), Norway (1986), Sweden (1983), Switzerland (1987), United Kingdom (1984), United States (1981).

*, †, and ‡ denote significance at the 0.01, 0.05, and 0.10 test levels, respectively.

For the model of the "early" measure of retrenchment, whose average year for retrenchment is 1980, 99.67 percent of non-retrenchment points are correctly predicted, but a mere 41.18 percent of "retreat points" are predicted correctly. (More technically, the log-likelihood statistic gauging goodness of fit is a barely acceptable 64.49.) Despite the disappointing ability of the "early" model to pinpoint moments of retrenchment, a greater number of significant contributors to the generation of retrenchment emerge for this model than for the "core" model. What arises in particular? Once again exclusive state structure emerges as a promoter of welfare retrenchment (R = 0.16) while Left cabinet participation emerges as an inhibiter of retrenchment ($R = -.14$). However, more political effects are found now. For this model of typically earlier and always first retrenchments, Christian Democratic cabinet participation ($R = 0.20$) is the greatest accelerator of retrenchment. Perhaps, given the Christian Democratic principle of "subsidiarity," which reduced state measures to market supplements of last resort, Christian Democrats' first responses to the shocks of openness were laissez-faire and market-oriented. In addition, neocorporatism emerges as a possible accelerator of retrenchment. The relevant effect is statistically insignificant, its R negligible though distinctly greater than 0.0. (Perhaps while social democracy is a force fending off spending retrenchment, mid-and-late-70s' neocorporatism is a modest source of spending restraint—as well as the source of wage restraint publicized by Lange and Garrett [1985] and others.) Consistent with Pierson's (1996) view that aged populations develop and advance vested interests in the social insurance programs of advanced welfare states, "Aged percent population" restrains retrenchment. Less predictably, per capita incomes appear to restrain retrenchment, perhaps because the costs of welfare expansion are more easily absorbed by the affluent. Pressure from unemployment for retrenchment is evident for the "early" as well as "best" datings of retrenchment. However, when retrenchment datings lean toward earlier years, unemployment is not the preeminent factor among the various accelerators and decelerators of retrenchment that it is for the more balanced "best" datings of Table 7.2 (or that it is, as we shall see, for "late" datings). Once again, trade openness has a quadratic relation to retrenchment: it first dampens retrenchment but beyond a point accelerates it. Once again, investment openness has a simple, inhibiting effect on retrenchment ($R = -.11$) that persists for all levels of investment openness. (The terms introduced for "Year" and "Year squared" to capture any time dependence are significantly positive and negative, respectively.)

For the model of the "late" measure of retrenchment, whose average year for retrenchment is 1985 (actually, "1984.6"), 99.20 percent of non-retrenchment points are correctly predicted, while over half (55.56 percent) of "retreat points" are predicted correctly. (More technically, the log-likelihood statistic gauging goodness of fit is 64.17.) The pattern of findings for "late" datings resembles that for early datings, especially for domestic as opposed to global variables. Still, surprises emerge. Exclusive state structure and social democratic government once more emerge as forces that, respectively, advance and inhibit retrenchment, although now they emerge supported by merely non-trivial Wald χ^2

(greater than |1.0|) and without statistical significance at conventional test levels. Fiscally conservative Christian democratic effects are gone, vanished by the shift toward later retrenchments, but fiscally restraining impacts of neocorporatism, statistically insignificant for the "early" measure (and utterly invisible for the "core" measure) are now significant and prominent (R = .07). Apparently, disproportionately rapid Christian Democratic retrenchments are limited to the first wave of 1970's shocks from the international system (aggravated by the OPEC price hikes and concurrent inflation in the price of food stuffs), while neocorporatism becomes (net of Left government) a fiscally conservative influence in the 1980s. Unemployment pressure for retrenchment again is the preeminent pressure among all pressures on retrenchment. Consistent with the view that aging populations pose a fiscally restraining threat to future fiscal solvency that inhibits spending—not a Piersonian force for the defense of past expansionary patterns—"Aged percent population" apparently exerts pressure for retrenchment. As in "early" models per capita income appears to restrain retrenchment (R = 0.05). However, inflation, a pro-cyclical variable that correlates positively with income, emerges as just about the promoter of retrenchment that believers in fiscal profligacy as a source of inflationary evils would warn against. (The two "Year" controls have no effects in this model.)

Trade and investment openness now reveal quadratic relations to rates of retrenchment. The trade quadratic is "U-shaped": openness retards retrenchment up to a point and subsequently accelerates it. This is the retrenchment analogue to a hump-shaped curve in an analysis of welfare effort in the sense that openness effects are "pro-welfarist" up to a point and then turn "anti-welfarist" (see Table A7B.1). The investment openness quadratic takes on a shape with opposite meanings: it is "hump-shaped": openness hastens retrenchment up to a point and subsequently decelerates its arrival. This is the retrenchment analogue of a U-shaped curve in an analysis of welfare effort, first "pro- welfarist" and then "anti-welfarist." In detail, these patterns conflict with earlier findings. As regards other retrenchment findings, the "trade" quadratic for "Late" datings, reverses patterns found for both the "core" and the "early" measures. As regards the "welfare effort" analyses of Tables 6.2 and 7.1, the presence of a trade openness quadratic is unprecedented. As regards the investment openness quadratic for the "late" model, this function reverses the quadratic pattern found for investment openness in models of welfare effort: now investment openness is first "anti-welfarist" and then "pro-welfarist." However, *findings are consistent across all "retrenchment" models if we discount estimates that fail to reach even the marginal 0.10 level of statistical significance.* All significant openness effects in models of retrenchment, like all significant trade openness ones in models of welfare effort, support compensatory conclusions either across the board or for higher level of openness. All significant findings are negative, indexing a tendency for welfare retrenchment to be held at bay, or welfare effort to be augmented, by either all levels or relatively high levels of trade openness. Across all models of either welfare effort or its retrenchment only once does a statistically significant quadratic pattern emerge that suggests otherwise. This occurs for investment openness and welfare effort and suggests a tendency for spending to decline relative to domestic income when flows of FDI have increased beyond a point. Overall, then, evidence of contradictory openness effects that pressure welfare policy first one way and then the other emerges. However, this pattern is statistically significant only for the case of declining welfare effort in response to increases in investment openness beyond some rather high level. Elsewhere, Rodrik's eventual "anti-welfarist" pressure from globalization are not found. Openness, though contradictory, tends to promote compensatory spending.

Culture/Welfare State

Culture as explicitly regarded (Steinmetz 1999) is missing here, yet it is present implicitly. First, institutions like party and neocorporatism are Janus-faced, both social relational and symbolic/expressive. Second, causes are channeled by actions issuing most immediately from subjects. Third, some prominent variables are amenable to cultural elaboration. For example, neocorporatism doubles well as an ideological dimension ranging tidily from Scandinavia social democracy through Austrian/Low-Countries Center-Left Christian democracy and its Continental Center-Right variant to English speaking laissez-faire (with Austrian leftism overstated and Japanese and Swiss guesstimates around the mean). It's a cogent scale, perhaps because ideology is carried by institutions like neo-corporatism. Still, the cultural roots of welfare states certainly merit much more study.

CHAPTER EIGHT

Employee Movement, Welfare Capitalism

[R]edistribution must not disappear from the agenda of social democracy. But . . . the "redistribution of possibilities" . . . should as far as possible replace "after the event" redistribution.

(Giddens 1996, 100–101)

I have examined the political sociology/economy of social insurance over the long run from a working-class perspective and with an eye to state institutions. What does such an examination tell us about the history of social insurance, the working-class social movement, and theories of politics and policy? What about current history and possible futures of the welfare state?

A Century of Social Insurance Politics

A revolutionary social democratic mobilization of German industrial workers provoked a series of social insurance reforms (unsought by social democrats) from a state vying with socialists for worker loyalty (Rimlinger 1971; Chapter 2). Politically moderate Danish industrial workers accommodated themselves to liberal parties as a voting block and gained satisfying, if again unsought, welfare and workplace policies in return (Luebbert 1990; Chapter 2). The emerging British Labour party struck a deal with Asquith's Liberals that joined both in a coalition government, bringing Labour some say in social insurance reforms that included a prominent early versions of unemployment compensation (Marwick 1967; Chapter 2). The Great Depression and postwar era Scandinavian Social Democrats led governments that extended programs of unemployment compensation, and postwar social democratic and Christian democratic governments (seldom without socialist partners) made family allowance programs commonplace (Esping-Andersen 1985; Misra 1994; Chapter 3). Governments of many varieties—Christian Democratic, Liberal, and conservative Catholic as well as social democratic—participated in extensions and deepenings of income-security policies in nations with labor-inclusive tripartite neocorporatist institutions (Chapters 5 and 6); indeed governments of all varieties found extant income-security programs similarly congenial during the neocorporatist heyday of the 1960s and 1970s (Chapter 6). Left parties battled Right parties over the retrenchment of social spending during the decades of economic troubles after the first OPEC oil embargo (Chapter 7). Working-class politics integrates the history of the welfare state.

Working-Class and Social Insurance Revisited

Table 8.1 provides a terse review of this work's account of one-hundred-plus years of working-class relevance to income security policy. In Panel A, which recounts analyses of which nations did or did not adopt three or more of the era's four major types of social insurance programs by 1920, we see that early working-class mobilization alone quite strongly differentiates 1920 consolidators from nonconsolidators. (The Yule' s Q, or phi, correlation is equal to 0.76). Indeed, if the Netherlands is shifted from being coded the most mobilized of *un*mobilized working classes to being coded the least mobilized of mobilized working classes, worker mobilization *almost perfectly* differentiates consolidators (Q = 0.89). In this light, the particular combinations of workers and political system—in brief, the Lib-Lab, the Catholic-worker, and Bismarckian conjunctures leading to 1920 program consolidation—are three historical vehicles transporting nationally differentiated segments of workers toward more secure material lives. True, these three historical vehicles—the one taken or *any* of the three—may still seem essential to each 1920 consolidator's transition to a strong early welfare state. However, extra-worker forces as varied as imperial states—Asquithian Liberals, and Catholic conservatives—seem to have chosen to exchange social insurance payoffs for worker allegiance (of one sort or another). Indeed, each specific non–working-class ally begins to look almost substitutable with the others, an instance of some general set of statist preconditions for working-class policy influence. The possibility emerges that, had workers gained the reigns of government before the 1920s, they

Table 8.1. Phases of Worker Organization and the Social Insurance Development

Panel A: 1920 Program Consolidation in Early Democracies[a]

Worker Mobilization	No Consolidation	Consolidation
High	Australia	Austria, Belgium, Denmark, Germany Italy, Sweden, United Kingdom
Low	Canada, France, New Zealand, Norway, Switzerland, US	Netherlands*

Correlation: 0.76. (*0.89 if the Netherlands scored high on worker mobilization)

Panel B: Major 1930s and 1940s Program Innovations[b]

	No Innovations	Innovations
Left party government participation		Australia, Austria, Belgium, Denmark, France, Finland, Italy, Japan, the Netherlands, Norway, Sweden, United Kingdom
No left government participation	Germany, Switzerland	Canada, United States

Correlation: 0.67. (Exceptions: nations without left parties)

Panel C: Midcentury Consolidation of Five Major Program Types[c]

	No Consolidation	Consolidation
Strong unions	Belgium	Australia, Austria, Denmark, the Netherlands, New Zealand Norway, Sweden, United Kingdom
Weak unions	Canada, Finland, France Germany, Italy, Japan, Switzerland, United States	

Correlation: 0.89. (Exception: Belgium for nonmandatory [but effective] workers' compensation program)

Panel D: 1980 Decommodification of Income through Social Insurance[d]

	Low Decommodification	High Decommodification
High neocorporatism (nine most)		Austria, Belgium, Denmark, Finland, Germany, Netherlands, Norway, Sweden, Switzerland
Low neocorporatism (9 least)	Australia, Canada, France, Italy, Ireland, Japan, New Zealand, Switzerland, United Kingdom, United States	

Correlation: 1.00.

[a] See Chapter 3, Appendix.
[b] See Chapter 4, Table 5.2.
[c] See Chapter 5, Tables 6.3–6.4.
[d] Neocorporatism is dichotomized into nine highest and lowest scores (Chapter 7).

might have adopted major social insurance policies as practical solutions to their needs. More primary worker goals might also have been realized, such as improved working conditions. Still, social insurance programs may have been more than expedient outcomes of particular working-class encounters with particular liberal, Catholic, or autocratic powers.

Social democratic participation in government during the 1930s and 1940s—the explanatory lever of Table 8.1's second cross-tabulation in Panel B—certainly is not inconsistent with the preceding speculations. When social democratic parties finally do enter an era of common governmental leadership (or junior participation), they invariably extend their nations' repertoires of basic programs (Panel B). Indeed, the correlation between a degree of Left governance and program adoption is a strong 0.67 for this period. The only democracies without notable Left government to adopt new programs are Canada and the United States, nations without notable national socialist parties.

Panel C indicates that consolidation of all five major programs, retirement, work-injury, illness, unemployment, and child-rearing compensation, is about as closely linked to working-class strength after World War II as it had been just after World War I. The correlation between a measure of 1919 to 1950 union strength and across-the-board program consolidation is a strong 0.89 (Table 8.1, Panel C).[1]

For a look at working-class development after the midcentury program consolidation, a turn to new measures is useful. Ideally, we could look at program development during this period of welfare-state maturation with measures of program outcomes and of program outputs sensitive to these—and look at details of program coverage, at benefit generosity per recipient, at benefit duration, and so on. Although such measures were not available with enough frequency to support "large N" analyses of program quality during the post-war war period, a good cross-sectional measure of quality is available for around 1980. This is Esping-Andersen's (1990) measure of decommodification, or the extent to which a citizen is freed from reliance on market remuneration for income, given some commitment to work (Table 8.1, Panel D). I relate neocorporatism to decommodification. Not only is neocorporatism a key variable in post–World War II analyses, it is the postwar era's key class-linked source of income security policy. (Social democ-

---

[1] Indeed, if we switch from the measure of union density, which helps establish the underlying force of unions themselves, to the measure of 1920 to 1950 social democratic reform and labor strength used earlier in Table 6.4 (Panel B), Belgium ceases to be an exception and we get a perfect relationship between midcentury program consolidation and working-class strength.

racy is, as I detailed in Chapter 6, the overriding cause of neocorporatism.) The relation between neocorporatism and decommodification, Esping-Andersen's (1990) core measure of social insurance quality, each measure divided at its 50th percentile, is a perfect 1.00.[2]

As the last chapter indicated, downward turns in the time plots of welfare effort, soaring since the early 1960s, begin to appear in 1976 to 1977 and proliferate across the 1980s; however, despite social policy retrenchments under Left governments in Australia and Sweden, Left rule tends to combat retrenchment. Although all nations experienced downturns in welfare effort at some time after the OPEC oil shock of 1973 to 1974, nations with strong Lefts were, as detailed in Chapter 7, more likely to have had relatively late, post-1982 retrenchment than were other nations (Table 8.2). Still, relations between working-class political capacities and retrenchment are only moderate.[2]

Of course, discontinuities in the types of working-class organization most relevant to social policy success are manifest here. Modes of working-class mobilization relevant to social insurance policy change with historical context. Union and Left governmental strength are facets of a single, Janus-faced force precipitating cooptive and opportunistic favors from more powerful political forces during the era before the emergence of durable governments led by social democrats (see Chapter 3). With this emergence, social democratic government becomes a force behind social policy reform. Neocorporatism arises as a major pro-welfarist institution. Selection of worker mobilization, rather than government, was an obvious choice for years preceding ample working-class participation in government; however, the non-class contingencies for nation-specific working-class relevance largely were identified inductively, albeit with theoretical help, from historical readings and data analyses. Without being more formulaic than a respect for history will bear, what—besides German autocrats and centrist-led governments—are some more of the contingencies?

Within particular nations, the working-class forces driving social reform change vehicles over time. Under conditions of accentuated need and demand brought on by the Great Depression and the postwar opportunity to prepare for any like occurrence of economic disaster, social democrats across Scandinavia gain votes and willing junior partners for the formation of governments in the form of agrarian parties. Following the brief prewar Dutch precedent set by the Catholic-Socialist government of Paul-Henri Spaak, Christian demo-

[2] Esping-Andersen's (1990) other dimensions (and measures) of social insurance program quality are discussed and further related to neocorporatism in Appendix A8.1.

Table 8.2. Worker Organization and the Social Insurance Retrenchment

| | Postwar Retrenchment | |
	Late (post-1982)	Early (by 1982)
High Left government (nine most)	Austria Belgium Finland France Germany Netherlands Norway Switzerland Sweden	Australia
		Canada
		Denmark
Low Left government (nine least)	Japan New Zealand United Kingdom	Ireland Italy United States
	Correlation: −0.55	

cratic partners, sometimes junior and sometimes senior, become crucial allies in the low countries and Austria (as well as most briefly in France and Italy). Only allies, and depression conditions themselves, best appreciated by Gourevitch (1986), seem like essential contingencies for the period of social democratic ascendence stretching from the early 1930s through 1950 (see Chapter 5). In recent decades, the neocorporatist institutionalization of union participation in labor market governance becomes a key contingency for a range of socioeconomic forces—unemployment, age structure and, once again, affluence—driving a great deal of social policy.

Perhaps the most manifest discontinuity in Table 8.1 is the rise and fall of Australia, Britain, and New Zealand to and from welfare-state leadership, a phenomenon already alluded to in Chapters 5 and 7. (Note the drop across Panel C and Panel D of Table 8.1.) These nations became welfare-state leaders during the 1930 to 1950 Social democratic ascendancy (Panel C), only to fall back toward laggard status during the postwar era in which they failed to consolidate neocorporatist institutions. Interestingly, Labour Party governments helped move these nations into belated neocorporatist development with the introduction of substantial national wage coordination during the 1980s. However, these neocorporatist developments were short-lived ones that were followed up by neoliberal turns (Labour-led in New Zealand).

Underlying the history of working-class politics just reviewed are a number of changes in the types of power exercised by the working class. Social democratic impacts on Bismarckian-era social insurance evoke the unintentional and indirect effects on welfare policy described by Lipsky (1968) and Piven and Cloward (1977) for Afro-American protesters. Bismarckian-era worker mobilization exercised a sort of inadvertent systemic power: it provoked palliative measures tangental to the social democratic agenda such as income transfers instead of better working conditions and social insurance instead of social and political rights. Labor impacts upon Liberal government evoke forms of power from group influence to shared governmental authority—that are all reminiscent of mainstream pluralist analyses (e.g., Dahl 1959). Left rule entails, of course, full state "authority." The rise of neocorporatism complements social democratic political authority with union economic power. The approximate sequencing of these transitions, from clout inadvertently exercised outside the corridors of state power to exercises of authoritative governance, from informal to institutionalized and outsider to insider, suggests the successful progression of a social movement. It suggests a progression that, although rather long on political institutionalizations and successes, resembles ones addressed by social movement theory. As I have referred recurrently to working-class actors as "movement" actors, perhaps it is time for some explicit social movement theory.

Working-Class Social Politics as Social Movement Politics

Although social movement theory indeed would seem very relevant, its relevance is complicated by the historical and sociological breadth of the social democratic working-class movement (or movements) in question. This movement straddles a range of organizations—interest groups and political parties as well as conventional movement organizations such as Student Non-Violent Coordinating Committee (SNCC) or National Organization for Women (NOW). It involves a degree of political institutionalization and policy-making success quite beyond the range of most self-termed social scientific movement theory. Despite its attainment of advanced degrees of political institutionalization (e.g., extended periods of rule), dynamic relations among parties and unions and citizens—wildcat strikes, electoral migrations, and rebellions—recur (see Swenson 1989; Pontusson 1992; and Western 1997, on worker collective behavior; Kitschelt 1994 on electoral dynamics; Przeworski 1985, on social democratic dynamics generally). These dynamics evoke something very much like a working-class social movement despite their entwining with political economic institutions.

I dub my social democratic working-class movement a *sociopolitical supermovement*. By this I mean an assembly of conventionally regarded social movements and movement organizations and of interest groups and political parties that is oriented (whether intentionally or functionally) toward common ends over extended periods. Unlike all but a few recent social movement dissidents such as Brustein (1998), I allow for movement progress, not only from disorganized collective actions to movement organizations, but from inexperienced support organizations to interest associations (e.g., labor union formation) and political representation (e.g., Social Democratic party incorporation) at the point of political practice. I allow for movement progress not only up to first policy successes, but beyond them through spells of policy development, through modifications in goals and reversals of fortune, and on into newly disruptive and uncertain ventures. (Criteria such as continued duration after success and recurrent Tarrowian "protest cycles" might be developed to define supermovement existence over extended periods.)

Here I am working in what might be called the "shadow" tradition of supermovement studies. This is the tradition of Claudin (1976) and Blackmer and Tarrow (1975) on the Communist movement, and Foner (1947) and Goldfield (1987) on the U.S. labor movement. It is a tradition outside that of self-termed social movement theory. As my approach will prove controversial to most social movement scholars, I devote Appendix 8.B to its justification. As the controversy will seem highly academic to most other readers, I now proceed directly to a social movement reading of social democracy and the welfare state. (Theorists may turn to Appendix 8.B.)

Some core categories of contemporary social movement theory can help here. Their application to my findings can illustrate the relevance of social movement theory beyond social movements conventionally regarded to the study of politically institutionalized extensions of such movements—in short, to sociopolitical super-movements. It might also help illuminate the promise of systematically expanding social movement analysis to the topic of working-class social politics in particular.

I apply the three principal sets of contemporary social movement variables (or sets of variables) to the findings of this work, era by era. These variables are movement organization, political opportunity, and cultural frame (Gamson and Meyer 1996; McAdam, Tarrow, and Tilly 1996; McAdam, McCarthy, and Zald 1996). Consensus on these three sets of explanatory factors is explicit across such prominent social movement authors as William A. Gamson, Douglas McAdam, John D. McCarthy, Sidney Tarrow, Charles Tilly, and Mayer Zald (e.g., Gamson and Meyer 1996; McAdam, Tarrow, and Tilly 1996; McAdam, McCarthy, and Zald 1996).

McCarthy (1996, 141) describes *organizational structures* as "agreed upon ways of engaging in collective action that include particular 'tactical repertoires,' particular 'social movement organizational' forms, and 'modular social movement repertoires.'" Within these "modular repertoires" McCarthy (1996, 141) includes such "macro-mobilization social locations" as "family units, friendship networks, voluntary associations, work units" and the like—in short, all of the "many varieties of enabling institutional configurations." (Indeed, such relatively contingent, situationally specific factors as these—traditional Black southern churches and residual "old Left" networks during the early U.S. civil rights movement—are what McCarthy refers to as "modular.") Writing in a similar vein, McAdam (1996, 4) stresses a confluence of "resource mobilization" theorizing and the "political process model" into one unifying focus on "organization dynamics of collective action," a move that parallels McCarthy's joining of tactical and organization movement resources. Just as earlier resource mobilization theorists incorporated movement tactics (e.g., "disruption") into their repertoires of movement resources (Jenkins 1983, 527–553; Lipsky 1968, 1144–1158), so more recently contemporary theorists have joined dynamic, path-dependent conception of process to more statically conceived, strictly structural conceptions of organization (McAdam 1996, 2–4). As McCarthy's (1996, 141) use of "enabling" institutions suggests, the focus of organizing structures is still very much on resources broadly construed—nonorganizational as well as organizational, informal as well as formal, processual as well as structural. Such organizing structures as unions and parties, as well as such less structured entities as strikers and voters, come to mind as examples of worker-movement resources.

This stress on wide-ranging resources, or an "encompassing scope of mobilizing structures," is used with close attention to the "reciprocal interrelationships" these have with "both political opportunity structures and framing processes" (McCarthy 1996, 141). *Political opportunities* refer to aspects of "the broader political system" that are important for "structuring the opportunities for collective action" (McAdam et al. 1996). In Jenkins and Klanderman's (1995, 7) words, this theme of political opportunities "elaborates on the impact of the state and the electoral system"—the polity—upon social movements.

Some principal elements of such opportunities are, according to Tarrow (1996, 54–56), the "opening up of political access," "unstable alignments," "influential allies," and "divided elites." Such "opportunities" as the uncertainty of Bismarck's working-class support, as the need of Herbert Asquith's Liberals for coalition allies, and as new centrist (Green and Black) allies for social democratic governance all jump to mind.

Cultural frames refer to groups' "shared understandings of the world and of themselves that legitimate and motivate collective action," as well as to "strategic efforts to fashion" these (McAdam et al. 1996, 6). Framings may be relatively taken for granted or self-conscious, internal to movements or tied to their contexts (McAdam et al. 1996, 16–17). They may consist of cultural toolkits or schemas, cognitive processes of group members, or strategic framings of inter-group negotiators (Gamson and Neyer 1996; Zald 1996). As regards instances of working-class "cultural frames"—the various social democratic ideologies from Kautsky via Per Albin Hansson and Olaf Palme to today's Gerhard Schroeder come to mind.

All three of these aspects of social movement thinking—organizations and resources, political opportunities, and cultural frames—are employed in Table 8.3, alongside political eras and their characteristic income security policy outputs, to restate the story of worker movement social politics over the last six-score years.

In Austro-German states before World War I, Social democratic party–union mobilizations, energized yet politically detached by revolutionary ideological "frames," provoked social insurance reforms from state autocrats. Autocratic leaders like Bismarck and Eduard Van Taaffe did so because they feared realignments of worker loyalty from state to social democratic movements (political alienation of potential conscripts, in particular). Here party-union organization and membership figure as organizational structures and resources; revolutionary ideologies figure as cultural frames; and autocratic competitions for working-class loyalty figure as political opportunities (Table 8.3, row 1).

In Lib-Lab and Catholic-worker–led polyarchies of early in the century, labor voters and parties exploited opportunities provided by competitive electoral politics to parlay the electoral and even parliamentary clouts of growing memberships into social insurance reforms (Table 8.3, **2**). During the 1930s and 1940s crises of world depression, world war, and postwar adjustment, social democratic parties parlayed their electoral clout and reformist and coalitional opportunism into government participation and leadership. On these bases they introduced unemployment compensation, family allowances, and, where

Table 8.3. Working Class Social Politics as Social Movement Politics

Key Eras	Social Movement Dimensions			Social Reforms
	Organization/Resource	Political Opportunities	Cultural Frames	
1. Pre-WWI autocratic (protodemocracy)	**Movement party-union organization & membership**	**State competition for working class loyalty**	**Ideology of socialist revolution**	Early social insurance innovation and adoption
2. Pre-WWI democracy	**Movement votes, legislative votes;** governmental participation	**Party competition for worker vote and governmental allies**	**Revolutionary ideology; electoral mobilization strategy**	Early social insurance innovation and adoption
3. Crisis-era (Great Depression, WWII, postwar)	**Movement votes** & legislative seats, governmental participation, leadership	Electoral access to government; class compromise	Ideology of popular/socialist reform: social amelioration, economic management and class compromise	Adoptions of family allowance and unemployment compensation; upgrades of other programs
4. 1950s to 1970s	**Movement votes** & legislative seats; governmental participation and leadership; union neocorp economic policy inclusion	Societal openness to Keynesian and complementary interventions in economy (Keynesian & progressive politics), economic prosperity	Reformist socialism aided by Keynes-plus and progressive tools (rationales for spending and for specific public goods)	Social insurance benefit and coverage upgrades and complements to supply-side goods (training, etc.)
5. Post-OPEC troubles and neoliberal reaction to welfare state	**Votes/seats, union density, neocorporatism** (all somewhat weakened) **Wildcat strikes** (pro and con neocorporatism) **Workers' councils**	Economic troubles and societal neoliberalism; contraction of pre-OPEC	Neoliberal skepticism of and supply-side compensations for spending opportunities	Program catch up, upgrading, and retrenchment

still lacking, national health insurance throughout most of the affluent democratic world (Table 8.3, **3**).

Starting roughly in the 1930s and extending on through World War II and the postwar era, labor movement union and party organizations helped construct neocorporatist institutions of labor market and macroeconomic coordination (Table 8.3, **4**). On the basis of quasi-governmental bargaining positions within these institutions (not infrequently reinforced and safeguarded by Left government), the social democratic movement forged ahead with the upgrading of social insurance programs and with such complementary programs as Gosta Rehn's "active labor market policy." It did so aided by Keynesian and progressive frameworks for economic steering and fruitful social spending. It did so guided by its own amplified Keynes-plus visions and by the abundant economic resources of the 1950s and 1960s booms.

After the 1970s onset of economic troubles—heightened natural rates of unemployment, increased corporate policy leverage, and so on—world economic globalization ushered in an era of challenges to welfare state evolution (Table 8.3, 5). Intensifications of international economic competitiveness increased pressures for enhanced flexibility and efficiency. These pressures, made writ by neoliberal economic orthodoxy, depressed state taxing, spending, and regulatory activity. They not only pressured against such state interventions, but they also undercut worker resources (e.g., electoral support, union density, bargaining authority), constricted opportunities (e.g., affluence and the revenue base), and shook traditional state-friendly (e.g., Keynesian) cultural frames to their foundations (Table 8.3, 5). Still, ruling Left parties (aided by new supply-side human and capital investment policies) tended to combat these reversals, even as Right governments (buoyed by a free-market fundamentalist revival) pressed for the reversal of welfare-state development. Electoral, union, and corporatist resources remained substantial (Garrett, 1998a, Tables 1.1, 1.2; Western, 1997, Table 10.2). On the policy front, Left parties increasingly turned to programs that did not just transfer income but invested it in public infrastructure, research the development of human capital, and the like (Boix, 1998; Garrett 1998a).

Although this tale of a working-class movement is a class story, it should not silence other accounts of social action, such as "gray" lobbies and centrist ("Black" and "Green") partisan allies and substitutes. As Dahrendorf (1959, 115–164, 215–279) has clarified, the militant working-class story is tied to the emergence and life course of industrial capitalisms. Indeed, as Giddens (1973, 202–215) has compellingly suggested, the working-class political narrative of revolutionary and then reformist (conflict) politics may be one that is primarily propelled by the explosive "clash of industrial capitalism with (post) Feudalism" and is doomed to entropy as that high conflict recedes into history (1967, 215). Class structures do not predetermine vigorous working-class (e.g., as opposed to sectoral) politics (Mann 1993).

Still, the working-class movement has been persistently important for income security policy. If it has been most important in the understudied 1930s and 1940s, it has remained prominent since midcentury. Since then, neocorporatist institutions, largely constituted and sustained by labor actions, have remained pivotal to the politics of income security policy. This is so even though, since midcentury, worker clout has been largely transmitted via neocorporatist institutions (Chapter 6).

Theoretically, the workers movement actors—the unions, Left-party governments, and neocorporatist labor representatives—in the tales of Table 8.3 may be too "institutionalized" for orthodox "social movement" tastes. Nevertheless, core social movement concepts articulate their story quite well. Relatively bottom up, grass root elements prominent in conventional social movement analysis play a part. (These elements are the ones in bold print in Table 8.3.) So far as social movement theory is concerned, the challenge is not only to complement such dynamic movement moments with new interest group and party data as Brustein (1998) recommends, but also to draw on them so that a dynamic fusion of movement elements is attained. Intimations of such a dynamic extension of social movement theory can be found in a number of explicitly social scientific social movement studies (e.g., Fainsad Katzenstein 1992; Jenkins and Klanderman 1995) and essays (Brustein 1998), as well as in some more theoretically removed or tacit works (e.g., Blackmer and Tarrow, 1975; Claudin 1976; Goldfield 1987; and Gallenson 1996).

Substantively, the current, real world chapter of Left-Right and worker-business contestation of policies affecting worker material security and positions of institutional power has still to be written. When this chapter is finished, the working-class narrative may emerge revived, its conclusion still far off.

Class, State, and Welfare State

What of the class politics framework? Certainly this work's state-contingent class politics framework directly mapped the early consolidation of major types of welfare programs (see Chapter 2). Consolidation of welfare-state programs through around 1920 generally involved Bismarckian, Lib-Lab, and Catholic entwinings with class mobilization. More subtly, 1930s and 1940s program adoptions by social democratic governments involved fusions of party programs and state authority (Chapter 3). Recent Left-Right struggles over retrenchment did so as well (Chapter 7). All these historical patterns match the initial class politics heuristic of Figure 1.1 (Panel G) now re-presented in Figure 8.1, Panel A. However, neocorporatist mediation of the

Figure 8.1 Class politics perspective on the welfare state.

Panel A   Class politics theory

Panel B   Revised class politics theory

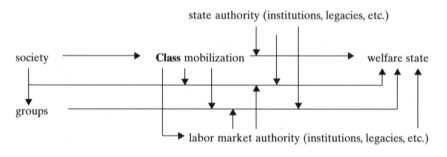

welfarist impacts of such societal and group forces as aging and the aged and unemployment and the unemployed requires revision of the class politics model of Figure 8.1. A place must be added for "labor-market institutions." Other elaborations are needed, particularly depictions of class, state, and labor-market mediations of societal and group forces. Requisite revisions are sketched out in Figure 8.1, Panel B. Of course, Figure 8.1 is only heuristic, a source of working hypotheses. This is as it should be, for although general theory should frame the construction of historical explanation, it can seldom precisely prefigure it.

The accuracy of the framework and the extent of its applicability can be assessed by its application to further, finer policy outputs: program-specific spending, income-replacement rates, and both de-commodification indexes and refined measures of welfare as a stratification system like those devised by Esping-Andersen (1990; 1999). Application to the last decades' additions to developed democratic capitalism—an easy doubling of nations studied—would also advance such assessment, improving theoretical generality and nuance.

Explanations of social insurance policy already advanced here for the first welfare states would be enriched by more qualitatively detailed and comparatively exhaustive case work. Further adjudication of the differences between Esping Andersen's "three worlds of welfare capitalism" and my sequence of more dichotomous worlds—social democratic or not? neocorporatist or not?—is wanted.[3] So are theoretical extensions back to the origins of social democratic strength and forward to its ongoing transformation.

Current History: Quo Vadis?

This work's account of a class movement seen through a welfare-state prism is incomplete. Not only can social movement theory not be reconstructed here for application to the *longe duree* and the actual corridors of power, but the real world story is very much in progress. The present narrative left off in the last chapter with income security policies and their neocorporatist bulwark at issue—battered by some international pressures, beleaguered by Right parties, but defended by some Left (and Left-Center) parties. Preconditions for neocorporatism, which include social democratic governments, were analyzed in the previous chapter. But what of the ongoing vitality of social democracy in the current context of societal aging, unemployment, and globalization?

Social Democratic Futures

On these issues, Kitschelt (1994, 295–301) has pointed to the potential for social democratic longevity in a turn to Left-libertarian constituencies and ideals such as those of environmental and women's movements. Continued social democratic electoral success calls for some mixture of retreat and conservation where such economic policy legacies as public investment, corporate governance, and income redistribution are largely discarded. New rights for a new labor force, buoyed by prosperity and globalization, are, with environmentalism, now key. The working class is a thing of the past.

Garrett (1998a) and Boix (1998), however, suggest that Kitschelt (1994) may have gone too far in relinquishing social democratic economic policy (distributive as well as competitive) to free-market critics of the welfare state. They find that social democratic supply-side policies involving, for example, public investment in infrastructural renovation, technological innovation, and human capital upgrading—*re*commodification instead of *de*commodification—are quite extensive

[3] Recall that neocorporatism and 1980 decommodification are just about perfectly correlated (see Table 8.1 and Chapter 7, n.13). For more detailed attention to social democracy's ongoing transformation—a key question, see Boix (1998), Garrett (1998), Stryker, Eliason, Fritsma and Pampel (1998).

and effective. Such supply-side policies aid economic performance.[4] They relax the pressures of competitiveness on traditional income security programs. They complement them, aiding worker placement and pay and earnings equality. They are distinct from conservative economic policies, although these may adopt a particular instrument of industrial training or public investment. They indicate how security concerns can complement efficiency ones. Thus, the tilt to Kitschelt's libertarian reforms might perhaps be more offset by egalitarian, security, and economic governance policies than Kitschelt (1994) has suggested. The social democratic economic agenda is by no means clearly exhausted, electorally or technically.

Moreover, the opposition of worker and Left-libertarian centers of gravity is partly an artifact of a premature abandonment of the working class, specifically of a false equation of working class with industrial worker or blue collar class. This formula, long challenged, is now revised. The class analytical tradition that once equated worker with industrial worker or wage earner has been vigorously challenged since the mid-1970s, most particularly by the scholarship of Erik Olin Wright (1978, 1985; 1997). One implication of this lucid, if complex, body of rational Marxist class analytical work is that working-class consciousness extends beyond wage earners into the larger category of wage *and* salary employees. The degree of this extension is furthered by the degree of class mobilization in an employee's nation. It is limited by an employee's possession of organizational assets (or authority) and financial assets and by educational capital (Wright 1997).

Przeworski (1985, chaps. 1–2) makes a good case for the primacy of an industrial-worker conception of working-class economic position during the period of industrialization. Today, however, "non-expert managers and non-managerial experts" have "ideological positions somewhere between" ideological extremes and are similar to non-expert, nonmanagerial employees (simple workers) in class consciousness in proportion to the national strength of workers' movements (Wright 1997, 537). In these terms, Left-libertarian appeals are most relevant at the margins of large extant social democratic constituencies. Such appeals may be increasingly relevant, but their relevance nevertheless is concentrated on employees with ample managerial authority or expert credentials, or both. Moreover, feminist appeals may largely be cast as appeals to female *employees*.

---

[4] Note that this use of supply side is not confined to cuts in tax rates as in the supply side of Arthur Laffer and Jack Kemp Republicans in the United States. It encompasses all of production.

Similarly, environmentalist appeals may be pitched disproportionally to employee citizens, likely, on average, to be less tied to the "benefits" of environmental degradation and depletion than employer citizens. Insofar as such appeals are central, the opposition between economic and Left libertarian interests collapses. Discussions of economic and class dimensions of politics are obscured by narrow—industrial, blue collar—usages for working class. Increasingly, employee class seems more suitable.[5] Insofar as this social category is more drawn to popular collective goods than employers, society is primed for employee class movements of working families (Greenberg and Skocpol 1997).

In the 1912 United States, Theodore Roosevelt brought an advanced progressive agenda onto the national political stage with his failed Bull Moose Party platform. This wide-ranging platform, including planks advocating social insurance, union rights, industrial corporatism, and consumer and environmental regulation (Roosevelt, 1967; Sklar 1988), gained support from just over a quarter of the electorate. By 1972, social democrats across northern and central Europe had implemented most of the Progressive planks of sixty years earlier. If as Przeworski (1985, postscript) indicates, social democracy has largely been reduced to the realization of an agenda of worker prosperity and security (e.g., wage increases, full employment and the like), it has become (to turn the coin over) the most effective, if not sole, proponent of the progressive liberal agenda of capitalist reform. The social democratic working-class movement has realized the agenda of the classically middle-class, progressive politics of the public interest (Kloppenberg 1986; Greenberg and Skocpol, 1997). The twentieth century's (characteristically blue collar) employee class has been its premier provider of public goods.[6]

In short, not only are social democratic economic politics alive, they

[5] Although employees with economic assets beyond their earnings or with compensational expertive or managerial assets (or any combination of the three) are candidates for relatively "capitalist" as well as "worker" identities and interests, they are within the ambit of working-class mobilization.

[6] These, although well theorized by the Progressives and Progressive Liberals in the United States and Britain, Radicals in France, and otherwise labeled intellectuals of the *via media*, would appear to have found their strongest constituencies elsewhere (see Kloppenberg 1986). Progressive Teddy Roosevelt was able to map out an agenda that encompassed a broad range of social insurance programs, a protocorporatist system of industrial regulation, and much else for his Bull Moose platform of 1912 (Gable 1978; Sklar 1988). Social democracy began to realize similar platforms beginning in the mid-1930s.

blend into classically middle-class progressive politics. Indeed, social democratic policy achievements have included many consumerist, environmentalist, and feminist planks (Kitchelt 1994; Ruggie 1985) that resemble Kitchelt's (1994) postmodern or Left-libertarian appeals without any fundamental shift in constituency or philosophy. All this is integral to the politics of an employee class.[7] The current chapter of Left-Right, worker-business contestation of policies of worker material security and institutional power has still to be written; however, when the chapter is done, the social democratic working-class narrative may emerge strongly revived, its last chapter still far off. Alternately, the narrative might devolve into a collection of only intermittently consequential stories, proto–social democratic at most, like that of the Second New Deal. Whether within a decade social democratic movements and welfare states appear revitalized or atrophied, their histories over the last five-score years provide the important precedent of citizen welfare enhanced by democratic movements of employees or working families.[8]

Even Center party governments that are outside neocorporatist arenas, but within proto–social democratic "moments" like the New Deal and Great Society, have helped insure poorer citizens (see Chapter 3, especially Fig. 3.1). For example, non-Southern Democratic majorities did so for the U.S. Democrats during the 1930s. Thus, if little progressive state income security reform is to be expected

[7] The call of Giddens (1994, 1996) for a radical politics that moves beyond class redistribution and security to the empowerment of self-reliant individuals may offer some general electoral tips but seems best suited to Left politics in relatively liberal, English-speaking societies where working-class politics have been precarious, at best, since postwar failure at neocorporatist development. They may even be thought of as post–Margaret Thatcher (and post–Ronald Reagan) adjustments.

[8] Allow me, by way of a postscript, to note that today, Bruno Ricci's children, grandchildren of DeSica's bicycle thief, would be in their third or fourth decades and concerned for the prospects for their children. These would be auspicious. Not only would Italian social insurances provide them with something better than the unserviceable safety net described for Bruno at the end of the introduction to this work, Bruno's children would be the beneficiaries of a dynamically open economy, especially in northern Italy, prosperous as never before, a European center of high tech with opportunities to rival any ever offered a Ricci who might have migrated to the Silicon Valley or Greater Boston (Piore and Sabel 1984, Priore 1995). Despite the long diaspora of the Italian Left, and the brief rise of Burlusconni's Right, Italian income security, in the hands of the (at-long-last) social democratic metamorphosis of *Il Partido Communista*, would seem to be in relatively promising hands for a line of Ricci employees.

from such marginal centrist majorities as were held by, say, the 1993 to 1996 Bill Clinton Democrats, neither are eventual extentions of social security (e.g., National Health Care) precluded by a merely nominal absence of social democracy. As New Deal and Great Society innovation indicate, income security reforms "can happen here"; but such U.S. policy breakthroughs may be as rare as proto–social democratic "moments," and their legacies are likely to be especially embattled.

The famous question "Why no socialism in America?" with its multitude of answers is elegantly followed up by the question "Why so little welfare state in America?" This has the simple answer "No social democracy,"[9] which might suffice as an answer to the more general question "Why so little Progressive liberalism in America?" If Progressive liberalism has developed the agenda that social democracy ultimately realizes, social democratic party and labor movements have typically provided the Progressive liberal agenda with the constituencies which the agenda's passage requires.

Questions about the failure of social democracy as a quest for socialism litter scholarship, obscuring perception of the success of social democracy—broadly construed—as an engine of capitalist reform. Przeworski (1985, 248) has written, "The struggle for improving capitalism is as essential as ever. But we should not confuse this struggle with the quest for socialism." The consequences of social democracy for this quest remain vague, contingent as ever on future events. Hopefully, the relevance of income security to the improvement of capitalism and of social democracy to the improvement of income security are now clear.[10]

---

[9] A more complex answer would be "no prominent social democratic party due to such fortuitous circumstances as Bismarckian or Catholic preemptive politics; or Liberal, "Green" or "Black" (farmer or Catholic) alliance; or sustained conservative marginalization and center proto-social democracy; or neocorporatist institutional progeny."

[10] The viability of future income security innovations (not to speak of sustained income security achievement) within the preeminent European family of nation states may lie, within the globalizing subworld of "European integration," in a matter so precise as the realization of a viable mode of general socioeconomic governance for the European Union. This proto-nation is now hamstrung by an inconsequential parliament, by the unanimity rule needed for most policy making within the Council of Ministers, and by all things that bar formation of a European state that can hope to internalize, and then address the externalities of the European political economy rather than devolve into a regional IMF (e.g., Scharpf 1999). A specter is haunting Europe, and that specter is Confederalism. "Nations of Europe unite!" You have...But that is another story.

A. Beyond Decommodification into the "Worlds" of Welfare Capitalism

I do not proceed with further analyses of Esping-Andersen's measures of program qualities—the best currently available—for several reasons. Time and space counsel against such elaborations here and now. I stick with decommodification (see Table 8.3).

More importantly, decommodification seems to me the most central of Esping-Andersen's program measures. True, an entire chapter is devoted to "The Welfare State as a System of Stratification," to the identification of "socialist," "conservative" and "liberal" dimensions of welfare capitalism and to derivative clusters, regimes, or "worlds" of welfare capitalist state. These are all of some interest and are related to neocorporatism below. Nevertheless, decommodification, as a measure of income-security, constitutes a far more summary and final measure of welfare consequences than do the three ideological axes of stratification. First, as a measure of income-security, decommodification taps the overriding "safety net" goal of social transfers and services as argued here in my Introduction and Chapter 1. Second, the three ideological dimensions emerge as two dimensions if they are factor analyzed— "socialism" and "liberalism" loading high on one factor, conservativism on the other; and decommodification emerges as the dominant component of a dominant welfare-quality dimension when it is factor analyzed along with the three ideological dimensions. This done, we get a first factor (e.g., a first unrotated principal component explaining 48 percent of item variance) with a decommodification loading of 0.826, "socialist" and "liberal" loadings of 0.786 and –0.759, respectively, and a "conservative" loading of 0.213—a factor I'll call "Progressivism." (A second notable factor with an eigenvalue greater than 1.0 has a conservative-scale-item loading of 0.947, a socialist loading of –534 and negligible other loadings.) Third, the preponderance of a welfare policy dimension combining qualities of decommodification, "socialism" and (low) liberalism casts doubt on the "balance" of a categorization of welfare regimes that neglects decommodification, disperses "socialism" and "liberalism" from poles of a single dimension to caps for two separate dimensions, and that then clusters nations on the doubtfully proliferated and decommodification-less dimensions. Fourth, we have already seen that conservative and liberal worlds are more historically concentrated and discontinuous than is suggested by Esping-Andersen (1990). In particular, we've seen that traditional conservativism may be more significant as an element in the multifaceted "Bismarckian" emergence of social insurance and that its Catholic cousin may be most notable for its coalitional contributions to the 1940-like social democratic ascendance than for any marked post-War Christian Democratic social reformism. Similarly, we have seen that "liberalism" both lays 1910-ish "Lib-Lab" foundations for 1930s and 1940s social democratic reforms and succumbs to a strong if short-lived Social Democratic phase in the United Kingdom and Antipodes of the 1940s.

This is not to say that Esping-Andersen's "regimes" fail to illuminate social policy (e.g., gendered labor-market policies, which do differ in so-called conservative regimes). (Certainly they do not fail to stimulate discussion and inquiry.) It is to say that these regimes are less "worlds" than shadings along a principal "decommodification" or "progressive-laissez-faire" policy axis running the length of a single capitalist world. The "regimes" involve not distinct historical routes to welfare states but retrospective projections of such routes on to a more complex etiology than a mere three regime-specific routes can describe. Relations of neocorporatism to a fuller range of Esping-Andersens' dimensions and of welfare capitalism are of interest. Thus, correlations between neocorporatism and a variety of these dimensions are noteworthy. Correlations between neocorporatism and Esping-Andersen's socialist, conservative and liberal dimensions are 0.490, −0.575 and 0.253, respectively. More important, correlations between between neocorporatism and the Progressivism factor and its "conservative" partner are 0.667 and 0.107 respectively. What I capture with the above factor analytical results are not distinct socialist, liberal and conservative "worlds," but one preeminent Progressive/laissez-faire dimension of a single, heterogeneous, liberal-capitalist world.

B. Social Movement Theory and the Social Democratic Income Security Movement

Unfortunately, self-proclaimed social movement theory in the social sciences is inclined to resist consideration of "supermovements." It is reluctant to follow movements beyond early compromise into the corridors of (conventionally institutionalized) power. Fortunately, there are traditions of scholarship for which a social movement framing of social democratic development should come as little surprise: Radical scholars have referred to workers, union, communist, and other labor "movements" quite routinely (Foner 1947; Gallenson 1960; Przeworski 1985; Goldfield 1987; Dubofsky 1994). Still, prevailing conventions of the social movement literature in sociology and political science make an explicitly social movement interpretation of working-class politics—at least once they have passed the institutional markers of success—problematic (see Jenkins and Klanderman 1995; McAdam, Tarrow and Tilly 1996). As Brustein (1995, 277) has written, "Once a movement begins to succeed . . . it ceases to be a movement."

Writings by sociologists and political scientists that are tied to the development and application of a social science theory of social movements confine themselves to "social movements" as newly mobilized, "challenger" groups committed to "social and political change" outside "established political institutions" (Brustein 1995, 277; Gamson 1975; McCarthy and Zald 1977; Tarrow 1994, 138–148). These writings typically eschew consideration of political parties and interest groups (unless spawned or swept up by a surrounding sea of collective action). They typically neglect the mainstream literatures on such actors, even though boundaries among them are so porous that they hardly constitute definable boundaries at all (Burstein 1998).

Such theoretical restrictiveness, however, underestimates the extent to which parties confront new opinion and ideology and absorb new challenges and challengers—indeed the extent to which they are oriented by the grass roots as well as the *status quo*" (Wilson 1990, on protester support from Left parties when out of office; Kitschelt 1994, on Left-libertarian pressures, partisan and grass roots; Wallace and Jenkins 1995, on "conventional" and "Left" as well as "new class" and "post-modern" resorts to varieties of nonviolent protest in "neo-corporatist" as well as affluent democracies). From 1930s incorporations of the nonunionized poor through 1970s and 1980s incorporations of the women's (and other "new social" and "libertarian") movements to present-day "wild cat" insurrections and "work council" interventions, exceptions to the sociological assumption that institutionalization kills social movements may be more notable than the rule (see Esping-Andersen 1985, on the 1930s; Swenson 1989, on the turbulent 1940s and 1960s; Pontusson 1992, on the turbulent 1960s and beyond; Kitchelt 1994, and Western 1997, on recent voter and worker unrest, respectively). True, mass movements reach such pinnacles of success as the Swedish active labor market policy of the 1950s and 1960s only via a diaspora of "institutionalization" (Janoski 1992). And "institutionalization" has the cooptive, self-binding facet stressed by Selznick (1967). Nevertheless, many institutions are both rooted in, and periodically revitalized by, grass roots action (see Swenson 1989, on neocorporatist institutions).

Academic students of social movements tend to avoid the slippery slope of movement cooption by the political establishment, without—unlike activists themselves—showing much aversion to the second slippery slope of principled irrelevance. They tend to hold fast to an underlying morality of principle in the face of a political world that, as Weber wrote in his "Politics as a Vocation," requires a "morality of responsibility" that is sensitive to consequence and to effectiveness (Weber [1926] in Hardin 1988). (The "art of the possible" rather than, "Here I stand though the whole world burn.") In every sense of "success"—and not merely Gamson's (1975) ironic coding of movement success as virtual movement death—a history of political "success" is almost invariably a history of historical institutionalization and beyond. Dissent and institutionalization both qualify as possible necessary conditions for successful social change. Neither suffices.

Respecting the imperatives of a mix—a balance—of dissent and institution, social movements need more fair weather friends, scholars who will stick with social movements through good times as well as bad (e.g., Claudin 1976; Smant 1996). Or, as prescribed with incomparable ambition by Sartre (1976), from ground zero through success to failure. Again, they should not only accept Burstein's (1998) challenge that they encompass interest groups and political parties, but seek to integrate these in a way that stresses their relations to a dynamic movement whole.

Bibliography

Abbott, A., and S. DeViney. 1992. "The Welfare State as Transnational Event: Evidence from Sequences of Policy Evaluation." *Social Science History* 16:245–274.

Alber, Jens. 1982. *Vom Armenhaus zum Wohlfahrtstaat*. Frankfurt: Campus.

——. 1986. Germany. In *Growth to Limits*: Vol. 2, *Germany, United Kingdom, Ireland, Italy*. Edited by P. Flora, 1–154. Berlin: de Gruyter.

Alapmo, R. 1988. *State & Revolution in Finland*. Berkeley: University of California Press.

Alesina, A., and R. Perotti. 1997. "The Welfare State and Competitiveness." *American Economic Review* 87:921–939.

Alford, R. R., and R. Friedland. 1975. "Political Participation and Public Policy." *Annual Review of Sociology* 1:429–479.

——. 1985. *Powers of Theory*. New York: Cambridge University Press.

Allison, P. 1982. *Event History Analysis*. Beverly Hills, Calif.: Sage.

Alvarez, M. R., G. Garrett, and P. Lange. 1991. "Government Partnership, Labor Organization and Macroeconomic Performance, 1967–1984." *American Political Science Review* 89:539–556.

Alwin, D., and R. Hausar. 1975. "The Decomposition of Effects in Path Analysis." *American Sociological Review* 40:37–52.

Amenta, E. 1998. *Bold Relief*. Princeton: Princeton University Press.

Amenta, E., and B. G. Carruthers. 1988. "The Formative Years of U.S. Social Security Spending Policies." *American Sociological Review* 53:661–678.

Amenta, E., and S. Parikh. 1991. "Capitalists Do Not Want Social Security, Etc?" *American Sociological Review* 56:891–909.

Amenta, E., and T. Skocpol. 1988. "Redefining the New Deal: World War II and Public Social Provision in the United States." Chapter 2 in *Politics of Social Policy in the United States*, edited by Margaret Weir, Ann Shola Orloff, and Theda Skocpol.

Princeton, N.J.: Princeton University Press.

Anderson, J. E. 1984. *Public Policy Making*. New York: Holt Rinehart Winston.

Ashford, D. E. 1986. *The Emergence of the Welfare State*. Oxford: Basil Blackwell.

Baldwin, P. 1990. *The Politics of Social Solidarity: Class Bases of the European Welfare State, 1875–1975*. New York: Cambridge University Press.

Bean, C. 1994. "European Unemployment: A Survey." *Journal of Economic Literature* 32:573–619.

Beck, N., and S. Katz. 1995. "What to Do (and Not Do) with Time-Series Data." *American Political Science Review* 89:634–647.

Berghman, J., J. Peters, and J. Vranken. 1987. Belgium. In *Growth to Limits*. Vol. IV. Edited by P. Flora, 751–810. New York: de Gruyter.

Berkling, A. L. (ed.) 1982. *Fran Frram till Forkhemmet: Per Albin Hansson Sotidningsman Och Talare*. Stockolm: Metodica Press.

Blackmer, D. L. M., and S. Tarrow, eds. 1975. *Communism in Italy and France*. Princeton N.J.: Princeton University Press.

Blank, R. M. 1994. *Social Protection vs. Economic Flexibility*. Chicago: University of Chicago Press.

Block, F. 1977. "The Ruling Class Does Not Rule." *Socialist Revolution* 33:6–27.

——. 1979. "Beyond Relative Autonomy: State Managers as Historical Subjects." *New Political Science*. Vol. 1:33–49.

Blondel, J. 1969. *An Introduction to Comparative Government*. London: Weidenfeld and Nicolson.

Boix, C. 1998. *Political Parties, Growth, and Inequality: Conservative and Social Democratic Party Strategies in the World Economy*. New York: Cambridge University Press.

Boswell, J. 1990. *Community and Economy*. London: Routledge.

Brown, C., ed. 1987. *The Illustrated History of Canada*. Toronto: Lester and Orpen Dennys.

Browne, E., and J. Dreijmanis. 1982. *Government Coalitions in Western Democracies*. New York: Longman.

Bruno, M., and J. D. Sachs. 1985. *Economics of Worldwide Stagflation*. Cambridge: Harvard University Press.

Burstein, P. 1995. The Success of Social Movements. In *The Politics of Social Movements*, edited by J. Craig Jenkins and Bert Klandermans. Minneapolis: University of Minnesota Press.

——. 1998. Social Movement Organization, Interest Groups, Political Parties and the Study of Democratic Politics. In *Social Movements and American Political Institutions*, edited by Anne Costain and Andrew McFarland. New York: Rowman and Littlefield.

Cameron, D. 1978. "The Expansion of the Public Economy: A Comparative Analysis." *American Political Science Review* 72:1243–1261.

——. 1984. Social Democracy, Corporatism and Labor Quiescence. In *Order and Conflict in Contemporary Capitalism*, edited by John H. Goldthorpe, 143–178. New York: Oxford University Press.

Carroll, E. 1994. "Unemployment Rights." Paper Presented at the Meetings of the International Sociological Association, Beilefeld, Germany, September, 1994.

Castles, F., ed. 1982. *The Impact of Parties*. Beverly Hills, CA: Sage.

——. 1985. *The Working Class and Welfare*. London: Allen and Unwin.

——. 1991. "The Shere Awelfulness of the English." *Journal of Theoretical Politics* 3:124–139.

——. 1998. *Comparative Public Policy: Patterns of Post-War Transformation*. Cheltenham: Edward Elgar.

Castles, F. G., and S. Dowrick. 1990. "The Impact of Government Spending Levels on Medium-Term Economic Growth in the OECD, 1960–85." *Journal of Theoretical Politics* 2:173–204.

Castles, F., and P. Mair. 1984. "Left Right Political Scales: Some Expert Judgements." *European Journal of Political Research* 12:73–88.

Castles, F., and R. McKinlay. 1978. "Public Welfare Provision and the Sheer Futility of the Sociological Approach to Politics." *British Journal of Political Science* 9:157–172.

Castles, F., and V. Merrill. 1989. "Toward a General Theory of Policy Outcomes." *Journal of Theoretical Politics* 1:177–212.

Castles, F. F., and Deborah M. 1990. "Three World of Capitalism or Four?" Discussion Paper No, 21, National University of Australia, October, 1990.

Claudin, F. 1976. *The Communist Movement*. London: Verso.

Crepaz, M. M. L. 1992. "Corporatism in Decline? An Empirical Analysis of the Impact of Corporatism on Macroeconomic Performance and Industrial Disputes in 18 Industrialized Countries." *Comparative Political Studies* 25:139–168.

——. 1998. "Inclusion versus Exclusion—Political Institutions and Welfare Expenditures." *European Journal of Political Research* 29:61–84.

——. 1996. "Consensus versus Majoritarian Democracy—Political Institutions and their Impact on Macroeconomic Performance and Industrial Disputes." *Comparative Political Studies*, 29:4–26.

Crepaz, M. M. L., and V. Birchfield. (1998). Global Economics, Local Politics." Typescript. Department of Political Science, University of Georgia, Athens.

Crouch, C. 1985. Conditions for Trade Union Wage Restraint. In Lindberg, *The Politics of Inflation and Economic Stagnation*, edited by Leon Lindberg and Charles S. Maier. Washington: Brookings Institution.

——. 1993. *Industrial Relations and European State Traditions*. Oxford, England: Oxford University Press.

Cutright, P. 1965. "Political Structure, Economic Development and National Social Security Programs." *American Journal of Sociology* 70:539–55.

Czada, R. 1983. "Konsensbedogungen und Auswirkungen neokorporatistischer Politikentwicklung." *Journal fur Sozialforschung* 33:435.

Dahl, R. 1971. *Polyarchy*. New Haven: Yale University Press.

——. 1982. *Dilemmas of Pluralist Democracy*. New Haven: Yale University Press.

Dahrendorf, R. 1959. *Class and Class Conflict in Industrial Society*. Stanford, Calif.: Stanford University Press.

Draper, H. 1977. *Karl Marx's Theory of Revolution*. New York: Monthly Review Press.

DeViney, S. 1984. "The Political Economy of Public Pensions." *Journal of Political and Military Sociology* 12:295–310.

Domhoff, G. William. 1967. *Who Rules America?* Englewood Cliffs, N.J.: Prentice-Hall.

Dowrick, S., and Nguyen, D. T. 1989. "OECD Comparative Growth in the Post-War Period." *American Economic Review* 77:1010–1030.

Doyal, L., and I. Gough. 1991. *A Theory of Need*. London: Macmillan.

Dubofsky, M. 1994. *State and Labor in Modern America*. Chapel Hill: University of North Carolina Press.

Dye, T. 1979. "Politics Versus Economics: The Development of the Literature on Policy Determination." *Policy Studies Journal* 7:652–662.

Ebbenhaus, B. 1992. The Transformation of Cleavage Structures into Western Trade Union Systems. Paper for ECPR Workshop on Trade Unions and Politics, University of Limerick, April 1–4.

Engels, F. [1890] 1960. Introduction. In *The Civil War in France, 1848–1850*, by Karl Marx. Moscow: Progress Publishers.

——. [1891] 1968. Introduction to Selected Works of Karl Marx & Frederick Engels. In *The Civil War in France, 1848–1850* by Karl Marx, 252–262. Moscow, Russia: Progress Publishers.

Erikson, R., et al., eds. 1987. *The Scandinavian Model Stockholm*. Armonk, NY: M. E. Sharpe.

Esping-Andersen, G. 1985. *Politics Against Markets*. Princeton, N.J.: Princeton University Press.

——. 1990. *The Three Worlds of Welfare Capitalism*. Princeton, N.J.: Princeton University Press.

——. 1996. After the Golden Age: Welfare State Dilemmas in a Global Economy. In *Welfare States in Transition: National Adaptations in Global Economies*, edited by G. Esping-Anderson. Thousand Oaks, CA: Sage.

——. 1999. *Social Foundations of Postindustrial Economies*. New York: Oxford University Press.

Esping-Andersen, G., and R. Friedland. 1982. "Class Coalitions in the Making of Western European Economies." *Political Power and Social Theory*.

Esping-Andersen, G., R. Friedland, and E. O. Wright. 1976. "Modes of Class Struggle and the Capitalist State." *Kapitalistate* 4/5:186–220.

Evans, P. M., D. Rueschemeyer, and T. Skocpol, eds. 1985. *Bringing the State Back In*. New York: Cambridge University Press.

Feldstein, M. 1997. "Supporting Retirees: The Case for Privatization." *Foreign Affairs* 76:24–37.

Ferarra, M. 1986. Italy. Vol. II of *Growth to Limits*, edited by Peter Flora. Berlin: de Gruyter.

Finegold, K., and T. Skocpol. 1995. *State and Party in America's New Deal*. Madison: University of Wisconsin Press.

Fitzmaurice, J. 1989. "Belgium." In *Western European Political Parties*, edited by F. Jacobs, 2–19. London: Longman.

Flora, P. 1983. *State, Economy and Society in Western Europe*, Vols. 1 and 2. Chicago: St. James Press.

——. 1986a. *Growth to Limits: The Western European Welfare State since World War II*. Vols. 1–4. New York: de Gruyter.

——. 1986b. Introduction. In *Growth to Limits*, edited by P. Flora, xi–xxxvi. New York: de Gruyter.

Flora, P., and Alber, J. 1983. Modernization, Democratization, and the Development of Welfare States in Western Europe. In *The Development of the Welfare State in Europe and America*, edited by P. Flora and A. J. Heidenheimer, 37–80. New Brunswick, N.J.: Transaction.

Flora, P., and A. J. Heidenheimer, eds. 1982. *The Development of the Welfare State in Europe and America*. New Brunswick, N.J.: Transaction.

Foner, P. 1947. *History of the Labor Movement in the United States*. New York: International Publishers.

Friedland, R., F. F. Piven, and R. R. Alford. 1978. "Political Conflict, Urban Structure and the Fiscal Crisis." *International Journal of Urban and Regional Research*. 13:447–470.

Friedland, R., and J. Sanders. 1985. "The Public Economy and Economic Growth in Western Market Economies." *American Sociological Review* 50:421–437.

Gable, J. A. 1978. *Theodore Roosevelt and the Progressive Party*. Port Washington, NY: Kennikat Press.

Gallenson, Walter. 1996. *The American Labor Movement*. Westport, Conn.: Greenwood Press.

Gamson, W. A. 1975. *The Strategy of Social Protest*. Homewood, IL: Dorsey.

Gamson, W. A., and D. S. Meyer. 1996. Framing Political Opportunity. In *Comparative Perspectives on Social Movements*, edited by Doug McAdams, John D. McCarthy, and Mayer N. Zald. New York: Cambridge University Press.

Garon, S. 1987. *The State and Labor in Modern Japan*. Berkeley: University of California Press.

Garrett, G. 1998a. *Partisan Politics in the Global Economy*. New York: Cambridge University Press.

———. 1998b. "Global Markets and National Politics: Collision Course or Virtuous Circle?" *International Organization* 52: forthcoming.

Garrett, G., and P. Lange 1986. "Performance in a Hostile World." *World Politics* 38:517–545.

Garrett, G., and D. Mitchell. 1997. Globalization and the Welfare State. Typescript. Department of Political Science, Yale University, New Haven, Conn.

George, V., and P. Taylor-Gooby, eds. 1996. *European Welfare Policy: Squaring the Circle*. New York: St. Martin's Press.

Giddens, A. 1973. *The Class Structure of Advanced Societies* New York: Harper.

———. 1994. *Beyond Left and Right: The Future of Radical Politics*. Stanford, CA: Stanford University Press.

———. 1996. *The Third Way: The Renewal of Social Democracy*. London: Polity Press.

Gill, S., and D. Law. 1988. *The Global Political Economy*. Baltimore: Johns Hopkins University Press.

Gilson, E. 1954. *The Church Speaks to the Modern World*. New York: Image Books.

Golden, M., P. Lange, and M. Wallerstein. 1993. Trends in Collective Bargaining and Industrial Relations in Non-Corporatist Countries. Paper Prepared for Presentation at the 1993 Annual Meetings of the American Political Science Association, Washington, September 3–5.

Goldfield, M. 1987. *The Decline of Organized Labor in the U.S.* Chicago: University of Chicago Press.

———. 1989. "Worker Insurgency, Radical Organization and New Deal Labor Legislation." *American Political Science Review* 4:1056–1080.

Gordon, A. 1998. *The Wages of Affluence: Labor and Management in Post-War Japan*. Cambridge, MA: Harvard University Press.

———. 1988. *Social Security Policies in Industrial Countries: A Comparative Analysis*. Cambridge, Mass.: Cambridge University Press.

Gourevitch, A. P. 1986. *Politics in Hard Times*. Ithaca, N.Y.: Cornell University Press.

Granatstein, J. L. 1975. *Canada's War: The Politics of the MacKenzie King Government, 1939–1945*. Toronto: Oxford University Press.

Greenberg, S. B., and T. Skocpol, eds. 1997. *The New Majority: Toward a Popular Progressive Politics*. New Haven: Yale University Press.

Grieder, William. 1997. *One World, Ready or Not*. New York: Touchstone Books.

Griffin, L. J., J. Devine, and M. Wallace. 1983. "On Economic and Political Determinants of Welfare Spending in the Post-World War II Era." *Politics and Society* 12:330–372.

Guest, D. 1985. *The Emergence of Social Security in Canada*. Vancouver: University of British Columbia Press.

Hage, J., E. T. Gargan, and R. A. Hanneman. 1989. *State Responsiveness and State Activism*. London: Unwin Hyman.

Hamerow, T. S. 1983. *The Birth of a New Europe: State and Society in the Nineteenth Century*. Chapel Hill: University of North Carolina Press.

Hardin, R. 1982. *Collective Action*. Baltimore, MD: Johns Hopkins University Press.

———. 1988. *Morality within the Limits of Reason*. Chicago: University of Chicago Press.

Heclo, H. 1974. *Modern Social Policy in Britain and Sweden from Relief to Income Maintenance*. New Haven: Yale University Press.

Heclo, H., and H. Madsen. 1987. *Policy and Politics in Sweden*. Philadelphia: Temple University Press.

Herf, Jeffrey. 1984. *Reactionary Modernism*. New York: Cambridge Univeristy Press.

Hewitt, Christopher. 1977. "The Effects of Political Democracy and Social Democracy on Equality in Industrial Societies: A Cross-Sectional Comparison." *American Sociological Review* 42:450–464.

Hibbs, D. A., and Jr. 1987. *The Political Economy of Industrial Democracies*. Cambridge: Harvard University Press.

Hicks, A. M. 1994. "Qualitative Comparative Analysis and Analytical Induction." *Sociological Methods and Research* 23:86–113.

———. 1998. Globalization and Reversals of Centralized Wage Bargains. Typescript. Department of Sociology, Emory University, Atlanta, Ga.

Hicks, A. M., and L. Kenworthy. 1998. "Cooperative Institutions and Political Economic Performance in Affluent Capitalism." *American Journal of Sociology* 103:1632–1672.

Hicks, A. M., and J. Misra. 1993. "Political Resources and the Expansion of Welfare Effort." *American Journal of Sociology* 99:668–710.

Hicks, A. M., J. Misra, and T. Ng. 1995. "The Programmatic Emergence of the Welfare State." *American Sociological Review* 60:329–349.

Hicks, A. M., and D. H. Swank. 1984a. "Governmental Redistribution in Rich Capitalist Democracies." *Policy Studies Journal* 13:265–286.

———. 1984b. "On the Political Economy of Welfare Expression." *Comparative Political Studies* 17:81–119.

———. 1992. "Politics, Institutions, and Welfare Spending." *American Political Science Review* 86:658–674.

Higley J., and M. G. Burton. 1989. "The Elite Variable in Democratic Transitions and Breakdowns." *American Sociological Review* 51:17–34.

Hofmeister, H. 1982. Austria. In *The Evolution of Social Insurance, 1881–1981: Studies of Germany, France, Great Britain, Austria and Switzerland*, edited by P. A. Kohler, H. F. Zacher, and M. Partington, 265–83. London: Frances Pinter.

Hollingsworth, J. R., and R. Boyer. 1997. *Contemporary Capitalism: the Embeddedness of Institutions*. New York: Cambridge University Press.

Hollingsworth, J. R., J. Hage, and R. A. Hannemann. 1992. *State Intervention in Medical Care*. Ithaca, N.Y.: Cornell University Press.

Hollingsworth, J. R., P. C. Schmitter, and W. Streeck, eds. 1994. *Governing Capitalist Economies: Performance and Control of Economic Sectors*. New York: Oxford University Press.

Huber, E., and J. D. Stephens. 1998. "Internationalization and the Social Democratic Welfare Model: Crisis and Future Prospects." *Comparative Political Studies* 31:353–397.

Huber, E., and J. D. John Stephens. Forthcoming. The Social Democratic Welfare State: Origins, Achievements, Crisis and Future. Typescript. Department of Political Science, University of North Carolina, Chapel Hill.

Huber, E., J. Stephens, and C. Ragin. 1993. "Social Democracy, Christian Democracy, Constitutional Structure and the Welfare State." *American Journal of Sociology* 99:711.

Immegut, E. *Health Politics*. New York: Cambridge University Press.

International Labor Organization, 1950–1995. *Cost of Social Security*. Geneva: ILO.

Isaac, L., and W. R. Kelley. 1981. "Racial Insurgency, the State and Welfare Expansion." *American Journal of Sociology* 86:1348–1386.

Jacobs, F. 1989. *Western European Political Parties*. London: Longman.

Janoski, T. 1992. *The Political Economy of Unemployment*. Berkeley: University of California Press.

Jenkins, J. Craig. 1983. *The Politics of Insurgency*. New York: Columbia University Press.

Jenkins, J. Craig, and B. Klanderman, eds. 1995. "The Politics of Social Protest." In *The Politics of Social Movements*. Minneapolis, Minn: University of Minnesota Press.

———. 1995. *The Politics of Social Movements*. Minneapolis, Minn: University of Minnesota Press.

Johnston, J. J. 1984. *Econometric Methods*. New York: McGraw-Hill.

Jones, Catherine, ed. 1993. *New Perspectives on the Welfare State in Europe*. New York: Routledge.

Kamlet, M. S., and D. C. Mowery. 1987. "Influences on Executive and Congressional Budgetary Priorities, 1955–1981." *American Political Science Review* 55:155–178.

Kangas, O. 1991. *The Politics of Social Rights*. Monograph 19. Stockholm: Swedish Institute for Social Research.

Katz, R. B. 1993. *Japan, the System That Soured*. Armonk, N.Y.: M. E. Sharpe.

Katzenstein, P. J. 1985. *Small States in World Market*. Ithaca, N.Y.: Cornell University Press.

Kenworthy, L. 1995. *In Search of National Economic Success*. Thousand Oaks, CA: Sage.

———. 1998. "Do Social Welfare Policies Reduce Poverty? A Cross National Assessment."

Kenworthy, L., and A. M. Hicks. 1999. "Welfare State Outcomes in Institutional Context." Typescript. Department of Sociology, East Carolina University.

Kerr, C., J. T. Dunlop, F. Harbison, and Charles A. Meyers. 1964. *Industrialism and Industrial Man*. New York: Oxford University Press.

Keynes, J. M. 1929. *Can George Do It? An Examination of the Liberal Pledge*. London: The Nation and Athenaeum.

———. 1929. "We Can Conquer Unemployment." *Evening Standard*, March 19, 1929.

Kersbergen, K. 1991. Social Capitalism: A Study of Christian Democracy and the Post-War Settlement of the Welfare State. Ph.D. diss. Department of Political/Social Sciences. European University Institute, Florence, Italy.

———. 1995. *Social Capitalism*. London: Routledge.

Kitschelt, H. H. 1994. *The Transformation of Social Democracy*. New York: Cambridge University Press.

Kloppenberg, J. T. 1986. *Uncertain Victory: Social Democracy and Progressivism in European and American Thought, 1870–1920*. New York: Oxford University Press.

Kmenta, Jan. 1988. *Elements of Econometrics*. New York: Macmillan.

Korpi, W. 1978. *The Working Class in Welfare Capitalism*. London: Routledge and Kegan Paul.

———. 1983. *The Democratic Class Struggle*. London: Routledge and Kegan Paul.

———. 1985. "Power Resource Approach vs. Action and Conflict." *Sociological Theory* 3:31–45.

———. 1988. The Politics of Employment Policy: A Comparative Study of Unemployment Insurance, Unemployment and Active Labor Market Policy in 18 OECD Countries. Working Paper Presented at the Workshop on Inequality and Distributional Conflict, Hasselby Slott, Stockholm, August, 1988.

———. 1989. "Power, Politics, and State Autonomy in the Development of Social Citizenship." *American Sociological Review* 54:309–28.

———. Forthcoming. *Contested Citizenship*. Cambridge: Cambridge University Press.

Lange, P., and G. Garrett. 1985. "The Politics of Growth." *Journal of Politics* 47: 792–847.

———. 1986. "The Politics of Growth Reconsidered." *Journal of Politics* 48:257–274.

Lange, P., M. Golden, and M. Wallerstein. 1995. The End of Corporatism? Wage Setting in Nordic and Germanic Countries. In *The Workers of the Nations*, edited by Sanford Jacoby. Oxford University Press.

Laumann, E., and D. Knoke. 1987. *The Organizational State*. Madison, Wisc.: University of Wisconsin Press.

Lehmbruch, G. 1984. Concertation and the Structure of Corporatist Networks. In *Order and Conflict in Contemporary Capitalism*, edited by John H. Goldthorpe, 60–80. New York: Cambridge University Press.

Lehner, F. 1988. The Political Economy of Distributive Conflict. In *Managing Mixed Economies*, edited by Francis Castles, Franz Lehner, and Manfed Schmidt. Berlin: de Gruyter.

Lenski, G. 1971. *Power and Privilege*. New York: McGraw-Hill.

Leone, R. C. 1997. "Supporting Retirees: Stick with Public Pensions." *Foreign Affairs* (July/August): 39–53.

Levine, A., E. Sober, and E. O. Wright. 1986. "Marxism and Methodological Individualism." *New Left Review* IXX: 67–84.

Lewin, L. 1988. *Ideology and Strategy*. New York: Cambridge University Press.

Levy, F. 1999. *The New Dollars and Dreams*. New York: Russell Sage Foundation.

Lewis, D. S., and Sagar (eds.). *Political Parties of Asia and the Pacific: A Reference Guide*. London: Longman.

Lieberson, S. 1991. "Small Ns and Big Conclusions." *Social Forces* 70:307–320.

Lijphart, A. 1984. *Democracies*. New Haven: Yale University Press.

Lijphart, A., and Markus M. L. Crepaz. 1991. "Corporatism and Consensus Democracy in 18 Countries: Conceptual and Empirical Linkages." *British Journal of Political Science* 21:345–356.

Lindblom, C. E. 1977. *Politics and Markets*. New York: Basic Books.

Lipset, S. M. 1982. "Radicalism and Reform: The Sources of Working Class Protest." *American Political Science Review* 77:1–18.

———. 1983. *Political Man*. Expanded ed. Baltimore: Johns Hopkins University Press.

Lipsky, M. 1968. "Protest as a Political Resource." *American Political Science Review* 62:1144–1168.

Longergan, B. 1957. *Insight*. London: Darton, Longman and Todd.

Lorwin, Val. 1966. Belgium: Religion, Class and Language in National Politics. In *Political Opposition in Western Democracies*, edited by R. Dahl. New Haven: Yale University Press.

Luebbert, G. 1991. *Liberalism, Fascism or Social Democracy: Social Classes and the Political Origins of Regimes in Interwar Europe*. New York: Oxford University Press.

Mackie, Thomas, and Richard Rose. 1982. *The International Almanac of Electoral History*. 2d ed. London: Macmillan.

———. 1982–1985. "General Elections in Western Nations." *European Journal of Political Research*.

Maddala, G. S. 1977. *Econometrics*. New York: McGraw-Hill.

Maddison, A. 1991. *Dynamic Forces in Capitalist Development*. New York: Oxford University Press.

Mahler, V. 1990. "Explaining the Growth of Social Benefits in Advanced Capitalist Countries, 1960–1980." *Government and Policy* 8:13–28.

Maier, C. S. 1984. Preconditions for Corporatism. In *Order and Conflict in Contemporary Capitalism*, edited by John H. Goldthorpe. New York: Oxford University Press.

Mann, M. 1993. *Sources of Social Power*. Vol. II. New York: Cambridge University Press.

Marcus, M. 1986. *Italian Film in the Light of Neorealism*. Princeton, N.J.: Princeton University Press.

Marks, G. 1986. "Neocorporatism and Incomes Policy." *Comparative Politics* 18:253–277.

Marx, K. 1968. [1852] *The Eighteenth Brumaire of Luius Bonaparte*. In *Selected Works*, edited by Karl Marx and Frederick Engels, pp. 95–180. New York: International Publishers.

———. 1968. [1871] *The Civil War in France*. In *Selected Works*, edited by Karl Marx and Frederick Engels, pp. 252–313. New York: International Publishers.

Marshall, T. H. 1964. *Class, Citizenship and Social Development*. New York: Doubleday.

Marwick, A. 1967. "The Labour Party and the Welfare State in Britain, 1900–1948." *American Historical Review* 73.

McAdam, D., J. D. McCarthy, and M. N. Zald. 1996. Introduction: Opportunities, Mobilizing Structures, and Framing Processes. In *Comparative Perspectives on Social Movements: Political Opportunities, Mobilizing Structures and Cultural Framings*, edited by Doug McAdams, John D. McCarthy, and Mayer N. Zald. New York: Cambridge University Press.

McAdam, D., S. Tarrow, and C. Tilly. 1996. A Comparative Synthesis on Social Movements and Revolutions. Paper Presented at the Annual Meetings of the American Political Science Association, San Francisco, August, 1996.

McKenzie, R., and D. Lee. 1991. In *Quicksilver Capital: How the Rapid Movement of Wealth Has Changed the World*, edited by Catherine Jones. New York: Routledge.

McOustra, C. 1990. *Love in the Economy: Catholic-Social Doctrine for the Individual*. Slough: St. Paul.

Miliband, R. 1969. *The State in Capitalist Society*. New York: Basic Books.

Mishra, Ramesh. 1993. *The Welfare State in Capitalist Society*. London: Wheatsheaf.

Misra, J. 1994. "The Emergence of Family Allowances: A Gendered Comparative-Historical Study of the Welfare State." Ph.D Dissertation, Department of Sociology, Emory University.

Moe, T. 1980. *The Organization of Interests*. Chicago: University of Chicago Press.

Mosca, G. 1939. *The Ruling Class*. New York: McGraw Hill.

Mueller, D. C. 1979. *Public Choice*. New York: Cambridge University Press.

Murray, C. A. 1982. "The Two Wars against Poverty: Economic Growth and the Great Society." *The Public Interest* 9:3–16.

Musgrave, R. A., and P. B. Musgrave. 1985. *Public Finance in Theory and Practice*. New York: McGraw Hill.

Myles, J. 1989. *Old Age in the Welfare State: The Political Economy of Public Pensions*. Expanded ed. Boston: Little, Brown.

OECD. 1985. *Economic Outlook: Historical Statistics, 1960–1983*. Paris: OECD.

———. 1986. *Reforming Public Pensions* Paris: OECD.

———. 1960–1995a. Labour Force Statistics. Paris: OECD.

———. 1960–1995b. Main Economic Indicators. Paris: OECD.

———. 1960–1995c. National Accounts of OECD Nations. Paris: OECD.

———. 1994. *The OECD Jobs Study: Evidence and Explanations, Part II. The Adjustment Potential of the Labour Market*. Paris: OECD.

———. 1994. *New Directions in Social Policy in OECD Countries*. Paris: OECD.

———. 1996. "Social Expenditures of OECD Member Countries." *Labour Market and Social Policy Occasional Papers*, No. 17. Paris: OECD.

———. Forthcoming. *OECD Database on Unemployment Entitlements and Replacement Rates*. Paris: OECD.

Offe, Clause. 1984–. *Contradictions of the Welfare State*. Cambridge, Mass.: MIT Press.

Ogus, A. I. 1982. Great Britain. In *The Evolution of Social Insurance, 1881–1981*, edited by P. A. Kohler, H. F. Zacher, and M. Partington, 150–264. London: Frances Pinter.

Olson, M. 1965. *The Logic of Collective Action*. Cambridge: Harvard University Press.

Orloff, A. S. 1992. *The Politics of Pensions*. Madison, Wis.: University of Wisconsin Press.

Orloff, A. S., and T. Skocpol. 1984. "Why Not Equal Protections?" *American Sociological Review* 49:726–750.

Padgett, J. F. 1981. "Hierarchy and Ecological Control in Federal Budgetary Decision Making." *American Journal of Sociology* 87:75–129.

Palme, J. 1990. *Pensions in Welfare Capitalism*. Monograph 14. Stockholm: Swedish Institute for Social Research.

Pampel, F. C., and J. B. Williamson. 1985. "Age Structure, Politics and Cross-National Patterns of Public Pension Expenditures." *American Sociological Review* 50:782–798.

———. 1988. "Welfare Spending in Advanced Industrial Democracies, 1950–1980." *American Journal of Sociology* 50:1424–1456.

———. 1989. *Age, Class, Politics and the Welfare State*. New York: Cambridge University Press.

Pampel, F. C., and R. Stryker. 1990. "Age Structure, the State and Social Welfare Spending: A Reanalysis." *British Journal of Sociology* 41:16–24.

Panitch, Leo. 1981. "Trade Unions and the Capitalist State." *New Left Review*, No. 125:21–44.

Pareto, V. 1962. [1935] *The Mind and Society*. New York: Dover.

Perry, R. 1986. United Kingdom. In *Growth to Limits*. Vol. I. Edited by P. Flora, 155–239. New York: de Gruyter.

Pfaller, A (with I. Gough). 1991. The Competitiveness of Industrialized Welfare States: A Cross-Country Survey. In *Can the Welfare State Compete?* edited by A. Pfaller, I. Gough, and G. Therborn, 15–43. London: Macmillan.

Pierson, P. 1994. *Beyond the Welfare State*. Cambridge: Polity Press.

———. 1996. "The New Politics of Welfare." *World Politics* 48(2):143–179.

Piore, M. 1995. *Beyond Individualism*. Cambridge: Harvard University Press.

Piore, M., and C. Sabel. 1984. *The Second Industrial Divide*. New York: Basic Books.

Piven, F. F., and R. A. Cloward. 1977. *Poor People's Movements*. New York: Vintage.

Plough, N., and J. Kvist. 1996. *Social Security in Europe: Development or Dismantlement*. Copenhagen: The Danish National Institute of Social Research.

Polanyi, K. 1944. *The Great Transformation*. Boston: Beacon Press.

Pontusson, J. 1992. *The Limits of Social Democracy: Investment Politics in Sweden*. Ithaca, N.Y.: Cornell University Press.

Poulantzas, N. 1973. *Political Power and Social Class*. London: New Left Books.

Przeworski, A. 1985. *Capitalism and Social Democracy*. New York: Cambridge University Press.

———. 1990. *State and Economy under Capitalism*. London: Harwood Academic Publisher.

Przeworski, A., and H. Teune. 1970. *The Logic of Comparative Social Inquiry*. New York: Wiley.

———. 1993a. Introduction to Qualitative Comparative Analysis. In *Methodological Advances in Comparative Political Economy*, edited by T. Janoski and A. Hicks, 299–319. New York: Cambridge University Press.

———. 1993b. A Qualitative Comparative Analysis of Pension Systems. In *Methodological Advances in Comparative Political Economy*, edited by T. Janoski and A. Hicks, 320–345. New York: Cambridge University Press.

Przeworski, A., and M. Wallerstein. 1988. "Structural Dependence of the State on Capital." *American Journal of Political Science* 82:11–31.

Quadagno, J. S. 1988. *The Transformation of Old Age Security*. Chicago: University of Chicago Press.

Quadagno, Jill. 1994. *The Color of Welfare*. New York: Oxford University Press.
Questiaux, N., and J. Fournier. 1978. "France." In *Family Policy: Government and Families in Fourteen Countries*, edited by S. Kamerman and A. Kahn. New York: Columbia University Press.
Quine, D. 1997. "The Origins of Financial Openness." *American Journal of Political Science* 82:11–30.
Ragin, C. 1987. *The Comparative Method*. Berkeley: University of California Press.
———. 1994a. Introduction to Qualitative Comparative Analysis. In *Methodological Advances in Comparative Political Economy*, edited by T. Janoski and A. Hicks, 299–319. New York: Cambridge University Press.
———. 1994b. A Qualitative Comparative Analysis of Pension Systems. In *Methodological Advances in Comparative Political Economy*, edited by T. Janoski and A. Hicks, 320–345. New York: Cambridge University Press.
Rao, P., and R. L. Miller. 1971. *Applied Econometrics*. Belmont, Calif.: Wadsworth.
Remmer, K. L. 1984. *Party Competition in Argentina and Chile*. Lincoln: University of Nebraska Press.
Reynolds, M. and E. Smolensky. *Public Expenditures, Taxes and the Distribution of Income*. New York: Academic Press.
Rhodes, M. 1997. "The Welfare State: Internal Challenges, External Constraints." In *Developments in West European Politics*, edited by M. Rhodes, P. Heywood, and V. Wright. London: Macmillan.
Rimlinger, G. V. 1971. *Welfare Policy and Industrialization in America, Germany and Russia*. New York: Wiley.
Rodrik, D. 1997. *Has International Economic Integration Gone Too Far?* Washington: Institute for International Economics.
———. 1998. "Why Do More Open Economies Have Bigger Government?" *Journal of Political Economy* 106:997–1032.
Roebroek, J., and T. Berben. 1987. Netherlands. In *Growth to Limits*. Vol. IV. Edited by P. Flora, 751–810. New York: de Gruyter.
Rogers, M. F. 1974. "Instrumental and Infra-Resources: The Bases of Power." *American Journal of Sociology* 79:1418–1433.
Rokkan, Stein. 1970. *Citizens, Elections, Parties*. Oslo: Universitets Forlaget.
Roosevelt, T. 1967. *The Writings of Theodore Roosevelt*, edited by W. H. Harbaugh. Indianapolis, Ind.: Bobbs-Merrill.
Rothstein, B. 1987. "Corporatism and Reformism: The Social Democratic Institutionalisation of Class Conflict." *Acta Sociologica*: 30:295–311.
———. 1990. "Marxism, Institutional Analysis and Working Class Power: The Swedish Case." *Politics and Society* 18:317–345.
———. 1991. Swedish Interest Organization. In *Svensk Democrati E Forandung*, edited by Johan P. Olsen. Stockholm: Carlson.
———. 1994. "Explaining Swedish Corporatism: The Formative Moment." *Scandinavian Political Studies* 15(3):173–191.
Roubini, N., and J. Sachs. 1989. "Fiscal Policy." *Economic Policy* 30:101–113.
Rueschemeyer, D., E. H. Stephens, and J. Stephens. 1991. *Capitalism, Development and Democracy*. Chicago: University of Chicago Press.
Ruggie, J. G. 1983. "International Regimes, Transactions and Change. Embedded Liberalism in the Post-War Economic Order." In *International Regimes*, edited by Stephen D. Krasner. Ithaca, N.Y.: Cornell University Press.
———. 1995. "At Home Abroad, Abroad at Home." *Millennium: Journal of International Studies*, 24:506–527.
———. 1996. Globalization and the Embedded Liberalism Compromise: End of an Era? Working paper 97/1. Cologne, Max Planck Institut fur Gessellschaftforschung.

Ruggie, M. 1985. *State and Working Women*. Princeton, N.J.: Princeton University Press.

——. 1996. *Realignments in the Welfare State*. New York: Columbia University Press.

Saint-Jours, J. 1982. France. In *The Evolution of Social Insurance, 1881–1981: Studies of Germany, France, Great Britain, Austria and Switzerland*, edited by Peter A. Kohler, Hans F. Zacher, and Martin Partington, 93–149. London: Frances Pinter.

Sartre, Jean-Paul. [1960] 1976. *Critique of Dialectical Reason*. Vol. I, *Theory of Practical Ensembles*. London: Verso.

Scharpf, F. 1987. *Crisis and Choice in European Social Democracy*. Ithaca, N.Y.: Cornell University Press.

——. 1999. *Governing Europe*. New York: Oxford University Press.

Schlesinger, A. Jr. 1958. *The Age of Roosevelt: The Crisis of the Old Order, 1919–1933*. Boston: Houghton Mifflin.

——. 1959. *The Age of Roosevelt: The Coming of the New Deal*. Boston: Houghton Mifflin.

Schmidt, M. 1982. Does Corporatism Matter? In *The Impact of Parties*, edited by Francis Castles. Beverly Hills, Calif., Sage.

——. 1983. "The Welfare State and the Economy in Periods of Economic Crisis." *European Journal of Political Research* 11:1–25.

——. 1986. "Politische Bedingungen erfolgriecher Wirtschaftpolitik." *Journal für Sozialforschung* 36:251–273.

Schmitter, P. C. 1974. "Still the Century of Corporatism?" *Review of Politics* 36:85–131.

——. 1981. Interest Intermediation and Regime Governability in Contemporary Western Europe. In *Organizing Interests in Western Europe*. New York: Cambridge University Press.

Selznick, P. [1949] 1967. *TVA and the Grass Roots*. Berkeley: University of California Press.

Shalev, M. 1982. "The Social Democratic Model and Beyond." *Comparative Social Research* 6:315–352.

Shepherd, W. 1994. *International Financial Integration: History, Theory and Applications in OECD Countries*. Brookfield, Vt.: Ashgate.

Skidelsky, R. 1967. *Politicians and the Slump: The Labour Government of 1929–31*. London: Macmillan.

——. 1983. *John Maynard Keynes: A Biography*. London: Macmillan.

Sklar, M. J. 1988. *The Corporate Reconstruction of American Capitalism*. Berkeley: University of California Press.

Skocpol, T. 1979. *States and Social Revolution*. Cambridge: Harvard University Press.

——. 1981. "Political Response to the Capitalist Crisis." *Politics and Society* 2:155–201.

——. 1985. Bringing the State Back In. In *Bringing the State Back In*, edited by Peter M. Evans, Dietrich Reuschemeyer, and Theda Skocpol, 3–37. New York: Cambridge University Press.

——. 1992. *Protecting Soldiers and Mothers*. Cambridge: Harvard University Press.

Skocpol, T., and E. Amenta. 1985. "Did Capitalists Shape Social Security." *American Sociological Review* 50:572–575.

——. 1986. "States and Social Policies." *Annual Review of Sociology* 12:131–157.

Slemrod, J. 1995. "What Do Cross-Country Studies Teach Us about Government Involvement, Prosperity and Economic Growth?" *Brookings Papers on Economic Activity* 2:373–431.

Smant, K. J. 1996. *How Great the Triumph: James Burnham, Anticommunism and the Conservative Movement*. Lanham, MD: University Press of America.

Soskice, R. 1990. "Wage Determination: The Changing Role of Institutions in Capitalist Industrial Society." *Oxford Review of Economic Policy* 6:36–41.

——. 1998. Divergent Production Regimes. In *Continuity and Change in Contemporary Capitalism*, edited by H. Kitschelt, P. Lange, Gary Marks, and John Stephens. New York: Basil Blackwell.

Steinmetz, G. (ed.) 1999. *State/culture*. Ithaca, NY: Cornell University Press.

Stephens, J. D. 1979. *The Transition from Capitalism to Socialism*. London: Macmillan.

Stimson, J. 1985. "Regression in Time and Space: A Statistical Essay." *American Journal of Political Science* 29:914–947.

Stockwin, J. J. A. 1992. Japan. In *Political Parties in Asia and the Pacific*, edited by D. S. Lewis and S. J. Sagar. London: Longman.

Streeck, W. 1984. "Neo-corporatist Industrial Relations and the Economic Crisis in West Germany." In *Order and Conflict in Contemporary Capitalism*, edited by J. H. Goldthorpe, 291–314. New York: Oxford University Press.

Strykes, R., S. Eliason, T. Fritsma, and F. Pampel. 1998. "Voting and the Welfare State." Paper presented at 10th International Conference on Socio-Economics. Vienna, Austria, July 13–16.

Summers, R., and A. Heston. 1988. "Improved International Comparisons of Real Product and Its Components, 1950–1984." *Review of Income and Wealth* 30:207–262.

Swank, D. H. 1983. "Between Incrementalism and Revolution." *American Behavioral Scientist* 26:291–310.

——. 1991. "Politics and the Structural Dependence of the State in Democratic Capitalism." *American Political Science Review* 86:38–54.

——. 1997. Global Markets, National Institutions, and the Public Economy in Advanced Market Economies. Paper presented at the Conference on Economic Internationalization and Democracy. Institute for Sociology, University of Vienna, December 14–15.

——. 1998a. "Funding the Welfare State: Globalization and the Taxation of Business in Advanced Market Economies." *Political Studies*.

——. 1998b. "Social Democratic Welfare States in a Global Economy." In *Globalization, Europeanization and the End of Scandinavian Social Democracy?*, Robert Geyer, Christine Ingebritsen and Jonathon Moses, eds. London: Macmillan.

——. Forthcoming. Diminished Democracy? Global Capital, Political Institutions, and the Welfare State in Developed Nations. Typescript. Marquette University, Milwaukee, Wis.

Swenson, P. 1989. *Fair Shares*. Ithaca, N.Y.: Cornell University Press.

——. 1991. "Bringing Capital Back In, or Social Democracy Reconsidered." *World Politics* 43:513–544.

——. 1996. "States and Opportunities: The Political Structuring of Social Movements." In *Comparative Perspectives on Social Movements*, edited by Doug McAdams, John D. McCarthy, and Mayer N. Zald. New York: Cambridge University Press.

Therborn, G. 1977. "Rule of Capital and the Rise of Democracy." *New Left Review*, No. 103.

——. 1979. *What Does the Working Class Do When It Rules?* London: Verso.

Tilton, T. 1990. *The Political Theory of Swedish Social Democracy*. New York: Oxford University Press.

Tingsten, H. 1973. *The Swedish Social Democrats: Their Ideological Development*. Toronto, Ontario: Bedminster Press.

Titmuss, Richard T. 1983. *Essays on the Welfare State*. London: Allen & Unwin.

Trevelyan, G. M. 1937. *British History in the Nineteenth Century and After: 1782–1919*. London: Longmans Green.

Truman, D. [1951] 1971. *The Governmental Process*. New York: Knopf.

Tsebelis, G. 1990. *Nested Games*. Berkeley: University of California Press.

——. 1995. "Decision Making in Political Systems." *British Journal of Political Science*, 25:289–325.

United Nations. Selected years. *Demographic Yearbook*. New York: UN.

U.S. Department of Health and Human Services, 1990. *The Cost of Social Security*. Washington: U.S. Government Printing Office.

——. 1990. *Social Security Throughout the World*. Washington: U.S. Printing Office.

Usui, C. 1994. "The Origins and Development of Modern States." In *Comparative Political Economy of the Welfare State*, edited by T. Janoski and A. Hicks, 254–277. New York, NY: Cambridge University Press.

Van Arnheim, J., M. Corina, and G. J. Schotsman. 1982. "Do Parties Affect the Distribution of Income?" In *The Impact of Parties*, edited by F. Castles. Beverly Hills, Calif.: Sage.

Visser, J. 1990. "Trade Union Membership Database." Typescript. University of Amsterdam.

Wallace, M., and J. Craig Jenkins. 1995. The New Class, Post-Industrialism, and Neo-Corporatism. In *The Politics of Social Movements*, edited by J. Craig Jenkins and Bert Klanderman. Minneapolis: University of Minnesota Press.

Wallerstein, M. 1987. "Unemployment, Collective Bargaining and the Demand for Protectionism." *American Journal of Political Science* 31:729–752.

Wallerstein, M., and M. Golden. 1998. "The Fragmentation of the Bargaining Society: Wage Setting in the Nordic Countries." *Comparative Political Studies* 31: forthcoming.

Weber, M. [1919] 1958. Politics as a Vocation. In *From Max Weber: Essays in Sociology*, edited by H. Gerth and C. W. Mills. New York: New Press.

Weede, E. 1984. "Democracy, Creeping Socialism and Ideological Socialism in Rent-Seeking Societies." *Public Choice* 44:349–366.

——. 1986. "Sectoral Relocation, Distributional Coalition and the Welfare State as Determinants of Economic Growth Rates in Industrialized Societies." *European Journal of Political Research* 14:501–514.

Weir, M., A. S. Orloff, and T. Skocpol. 1988. *The Politics of Social Policy in the United States*. New York: Cambridge University Press.

Weir, M., and T. Skocpol. 1985. State Structures and the Possibilities for Keynesian Responses to the Great Depression in Sweden, Britain and the United States. In *Bringing the State Back In*, edited by P. M. Evans, D. Reuschemeyer, and T. Skocpol, 107–163. New York: Cambridge University Press.

Wennemo, I. 1992. "The Development of Family Policy." *Acta Sociologica* 35:201–217.

——. 1994. *Sharing the Costs of Children*. Stockholm: Swedish Insitute for Social Research, Monograph 25.

Western, B. 1991. "A Comparative Study of Corporatist Development." *American Sociological Review* 56:283–294.

——. 1997. *Between Class and Market*. Princeton, N.J.: Princeton University Press.

White, K. J. 1997. Shazam Econometrics Computer Program, Ver. 7.2. New York: McGraw Hill.

Wilensky, H. L. 1975. *The Welfare State and Equality*. Berkeley: University of California Press.

——. 1976. *The New Corporatism*. Beverley Hills, Calif.: Sage.

——. 1981. Leftism, Catholicism, and Democratic Corporatism. In *The Development of the Welfare State in Europe and America*, edited by Peter Flora and Arnold Heidenheimer, 341–378. New Brunswick, N.J.: Transaction.

——. 1998. Globalization: Does It Subvert Labor Standards, Job Security and the

Welfare State? Paper Presented at the Meetings of the American Sociological Association, San Francisco, August 21–25.

——. Forthcoming. *Tax and Spend*. Typescript. Department of Political Science, University of California, Berkeley.

Wilensky, H., and C. N. Lebeaux. 1958. *Industrial Society and Social Welfare*. New York: Russell Sage Foundation.

Williamson, J. B., and F. C. Pampel. 1993. *Old Age Security in Comparative Perspective*. New York: Cambridge University Press.

Wilson, G. K. 1979. *Unions in American National Politics*. New York: St. Martin's Press.

Wonnacott, R., and T. Wonnacott. 1985. *Regression: a Second Course*. Malabar, Fla.: Krieger.

Wright, E. O. 1978. *Class, Crisis and the State*. London: New Left Books.

——. 1985. *Classes*. New York: Verso.

——. 1997. *Class Counts: Comparative Studies in Class Analysis*. New York: Cambridge University Press.

Zald, M. N. 1996. Culture, Ideology and Strategic Framing. In *Comparative Perspectives on Social Movements*, edited by Doug McAdams, John D. McCarthy, and Mayer N. Zald. New York: Cambridge University Press.

Zollner, D. 1982. Germany. In *The Evolution of Social Insurance, 1881–1981*, edited by P. A. Kohler, H. F. Zacher, and M. Partington, 1–92. London: Frances Pinter.

Znaniecki, F. 1934. *The Method of Sociology*. New York: Farrar and Rinehart.

Index

Page references followed by an italicized *t*, *f*, *or n* indicate tables, figures, and notes respectively.

Catholic government participation
in class politics theory, 46
and coverage and income
replacement, 1931–1950,
108
in Germany, postwar, 103
and income security adoption
1931–1950, 79t, 109–110, 119t
Depression-era, 90–91
interpretive formula for,
83–85
1940s era, 79t, 82, 96, 101–103
interpretive formula for, 96–97
and neocorporatism, 139, 150
in pluralist theory, 24
Red-Black coalitions and, 91, 96,
101–103, 109, 119t, 122t,
125–126
in Switzerland, postwar, 103
and welfare consolidation, early,
52t, 54, 56–66, 68–69
working class social movement
in, 239, 240t
Catholic-Left coalitions, 91, 96,
102–103, 109, 119t, 122t,
125–126
Catholic majorities, and income
security policy, 71–73, 72t
Catholic Mouvement
Republicaine Populaire
(France), 103
Catholic Partie Democrate
Populaire (France), 90, 91n
CCF (Canada). See Canadian
Commonwealth Federation
centrist government participation
in class politics theory, 46
and coverage and income
replacement, 1931–1950,
81t, 105–108
in early welfare consolidation,
52t, 54, 56–66, 68
and income security adoption
1931–1950, 78–80, 79t, 82, 110
in Depression era, 76, 91–94
theory of, 83–85
1940s era, 79t, 100–101
interpretive formula for,
96–97
in pluralist theory, 23
CFTC (France). See Catholic
Confederation Francais
des Travailleurs Chretiens;
Confederation Francais
des Travailleurs Chretiens
CGT (France). See Confederation
Generale du Travail
Chaplin, Charle, 3
Christian democracy
Christian democratic
government participation
and income security adoption,
in 1940s, 96, 101–103, 109,
125, 234–235
and welfare effort, 159t, 161
as explanatory variable, 179
cumulative measurement of,
174n, 189–193, 191t, 192t
measurement of, 169, 186
statistical findings, 172, 173t,
177t, 188t
retrenchment in, 216t, 226t, 227,
228
in class politics theory, 46
formation of, in 1940s, 96,

101–103, 109, 125
and neocorporatism, 139, 143t,
144, 146t, 147
in pluralist theory, 24
Churchill, Winston, 109
class. See also capitalist class;
employee class; working
class
in class politics theory, 15f, 27,
28–29
in neo-Marxist welfare state
theory, 14, 15f, 27–28
in political resource theory of
welfare effort, 160, 181–182
and working-class movements,
241
class analytical perspective, on
welfare state, 14, 15f,
17–21, 245
class-centered, state-mediated
theory
of welfare state, 15, 15f, 27, 29,
44
revision of, 242–244, 243f
of welfare state consolidation
economic development in
methodological preview of,
31–34
theoretical domain of, 29–31,
47–49
theory of, 45–47
class politics theory. See class-
centered, state-mediated
theory
Cloward, R. A., 236
communist parties. See also social
democratic government
participation
post-Depression era, 78
compensation view, of
globalization, 206–207, 218
competitiveness view, of
globalization, 204–206
Confederation Francais des
Travailleurs Chretiens
(CFTC; France), 89
Confederation Generale du
Travail (CGT; France), 89
configurative model, in class
analytical theory, 20
conservatism, and
neocorporatism, 150
conservative economic policy, 245
conservative governments, and
income security reform,
1931–1950, 76n, 78, 82, 109
Conservative Party (Canada), 82,
92–93, 109
conservative welfare regime, 117,
249–250
consolidation
early
analyses and findings in, 55–62,
74–75
Bismarckian route, 13–14, 58,
61–64
Catholic government
participation in, 52t, 54,
56–66, 68–69
data in, 50–55, 67–69
decommodification and, 25
economic development and,
25–26, 34–41, 35t, 36t, 37t,
40t
empirical patterns in, 62–66

Lib-Lab coalitions in, 19,
43–44, 62–64, 125
methods in, 49–50
state as variable in, 52t, 55–65,
57t
theoretical domain in, 47–49
theory of, 45–47
working class and, 26, 36t,
39–41, 40t, 114–117, 115t,
231–233, 232t
analyses and findings, 56–62
patterns of, 62–66
as variable in, 52t, 54, 68
laggards, 98, 100, 111, 120–121,
125–126, 154, 197–200, 233
by midcentury
decommodification and,
121–126, 123t
patterns of explanation for,
112–113
and welfare effort, 153–154,
154f, 155t, 182–186, 183f,
185f
and welfare retrenchment,
197–200, 198f–199f
and welfare effort, vs.
neocorporatism, 182–186,
185f
working class and, 114–117, 115t,
197–200, 231–233, 232t
consumerist policies, in social
democratic agenda, 247
cooperative veto points, in welfare
effort, 162–163, 172–173,
173t, 177t, 188t
corporatism, 128–129. See also
neocorporatism
cost of living allowances, as
policy-maker norm, in
welfare effort, 163–164, 170
Crepaz, M. M. L., 24, 141, 143t,
145n, 169
Crouch, C., 131–133, 137, 139, 141,
142, 148, 149n, 150
culture, and state, 223f, 229
cultural frames, in social
movement theory, 239
Czada, R., 141
Czechoslovakia, 31n, 84n

Dahl, R., 24, 25, 30, 48
Dahrendorf, R., 15n, 241
Daladier, Eduord, 90
DCI (Italy). See Democrazia
Cristian Italiana
decommodification
1980, 9, 10t
early consolidation and, 25
in Esping-Andersen's regime
stratification, 249–250
midcentury consolidation and,
121–124, 123t, 125–126
neocorporatism and, 232t,
233–234
and welfare effort, 10t
correlation with, 169n
deficit spending, in Depression
era, 77–78, 86
democracy
in early welfare state reform
in class analytical theories,
19–20
in pluralist theories, 23–24
economic development and, 26,
30–31

Social Democracy and
Welfare Capitalism